The Creators of Tomorrow

Homo Technologicus, Social and Ethical Futures

Editors

James Giordano, Niko Kohls, and John Shook

VOLUME 2

The titles published in this series are listed at *brill.com/htse*

The Creators of Tomorrow

An Interdisciplinary Perspective on Shaping the Future

Edited by

Paweł Fortuna and Anna Dutkowska

BRILL

LEIDEN | BOSTON

This publication is financed from the state budget under the program of the Minister of Education and Science (Poland) called "Science for Society II" (project number: NdS-II/SN/0477/2023/01, funding amount: PLN 636,158.00, total project value: PLN 636,158.00).

Ministry of National Education
Republic of Poland

SCIENCE FOR THE SOCIETY

The Library of Congress Cataloging-in-Publication Data is available online at https://catalog.loc.gov
LC record available at https://lccn.loc.gov/2025038484

Typeface for the Latin, Greek, and Cyrillic scripts: "Brill". See and download: brill.com/brill-typeface.

ISSN 2666-8769
ISBN 978-90-04-73717-4 (hardback)
ISBN 978-90-04-74819-4 (e-book)
DOI 10.1163/9789004748194

This book is printed on acid-free paper and produced in a sustainable manner.

Contents

The Transformative Power of Creativity in the Re-globalization Era: An Introductory Overview

Paweł Fortuna[1] *and Anna Dutkowska*[2]

In 1998, when the first universal USB 1.1 ports appeared on the market, Toyota introduced the first hybrid car, and Google registered its business, Hans Moravec published an article titled "When Will Computer Hardware Match the Human Brain?" in the Journal of Evolution and Technology (1998). The futurist, who had built one of the first autonomous vehicles in the 1980s, predicted that computers' processing power would reach a level comparable to the human brain around the year 2025 – the exact moment when we present this book to our readers. Although constructing a computer capable of functioning similarly to the neural architecture of the human brain remains challenging, the futurist's forecasts remain relevant today.

In the final part of his article, Moravec introduced the metaphor of the "Great Flood", describing technological advancement as the gradual flooding of successive areas of human activity (the landscape of human competence). Nearly two decades later, this metaphor was updated and expanded by Max Tegmark (2017). The physicist emphasized that the level of "cyber-fluid" is rising ever more rapidly, and areas of human activity previously considered safe – such as creativity – are now also experiencing "flooding". Tegmark observed that the threshold for task automation is dynamic, and artificial intelligence (AI) systems not only imitate but also exceed human capabilities in unexpected domains. At the time Tegmark was working on his text, skills such as playing Go and chess were already submerged beneath the "cyber-fluid", while abilities like translating languages and driving vehicles still existed as islands, with investing considered a peninsula. Technological progress continues today. The introduction of ChatGPT and other large language models (LLMs) in 2022 caused further "flooding", with AI becoming increasingly proficient in text generation, visual content and music creation, programming, data analysis, mentoring, and customer service.

1 The John Paul II Catholic University of Lublin, Institute of Psychology, Lublin, Poland, https://orcid.org/0000-0002-0633-4453

2 The John Paul II Catholic University of Lublin, Department of Philosophy of Nature and Natural Sciences, Institute of Philosophy, Faculty of Philosophy, https://orcid.org/0000-0002-6302-3651

Moravec's vision is materializing before our eyes. The pace of change is so rapid that soon, by the time we utter the word "technology", its first syllable will already refer to the history of technology. The ongoing digitalization process has become one of the most significant sources of global tension, shaping a reality described as the *Great Unsettling* (Steger & James, 2020; Steger et al., 2023). The unprecedented flow of information, ideas, data, digital assets, blockchain-based currencies, and cyber communication has led to the dominance of intangible globalization over traditional forms of global interconnectedness. As a result, Moravec's "cyber-fluid" takes on a new meaning – it is no longer merely a metaphor for job automation but rather a reflection of the real and dynamic shift of the global system toward a technology-driven reorganization of reality.

According to Roland Benedikter (2022), the world is entering an era of *re-globalization* – a new phase of global connectivity that differs both from the neoliberal globalization of the 1990s and from its regression observed between 2010 and 2020, driven by the rise of nationalism, protectionism, and economic fragmentation. Unlike previous stages, *re-globalization* is based on the increasing role of digital networks, automation, and AI, which are redefining the flows of capital, labor, and information. However, this does not signify a return to the traditional model of globalization. Instead of a uniform global system, a complex, multi-layered structure is emerging, where digital interactions prevail over physical ones, and states, corporations, and individuals adapt to the new realities to varying degrees.

How can we establish safe harbors for human agency within this dynamic process of intangible globalization? Moravec himself suggested that the best solution is to "build Arks as that day nears, and adopt a seafaring life" (1998, p. 12). The very human intelligence and creativity that contributed to the rise of the "Great Flood" must now become the tools for navigating this new reality. The key challenge of the *re-globalization* era is no longer merely adapting to the technological wave but consciously shaping its direction – wherever possible – toward well-being.

1 The Prospect of Halting the "Technological Flood"

It seems that halting the expansion of technology could only occur due to objective factors, such as inherent limitations in the development of artificial systems or unforeseen technological barriers. It is unlikely that humanity itself would voluntarily decide to stop technological progress. Few people remember, and even fewer are concerned with the fact that more than half a century ago, in 1972, 2,200 scientists from 23 countries signed the so-called *Menton Appeal* (UNESCO, 1971). This document called for caution in the introduction of new technologies without a full understanding of their consequences and emphasized the need to perceive Earth as a finite system in which all humans are interdependent. Today, similar calls for reflection are often drowned out by the media noise surrounding start-ups and technological innovations. The exponential growth of emerging technologies demonstrates that society operates under the *technological imperative* (Mumford, 1934) – the belief that every technically feasible innovation corresponds to some human need and therefore must be realized, regardless of its potential social, ethical, or environmental consequences.

Today, the role once played by the *Menton Appeal* is echoed in initiatives advocating for the development of so-called *friendly AI*. The concept of *AI Alignment* emphasizes designing artificial systems in a way that ensures their harmonious cooperation with humans while minimizing the risk of unintended consequences (Russell, 2019). The OECD guidelines (2019) on responsible AI development highlight the need for transparency, accountability, and privacy protection. Meanwhile, the *Artificial Intelligence Act* proposed by the European Commission (2021) calls for the regulation of high-risk technologies due to their potential societal impact. While such initiatives are met with understanding, they do not slow down the rapid advancement of systems that increasingly imitate – and in some cases surpass – human capabilities.

Awareness of the concept of artificial general intelligence (AGI) – a system capable of matching or surpassing human abilities – shifts the imagined level of Moravec's cyber-fluid to the peaks of the highest summits in the landscape of human competence. This vision is reinforced by pop culture narratives – films such as *Terminator*, *Blade Runner 2049*, *Ex Machina*, *Westworld*, and *NeXt* highlight fundamental questions about the boundaries of humanity, the extent of human control over machines, their ethical implications, and the long-term consequences for civilization. The debate on the future of AI is not merely a technical issue; it is also deeply philosophical, social, and moral. It does not concern only a narrow group of experts but increasingly engages broader segments of society. A sign of the growing public interest in this issue is, for instance, the rising number of internet searches in recent years for the phrase "What is the difference between human and AI?" (see Google Trends).

No one knows whether – and if so, when – the idea of AGI will become a reality. The primary obstacles to its realization remain the current limitations of computing power and the absence of algorithms capable of flexible adaptation across various domains. So far, AI development has been characterized by leaps of progress, with periods of rapid advancement alternating with so-called AI winters. Another significant factor that may slow progress is the lack of breakthroughs in understanding competencies based on emotions and intuition, including creativity. At present, it is easier to define what intuition is *not* than what it *is*. Weinberg (2007) aptly described it as "intellectual happenings in which it seems to us that something is the case without arising from our inferring it from any reasons that it is so, or our sensorily perceiving that it is so, or our having a sense of remembering that it is so" (p. 319). Of course, artificial systems can be designed to exhibit behaviors that may be interpreted as intuition, free will, or other complex cognitive abilities, but any positive human response to such behaviors would largely be a result of anthropomorphization rather than a reflection of actual rational agency. At this point, it remains impossible to develop systems that, like humans, can engage in creativity that transcends existing rules and paradigms – an activity that Margaret Boden (1990)) referred to as transformational creativity.

2 Managing the Force: Technology with the "WELL" Quality Mark

Many people are concerned about the expansion of technology, including the prospect of quantum computers, yet the "Great Flood" metaphor can also be viewed with optimism. According to Tegmark (2017), maintaining a course that benefits both humanity and the planet requires the development of a shared vision of the future through an extensive dialogue, which he described as "the most important conversation of our time". The significance of such discussions is immense – if humanity fails to agree on its priorities, there is a high probability that the future will unfold in ways misaligned with human needs and goals. This perspective finds justification in the field of cyberpsychology. Systematic literature reviews indicate that users' interactions with digital environments can lead to phenomena revealing the dark side of technology. Among the most frequently analyzed issues are digital addiction, technostress, cyberbullying, compulsive internet use, cyberpornography, cyberchondria, and FOMO (Ancis, 2020, Singh & Singh, 2019). This trend persists. The challenges faced by young smartphone users, often referred to as the anxious generation (Haidt, 2024), are drawing increasing attention from researchers. Scholars investigating problematic screen use, such as Agata Błachnio and Aneta Przepiórka, rank among the most frequently cited scientists in this domain worldwide.

The distinctly victimological character of cyberpsychology does not, however, imply a resignation – rooted in learned helplessness – from studying the beneficial interactions between humans and the technosphere. Evidence of this can be found in the development of positive cyberpsychology (Burke, 2021; Fortuna, 2021, 2023) – a research field focused on analyzing the conditions that foster well-being (flourishing, high-quality life, and optimal functioning) in interactions with and through technology. Positive cyberpsychology emerges at the intersection of cyberpsychology, positive psychology, and well-being design. Its intellectual capital is built upon numerous theories that mark a collaboration between psychologists and designers. A particularly noteworthy concept is Positive Technology (Riva et al., 2012), which distinguishes three categories of technology: hedonistic – enhancing well-being and amplifying positive experiences; eudaimonic – supporting personal growth, character strengths, and the pursuit of meaningful goals; social – facilitating relationship-building and strengthening social support. While designing such technologies is not yet the mainstream focus of innovation, the first steps in this direction have already been taken.

Introducing innovations to the market without testing their impact on user well-being makes the process of intangible globalization resemble an experiment with minimal variable control, where the stakes are the quality of life for individuals and, on a broader scale, the condition of the entire planet. Undoubtedly, SMART technology requires smart users whose interactions should be systematically studied to provide designers with tools for creating more responsible solutions. A shift in the approach to technology design could significantly influence the direction of its development. Much could change if the business world recognized the benefits of introducing a *WELL* quality mark, certifying the positive effects of specific innovations (see Fortuna, 2024). A source of hope and opportunity for business lies in approaches advocating for the expansion of standard UX research – traditionally focused on usability and ease of interaction – to include user well-being. For example, the creators of the Motivation, Engagement, and Thriving in User Experience (METUX) model (Peters et al., 2018) suggest that the starting point for designing innovations should be the fundamental psychological needs outlined in Self-Determination Theory (Ryan & Deci, 2000): the need for competence, autonomy, and relatedness. Measuring the fulfillment of these needs (using specially developed TENS scales) allows for a precise determination of which features of a given technology promote user well-being and can serve as the foundation for an effective feedback mechanism between users and designers.

3 *Futures Literacy* and Creative Competencies in the Process of *Re-globalization*

What competencies should the creator of the future possess to maintain control and agency in the process of *re-globalization*? According to Benedikter (2025), a key element of consciously shaping the future is futures literacy – the ability to anticipate upcoming changes and actively influence their direction through strategic and creative thinking about the future, designing it in a way that aligns with social values and human needs.

Futures literacy can be considered a meta-competency encompassing a broad set of skills, as it requires both analytical thinking and cognitive flexibility, along with the ability to integrate knowledge from various fields. Guidelines for shaping such a competency package can be found in Joseph E. Aoun's (2018) concept of *humanics*. He argues that in addition to traditional skills such as reading, writing, and arithmetic, modern individuals should develop three key competencies: (1) **data literacy** – the ability to analyze and interpret data; (2) **technological literacy** – an understanding of engineering fundamentals, programming, and the functioning of technology; and (3) **human literacy** – knowledge of the humanities, interpersonal communication, and social design. Both Aoun and Benedikter emphasize the importance of creative competencies. As long as humans can create, they can actively shape the future and maintain agency in the face of the "Great Flood". The very act of aligning technological development with human well-being exemplifies creativity with a capital C, but equally important are the small-scale creative acts that influence the quality of daily life and, consequently, the well-being of society, the environment, and the planet as a whole.

The development of creative abilities appears to be the most suitable mental resource for confronting the reality of the *Great Unsettling*. This is likely why creativity is recognized as one of the key competencies of the 21st century, as indicated by forecasts from the *World Economic Forum* (Collegium Da Vinci, 2024), analyses by *Youniversity* (2024), and the *EY Report* (2024). The way the creator of the future embraces these insights and applies acquired skills will be crucial for their well-being, particularly in maintaining agency amidst technological progress, socio-political transformations, and cultural hybridization. Undoubtedly, they can rely on the support of researchers whose intellectual efforts contribute to advancing futures literacy – not merely to keep pace with change and adapt effectively, but above all, to define the optimal direction in which the world should evolve.

4 Contributions

The book we present to our readers is a modest yet significant contribution to the interdisciplinary reflection on a creative approach to shaping the future. It focuses on the crucial role of the subject – the creator of the future – whose actions determine not only their own well-being but also the condition of the technology-saturated world in which they operate. Reading through the chapters enables a systematic analysis of who the creator of the future is, what factors shape their creativity, what outcomes they can achieve, and what consequences they must consider.

This publication consists of eight chapters written by experts from various fields, including psychology, behavioral economics, cognitive science, philosophy of nature, media studies, AI, and law. Each chapter explores a distinct aspect of human activity shaping the second quarter of the 21st century, addressing the challenges of digitalization, automation, hyperconnectivity, start-ups, globalization, as well as the issues of loneliness and alienation. The value of this book lies in the authors' creative and innovative approach to the topics discussed, with many of the ideas and research findings presented here for the first time. The authors carefully examine the future of designers, users, and AI-based systems–avoiding both catastrophic visions and excessive optimism, and inviting readers to a thoughtful, critical discussion about where we're headed.

The book opens with the chapter *Who are you really, the creator of the future? Forming identity in the age of 'Soft Cyborgization'*, authored by Paweł Fortuna, Małgorzata Puchalska-Wasyl, Łukasz Kaczmarczyk, Andrzej Cudo, and Monika MacNeil. The authors examine the impact of technology on the identity formation of young people, focusing on the concepts of identity, self, and dialogical self. They explore how interactions with multiple virtual realities influence online identity management and self-presentation. The chapter presents research findings on content personalization, the filter bubble effect, and, for the first time in the literature, results on the internal dialogical activity of gamers. The authors emphasize that online identity formation is one of the primary creative activities of young people and suggest that future research should focus on its relationship with well-being.

A person accustomed to modifying their own identity does not necessarily have to fear Moravec's vision of the "Great Flood". They can formulate their own predictions, subjectively assessing the significance of factors such as increasing computational power or the possibility of another *AI winter*. But are their predictions accurate? Can they trust their own intuitions? These questions are addressed by Piotr Zielonka and Sławomir Jakiela in the chapter *Unlocking the creative future: A framework for intuitive foresight*, where they explore how the human mind copes with uncertainty, highlighting both the advantages and pitfalls of relying on *gut feelings* when predicting the future. The authors analyze cognitive biases associated with predictive processes and introduce a theoretical model of intuitive foresight. The key elements of this model are well-documented in psychological research and form the foundations of contemporary cognitive psychology. By integrating these findings into a coherent framework, Zielonka and Jakiela provide a structured perspective on the mechanisms of intuitive forecasting and its effectiveness in an unpredictable and complex world.

The creator of the future can enhance their creativity with increasingly advanced generative AI systems. Their typology is presented by Michał Kalisz and Maksymilian Kulicki in the chapter *Creativity, reproduction, or co-creativity? The concept of friendly generative artificial intelligence*. This chapter outlines the fundamental technical principles behind generative models, explaining their mechanisms of operation. A particularly noteworthy and original aspect of the text is the introduction of the concept and principles of friendly GAI. The authors emphasize the necessity of responsible and conscious development of this technology to support human creativity rather than replace or constrain it. They also advocate for further interdisciplinary research and an open dialogue between creators, researchers, and policymakers to maximize the benefits and minimize the risks associated with the advancement of GAI.

As humans move toward a subjectively perceived future, they navigate between nature and culture, and understanding creative activity requires an exploration of fundamental emotional-motivational and cognitive processes. In the chapter *A journey through wonder: The creative power of epistemic emotions*, Anna Dutkowska examines the transformative role of epistemic emotions such as curiosity, surprise, and intellectual awe. Drawing on cognitive sciences, philosophy, and evolutionary biology, the author explores their impact on human creativity and their evolutionary roots in animals. She demonstrates that these emotions not only support exploration and problem-solving but also inspire philosophical and artistic endeavors. The chapter also addresses the potential of digital technologies in stimulating epistemic emotions. While reinforcement learning-based systems lack consciousness, they can simulate curiosity and create engaging educational environments. These findings point to new opportunities for unlocking creative potential in the era of digital revolution.

The analysis of epistemic emotions as a foundation of creative activity gains particular significance in the context of its potential effects. The following chapters direct this reflection in three different directions. The first explores the design of objects that support the well-being of the creator of the future, particularly in a eudaimonic sense. In the chapter *Imagination-Oriented Design: Why and how to create objects and environments with imaginative affordances?*, Monika Dunin-Kozicka introduces her original concept of Imagination-Oriented Design (IOD). This approach focuses on designing both physical and virtual environments that stimulate imagination. Rooted in ecological perception theory, the concept assumes that properly designed objects can activate mental affordances, or cognitive processes associated with imagination. The author highlights that within the framework of IOD, it is possible to design both objects that inherently encourage imaginative thinking and those whose material properties further intensify this effect. She also proposes a typology of such objects, representing an original contribution to the development of design theory.

The development of imagination plays a crucial role in designing phenomena that promote societal well-being. In the chapter *Creativity – A future competence for solidarity and sensitivity?*, Rafał Pastwa and Łukasz Sarowski examine how AI-based tools can support the development of future-oriented competencies such as solidarity and sensitivity. The authors argue that the effective use of technology can contribute to reducing social inequalities and improving the conditions of both individuals and societies, thereby addressing key contemporary challenges. In this context, they reference Richard Florida's concept of the *creative class* and Arthur J. Cropley's definition of creativity, expanding its significance beyond economic growth to include social and relational dimensions. Their discussion also incorporates Roland Benedikter's concept of the new global culture of the 21st century, emphasizing that creativity should not only serve as a tool for technological innovation but also as a mechanism for shaping a more just and sustainable world.

The likelihood of the "Great Flood" vision becoming a reality demands a proactive stance from the creator of the future, which implies that entities meeting the criteria of AGI should also be subject to design oversight. This issue is explored by Zbigniew Wróblewski in the chapter *Am I important to you? Designing the moral status of artificial general intelligence.* The author focuses on the challenge of identifying and designing the moral status of AGI systems, which could potentially become new members of the moral community. To define moral status, Wróblewski refers to a multi-criteria ethical theory in which cognitive criteria play a key role in determining the conditions for being both a moral subject and a moral patient. Complementing these criteria, the author develops a set of principles for designing moral status, tailored to the artificial nature of AGI. These principles encompass ontological, methodological, and meta-ethical aspects, essential for shaping the moral framework of future artificial entities.

Adopting a forward-looking perspective on innovation requires considering the legal aspects of creative activities. Kamil Muzyka, the author of the final chapter, *AI inventors and robotic infringers: Machine ingenuity and its products through the lens of patent law*, explores a future in which AI systems may become the creators of innovation, necessitating their recognition within the framework of patent law. The author explains that patent law is a branch of intellectual property law, encompassing utility patents granted for technical inventions applied across various industries. Traditionally, a patent can be obtained by an inventor or an entity assigned the rights, with the assumption that this entity is either a human or a corporation. However, the evolving role of AI in the invention process raises critical questions about whether AI systems could be recognized as inventors or co-inventors. This chapter introduces readers to key issues related to invention authorship, patent ownership, patentability criteria, and infringement, all within the context of the growing involvement of AI and robotics in creative processes.

We recognize that the considerations presented in this book represent only the tip of the iceberg when it comes to creativity in the context of *re-globalization*. While an interdisciplinary approach appears to be the most appropriate, it can never be entirely exhaustive. Beyond the topics covered, equally important questions remain: Does technology support or constrain the creative process? How does AI-driven creativity redefine the notions of authorship and originality? In what ways can creativity contribute to solving global challenges such as climate change or social crises? And how should the education system be transformed to prepare individuals for designing the future while upholding the principle of strengthening *futures literacy*? These questions are left open for further reflection and analysis in future studies.

We believe that the content of this book can serve as an inspiration for researchers, theorists, and practitioners alike. We hope it will encourage empiricists to design studies in the spirit of positive cyberpsychology, theorists to critically analyze the concept of creative thinking in the context of cyborgization, and educators and practitioners to foster in the creators of the future the ability to anticipate the consequences of their actions and take moral responsibility for them. Perhaps, through such a conscious approach, in a hundred years, humanity will become an expert primarily in the bright side of technology – developing solutions that promote well-being and harmonious cooperation between humans and technology.

References

Ancis, J. R. (2020). The age of cyberpsychology: An overview. *TMB, 1.* https://doi.org/10.1037/tmb0000009

Aoun, J. E. (2018). *Robot-proof: Higher education in the age of artificial intelligence.* MIT Press.

Benedikter, R. (2025). Futures thinking becomes a priority for all globalized societies. *Discover Global Society, 3*(1), 7. https://doi.org/10.1007/s44282-024-00128-7

Benedikter, R. (2022). Re-Globalization – Aspects of a heuristic umbrella term trying to encompass contemporary change. In R. Benedikter, M. Gruber, & I. Kofler (Eds.). (2022). *Re-Globalization: New frontiers of political, economic and social globalization.* Routledge.

Boden, M. A. (1990). *The Creative Mind: Myths and Mechanisms.* London: Weidenfeld & Nicolson.

Burke, J. (2021). Positive cyberpsychology: A conceptual framework of an emerging field. In A. Kostic & D. Chadee (Eds.), *Positive psychology: An international perspective* (pp. 85–101). Wiley-Blackwell.

Collegium Da Vinci (2024). *Przyszłość rynku pracy 2030: Jakie kompetencje będą najcenniejsze?* / The Future of the Job Market in 2030: Which Competencies Will Be the Most Valuable?. Retrieved from: https://cdv.pl/blog/rozwoj-osobisty/przyszlosc-rynku-pracy-2030-jakie-kompetencje-beda-najcenniejsze

European Commission (2021). *Proposal for a Regulation laying down harmonised rules on artificial intelligence (Artificial Intelligence Act) and amending certain Union legislative acts.* https://eur-lex.europa.eu/legal-content/EN/TXT/?uri=CELEX%3A52021PC0206

EY (2024). *Kompetencje przyszłości: Jakie umiejętności będą kluczowe w nadchodzących latach? / Future Competencies: Which Skills Will Be Key in the Coming Years?.* Retrieved from: https://www.ey.com/pl_pl/insights/workforce/kompetencje-przyszlosci

Fortuna, P. (2021). *Optimum. Idea cyberpsychologii pozytywnej / Optimum. The idea of positive cyberpsychology.* Wydawnictwo Naukowe PWN.

Fortuna, P. (2023). Positive cyberpsychology as a field of study of the well-being of people interacting with and via technology. *Frontiers in Psychology, 14.* https://doi.org/10.3389/fpsyg.2023.1053482

Fortuna, P. (2024). *Optimum 2.0. Idea cyberpsychologii pozytywnej.* Wydawnictwo Naukowe PWN.

Haidt, J. (2024). *The anxious generation: How the great rewiring of childhood is causing an epidemic of mental illness.* Penguin Press.

Moravec, H. (1998). When will computer hardware match the human brain? *Journal of Transhumanism.* Retrieved from: https://www.semanticscholar.org/paper/

When-will-computer-hardware-match–the-human-brain-Moravec/2f2f5dbfc9641e efa862bd6185877638598 9baeo

Mumford, L. (1934). *Technics and civilization*. Harcourt, Brace and Company.

OECD. (2019). *Recommendation of the Council on Artificial Intelligence*. Organisation for Economic Co-operation and Development. Retrieved from: https://legalinstruments.oecd.org/en/instruments/OECD-LEGAL-0449

Peters, D., Calvo, R. A., & Ryan, R. M. (2018). Designing for motivation, engagement and wellbeing in digital experience. *Frontiers in Psychology*, *9*, 797. https://doi.org/10.3389/fpsyg.2018.00797

Riva, G., Banos, R. M., Botella, C., Wiederhold, B. K., & Gaggioli, A. (2012). Positive technology: Using interactive technologies to promote positive functioning. *Cyberpsychology, Behavior, and Social Networking*, *15*(2), 69–77. https://doi.org/10.1089/cyber.2011.0139

Russell, S. (2019). *Human compatible: Artificial intelligence and the problem of control*. Viking.

Ryan, R. M., & Deci, E. L. (2000). Self-determination theory and the facilitation of intrinsic motivation, social development, and well-being. *American Psychologist*, *55*(1), 68–78. https://doi.org/10.1037/0003-066X.55.1.68

Singh, A. K., & Singh, P. K. (2019). *Recent trends, current research in cyberpsychology: A Literature review*. Retrieved from: https://link.gale.com/apps/doc/A622150365/AONE?u=anon~43107a07&sid=googleScholar&xid=8al9add

Steger, M. F., Benedikter, R., Pechlaner, H., & Kofler, I. (2023). Introduction. In R. Benedikter, M. B. Steger, H. Pechlaner, H., & I. Kofler, (Eds.). *Globalization: Past, present, future* (pp. 1–8). University of California Press.

Steger, M., & James, P. (2020). Disjunctive Globalization in the Era of the Great Unsettling. *Theory, Culture & Society*, *37*(7–8), 187–203. https://doi.org/10.1177/0263276420957744

Tegmark, M. (2017). *Life 3.0: Being human in the age of artificial intelligence*. Alfred A. Knopf.

UNESCO. (1971). Menton appeal. *The UNESCO Courier*.

Weinberg, J. M. (2007). How to challenge intuitions empirically without risking skepticism. *Midwest Studies in Philosophy*, *31*(1), 318–343. https://doi.org/10.1111/j.1475-4975.2007.00157.x

Youniversity (2024). *Kompetencje przyszłości: Top 10 / Future Competencies: Top 10*. Retrieved from: https://youniversity.be/blog/kompetencje-przyszlosci-top-10

CHAPTER 1

Who Are You Really, the Creator of the Future? Forming Identity in the Age of 'Soft Cyborgization'

Paweł Fortuna[*,1], *Małgorzata Puchalska-Wasyl*[*,2], *Łukasz Kaczmarczyk*[*,3], *Andrzej Cudo*[*,4] *and Monika McNeill*[*,5]

Abstract

Soft cyborgization refers to the increasing dependence of human functioning on technological innovations. In this article, we explore how these novel conditions shape the identity formation of young people. We begin by conceptualizing the following key terms: "identity," "self," and "dialogical self," which serve as the foundation for discussing how identity extends through engagement in multiple virtual realities. We then examine the technological factors that influence self-presentation in networked realities and the management of virtual identity. Following this, we review psychological research that underscores the strong connection between digital technology use and identity formation. Specifically, we investigate how website personalization, and the filter bubble effect can reinforce individual identity. We also address the significance of online self-presentation in maintaining identity coherence, the role of avatar creation and manipulation in fostering an authentic identity, and how gaming contributes to the expansion of the dialogical self. Finally, we conclude by considering future perspectives on identity formation that promote well-being.

Keywords

identity – self – virtual identity – dialogical self – identity coherence – Proteus effect

* The John Paul II Catholic University of Lublin, Institute of Psychology Lublin, Poland

1 https://orcid.org/0000-0002-0633-4453

2 https://orcid.org/0000-0003-4295-8308

3 https://orcid.org/0009-0001-9337-1251

4 https://orcid.org/0000-0001-7424-8576

5 Glasgow Caledonian University, Glasgow, United Kingdom, https://orcid.org/0000-0001-8936-8300

In 2020, when Pokémon Go had been installed on over 514 million devices worldwide, a teenage girl named Laura requested her father's company in locating a PokéStop in their city. She had a specific site in mind: the Marie Curie monument, where she anticipated maximizing the benefits of augmented reality, such as capturing Pokémon. Upon arriving at the location, her father observed the statue of the Nobel laureate and remarked, "There is a monument, so there should be a PokéStop here." Laura, while focusing on her smartphone screen, responded, "There is a PokéStop here, so there should be a monument of Marie Curie." This exchange illustrates two distinct approaches to identifying the target location. Laura, a *digital native* (Prensky, 2001), was born into an era of pervasive computer technology, seamlessly integrating and intuitively mastering digital innovations. In contrast, her father, a *digital immigrant*, adapts to technology at a slower pace, often consulting user manuals and relying on traditional sources of information.

Laura and her peers are growing up in an electronically enriched world, one that has been shaped through iterative processes by previous generations. They are deeply engaged with STARA technology – encompassing Smart Technology, Artificial Intelligence, Robotics, and Algorithms (Brougham & Haar, 2018) – and navigate virtual environments where individuals are represented by nicknames, avatars, and game characters. By actively participating in a reality that merges the virtual with the physical, they unconsciously traverse the human-cyborg continuum (Jupiter, 2016 Their cognitive processes increasingly integrate with AI-based systems, which, akin to smartphones and personal computers, serve as a form of electronic skin. The internet and computer games offer a *virtual cognitive niche,* defined as environments where information and tools are shared and distributed among users – sometimes by other users, and sometimes directly from digital platforms (Arfini et al., 2021, p. 200). This gradual and often imperceptible incorporation of technology into daily life, and even into the human body, which becomes a natural extension of oneself, is referred to as *soft cyborgization* (Kamieński, 2014). A key aspect of this phenomenon is the use of technological tools and available affordances to construct a virtual identity (also known as digital identity, online identity, virtual self, or digital self) – a crucial component of one's presence in cyberspace (Suler, 2017).

As the creators of the future transition into adulthood, they will assume diverse roles that will shape not only social reality and the technosphere but, most critically, their own identities. They will design and navigate their lives within the context of ambitious visions such as the Metaverse, mind uploading, and artificial selves, while also confronting the fears and challenges associated with advancements in artificial intelligence (AI), including superhuman AI. These individuals will come to understand that technological innovations do more than merely entertain – they have a profound impact on the quality of human life. Consequently, they will recognize the opportunity, and indeed the necessity, to participate in the crucial debate on how technology can best serve humanity – a discussion that Tegmark (2017) referred to as "the most important conversation of our time" (p. 37). A critical component of this dialogue must occur within the mind of each individual, starting with the fundamental question: "Who am I?" Continuous immersion in the dynamic landscape of digital worlds means that the quality of the answer to this question hinges on the self's ability to manage the polyphony – and often the cacophony – produced by various virtual identities.

1 The Multifaceted Nature of Identity

Digital natives are exposed to a vast array of ideas, meanings, and values, integrating elements from the virtual space that progressively become integral to their personal, multi-faceted world. Their identity, which consists of various roles adopted and transformed according to different contexts, is neither clear-cut nor stable. For instance, an individual might simultaneously assume the roles of a warrior in an electronic game, an influencer on Instagram, and a student in real life. Furthermore, they cultivate multiple group identities, which are shaped and developed through their affiliations with both real-world environments and virtual communities.

1.1 *Identity and Self*

The semantic fields of the concepts of "identity" and "self" often overlap, leading to their frequent interchangeability in discourse. When analyzing the relationship between these constructs, many researchers emphasize the superior status of the self (e.g., Soenens & Vansteenkiste, 2011). Conversely, some scholars argue that the self is subsumed within the broader concept of identity (Morf & Mischel, 2012) or view the self as a specific facet of identity (Sendyka, 2015). Generally speaking, while identity addresses the question "Who am I?", the self pertains to "What is my experience of being myself?" or "How do I perceive myself?" Identity is more closely related to an individual's positioning within social and cultural contexts, whereas the self focuses on personal experience and self-perception.

The close and intricate relationship between identity and self is notably articulated in William James' classical concept (1890). James' approach is comprehensive, distinguishing between two primary aspects: the "I" (pure/active self) and the "Me" (cognitive self). The "I" represents the subjective aspect of the self, responsible for present perceptions and encompassing the continuity of personal experience. In contrast, the "Me" includes all components perceived as part of one's identity, which can be observed and analyzed: (1) the material self – encompassing possessions such as the body, clothing, home, and close relationships; (2) the social self – varying according to the multiple social groups with which an individual identifies; and (3) the spiritual self – comprising the inner self, including thoughts, feelings, beliefs, values, and consciousness.

James' concept aligns with contemporary integrated models of identity. For instance, Vignoles et al. (2011) propose that identity includes selected or assigned personal characteristics, self-beliefs, roles, and positions relative to significant others, as well as membership in groups and social categories, and identification with valued possessions and a sense of belonging to particular spaces. In the process of identity formation, individuals cognitively construct a set of defining characteristics that delineate who they are, considering their attributes, reputation, values, and self-concept (Oleś, 2012).

1.2 *Extension of Identity*

James' distinction between the "I" and the "Me" serves as a primary inspiration for Hubert Hermans' development of the dialogical self theory (Hermans, 2001, 2002, 2003), which provides a valuable framework for examining how digital natives, operating within multiple virtual realities, extend their identities. Hermans (2003) defines the dialogical self as a dynamic multiplicity of relatively autonomous I-positions. The "I," akin to James' concept, represents the center of intentionality and can shift from one I-position to another based on situational and temporal changes, thereby adopting various, often opposing, perspectives. The "I" possesses the capacity to imaginatively endow each I-position with a distinct voice, resulting in each I-position narrating its own experiences. Additionally, I-positions can engage in dialogue with one another. These interactions, characterized by agreement, disagreement, questions, and answers, are akin to the dynamics observed within human societies, leading Hermans to describe the dialogical self as a "society of mind" (Hermans, 2002). Each I-position, by crafting a narrative about itself and its experiences, contributes to the formation of its own self-concept, paralleling James' "Me." As I-positions exchange information about their self-concepts and the world, they collectively contribute to a narratively structured self.

I-positions within the dialogical self can be categorized as either internal or external. Internal I-positions are perceived as integral parts of the self (e.g., "I-son," "I-older brother," "I-student," "I-player"), while external I-positions are experienced as components of the environment (e.g., "my father," "my younger brother," "my lecturer," "Geralt, the hero of the game"). Despite their external nature, all I-positions are considered part of what the individual regards as "one's own" (James' "Me") and are accessible to the "I" (Hermans, 2001; Hermans & Hermans-Jansen, 2001).

I-positions receive their importance as a consequence of mutual interaction. Internal I-positions gain importance through the relationships they enter into with one or more external I-positions (e.g., I have an internal I-position "I-older brother" because it is in a dialogical relationship with the external I-position "my younger brother"). External I-positions, on the other hand, are relevant from the perspective of one or more internal I-positions (e.g., my lecturer becomes an element of my dialogical self because it enters into a dialogical relationship with the "I-student" position). Interactions between I-positions can take the form of real or imagined: negotiation, cooperation, opposition, conflict, agreement, etc. (cf. Hermans, 2001; 2003).

The significance of particular I-positions fluctuates over time, influenced by situational demands that guide the course of dialogical processes within the self. For example, when engaging in a virtual reality game, the I-positions "I-player" and "Geralt, the hero of the game" become more prominent, while "I-older brother" and "my younger brother," as well as "my lecturer" and " I-student," recede into the background. Hermans (2001; Hermans & Hermans-Jansen, 2001) asserts that I-positions within the dialogical self are in constant flux; some positions may emerge while others recede, but background positions can be reactivated by personal intention or situational triggers.

Moreover, the movement of I-positions involves not only the activation of those previously in the background but also the introduction of new positions from the environment. For instance, when a child starts school, they encounter a teacher (an external I-position) who facilitates their experience as a student (an internal I-position). Similarly, entering new virtual realities can expand the dialogical self, incorporating new external and internal positions. This fluidity suggests that internal I-positions can become external, and vice versa. For example, a teenager might create a story with a protagonist that materializes as an extension of themselves (externalization). Conversely, a person might identify so deeply with a game character that they experience a form of internalization (Hermans, 2003; Hermans & Hermans-Jansen, 2001).

1.3 *Identity Coherence*

Identity can exhibit varying degrees of stability or fluidity (Vignoles et al., 2011). The variability, flexibility, and multifunctionality of identity are increasingly viewed as adaptive responses to a complex reality, aligning with the observation that "it is no longer fidelity to specific ideals and consistency in fulfilling life tasks, but change that becomes its content" (Oleś, 2012, p. 120). A multifaceted identity does not inherently conflict with living "in accordance with oneself," and identity can be strengthened by adapting to constantly emerging challenges. Maintaining mental health and well-being in the context of multiple identities is feasible through identity coherence (Erikson, 1968). This concept encompasses the overall consistency and stability of an individual's identity across various life domains, referring to the extent to which different roles and aspects of identity are integrated into a coherent self-image. According to James (1890), the sense of coherence is provided by the "I," which ensures continuity of the self despite the diversity of the "Me." Identity coherence fosters self-acceptance, emotional well-being, and psychological stability during adolescence and is associated with achievement motivation and commitment to life goals (e.g., Luyckx et al., 2006). Conversely, a lack of integration can lead to identity confusion, which is often accompanied by increased anxiety and withdrawal – symptoms increasingly observed among young individuals navigating networked realities (Haidt, 2024).

2 Managing Virtual Identities

The architects of the future shape and reconstruct virtual identities through the relative freedom afforded by self-presentation mechanisms. Virtual identity refers to the configuration of a person's defining characteristics within cyberspace, resulting from both self-creation and interaction with other users (Kim et al., 2011). It is distinct from digital identity, which denotes a collection of personal information used for online identification, such as names, dates of birth, and email addresses.

The shaping of virtual identity is facilitated by the unique features and affordances of different platforms, which provide a cognitive infrastructure enabling users to present themselves through profile creation, avatar selection, character choice in digital games, and the formation of personal networks. Decisions regarding these aspects are influenced by current preferences and goals, intertwining the search for "Who am I?" with considerations of "What do I care about?" (Archer, 2000). Within the dynamic environment of cyberactivity, users experiment with various images, engaging in continuous self-creation and self-verification. They may pursue different self-presentation motives, including strategic (e.g., crafting an image for career advancement), deceptive (e.g., creating an image to attract a partner), or false (e.g., designing an image to garner admiration) (Ranzini & Lutz, 2017). In the terms of James (1890) and Hermans (2001, 2003), this ongoing process involves the creation of various "Me" identities through a multiplicity of I-positions. Importantly, individuals are always engaged in self-presentation, even when attempting to conceal their authentic self.

2.1 *Users' Online Profiles*

Access to the internet facilitates the creation of personal profiles across a variety of platforms, including social networking sites (e.g., Facebook, Instagram, X, TikTok), career development portals (e.g., LinkedIn), creative platforms (e.g., Pinterest, Spotify, YouTube), and blogging and website platforms (e.g., Medium, WordPress). Users engage in self-presentation through a multitude of data entry modalities, including visual (e.g., selfies, vlogs), audio (e.g., voice messages, podcasts, compositions), and textual forms (e.g., posts, comments, articles), as well as by interacting with posted content (e.g., liking, subscribing, blocking users, sharing content).

The act of posting information about oneself not only affirms digital existence but also serves various functions, such as self-presentation, documentation of personal experiences, sharing knowledge, inspiring discussions, and, for influencers or podcasters, generating income. The diversification of online presence results in varied forms of expression, ranging from formal to informal, and necessitates adaptation to specific social contexts. Variability in self-presentation, autobiographical narrative development, and the depth of information shared can differ significantly. For example, young adults in China are less likely than their American counterparts to post optimistic content on online profiles and are more prone to discussing personal matters (Mazur & Li, 2016). Conversely, young adults in Japan tend to share more personal information on social media compared to their peers in the USA, often using pseudonyms (Acar, 2013).

2.2 *Avatars*

Avatars function as virtual proxies for the self, serving as stand-ins for the user's real-world identity (Friedenberg, 2020). Suler (2016) categorizes avatars into sixteen distinct types, including real-face, animal, cartoon, celebrity, idiosyncratic, and environmental avatars. Users often employ multiple avatars simultaneously, adjusting them according to their preferences, mood, and objectives. This selection and modification of avatars are integral to the broader process of virtual identity formation, influenced by motives such as self-presentation, self-exploration, impression management, partner-seeking, and the avoidance of criticism and shame (Huang et al., 2021).

In platforms like Second Life and VRChat, which can be considered precursors to the Metaverse, users have the capability to create and meticulously customize avatars, thereby showcasing their distinct identities, interests, and passions. While avatar customization in these environments often emphasizes elements such as clothing, accessories, and physical appearance, it generally does not extend to developing detailed backstories or intricate personality traits. Conversely, in contemporary open-world action-adventure games like GTAV Online, avatar customization remains a prominent feature, focusing primarily on visual appearance and attire, but does not typically encompass comprehensive identity development.

2.3 *Game Characters*

Game characters are often identified with avatars, but it is possible to point out characteristics that differentiate them. While avatars are usually static, a game character is controlled by the user (or by the computer), participates in the narrative, tasks, and interactions in the game. Additionally, game characters can have specific roles, skills, attributes, and stories that affect the way the game is played. As the game progresses, characters can develop, gain experience, items, and skills. Moreover, the gamer can, to a greater or lesser extent, give the game character different physical and mental characteristics.

Games facilitate diverse forms of character creation and manipulation, with distinctions emerging based on the nature of representation: narrative, simulation, and communication (Schröter & Thon, 2014). In the context of narrative representation, players engage with a game character designed by the developer, immersing themselves in the character's world and storyline with limited opportunities for customization (e.g., S.T.A.L.K.E.R., Far Cry). In contrast, simulation representation allows players extensive customization and development of their characters across multiple dimensions, significantly affecting gameplay dynamics (e.g., Skyrim, Diablo 3).

Communication representation, in addition to incorporating narrative and simulation aspects, involves interactive elements between gamers, which also impacts character customization and development (e.g., World of Warcraft, Guild Wars, Star Wars). It is noteworthy that these forms of representation are not mutually exclusive and may overlap. Some game characters evolve into transmedia figures, gaining independent life across digital media platforms (Thon, 2019) (e.g., Ezio Auditore da Firenze, Lara Croft). Furthermore, there can be a reciprocal relationship between the gamer's identity and the game character they embody or customize, reflecting a dynamic interaction between the player's self-concept and the virtual persona.

There are at least two theoretical approaches to understanding game characters customized by gamers. The first approach posits that game characters function as virtual projections or digital embodiments of the gamer's identity and self. In contrast, the second approach views game characters as mere artifacts for exploring identities that diverge from the gamer's actual self, thus not serving as embodiments of the gamer's identity (Castronova, 2003; Mancini & Sibilla, 2017). Sibilla and Mancini (2018), drawing from literature reviews, self-discrepancy theory (Higgins, 1987), and the virtual identity discrepancy model (Jin, 2012), identified two primary types of relationships between the self of Massively Multiplayer Online Worlds (MMOW) gamers and their game characters: idealization and actualization. Idealization refers to the portrayal of a game character as an embodiment of the gamer's ideal self, with no direct correlation to the gamer's actual self. In contrast, actualization involves the representation of a game character as an enhanced version of the gamer's real self. Actualization has been found to be positively associated with higher self-esteem, improved online social interactions, and more favorable gaming experiences (Sibilla & Mancini, 2018). Conversely, idealization has been linked to problematic game use (Leménager et al., 2013).

Additionally, Mancini and Sibilla (2017) described two further relationships between the self of MMOW gamers and their game characters: the negative hero, which represents an antithesis to the gamer's self, and the alter ego, which mirrors the gamer's actual self, incorporating both positive and negative traits. Moreover, Mancini et al. (2019) introduced the concept of the utopian game character, which transcends the gamer's ideal self. Thus, it can be posited that game characters may serve as a form of digital projection or virtual embodiment of the gamer's self, encompassing a range of relationships from idealized representations to enhanced or contrasting versions of the self.

3 The Impact of Technology Use on Identity Formation

Several decades ago, in the context of analyzing audio-visual media, McLuhan noted: "We shape our tools, and thereafter our tools shape us" (1964, p. 8). This dependency is particularly evident in the discourse surrounding cyborgization within the framework of transhumanism. A pertinent example is Neil Harbisson, who, through the integration of an antenna called Eye-borg into his skull – designed to convert visual images into auditory signals – has described himself as a trans-species entity (Łukaszewicz Alcaraz, 2020). In this context, the identity of an individual undergoing soft cyborgization is constructed in relation to the virtual identities they develop, and is shaped by the ongoing negotiation between these virtual constructs and their authentic self.

3.1 *Personalization and the Filter Bubble Trap*

Every person with intentional or unconscious contact with digital technology continuously provides data about themselves, creating a mathematical-statistical representation of themselves, which Deleuze described as a *dividual* (1990). The individual (a flesh-and-blood user) and the dividual form a pair of agents functioning in a loop of continuous feedback – a system pulsing to the rhythm set by the transfer of data in a brain-algorithmic loop. Each user's keystroke, voice recording, or image on personal profiles expands the dividual's resources, creating an invisible yet algorithmically accessible image of their individuality. Users are usually unaware of their role as data providers feeding the cyberbusiness (Zuboff, 2019). Internet portals appear more like a "common pasture," although in fact, they are owned by specific organizations that set the framework and rules of presence, and thus the possibilities of creating and expressing one's identity.

The algorithms that constitute the "mind" of the dividual systematically analyze user data, including browsing history, click patterns, and social interactions. This analytical process culminates in the personalization of content recommendations tailored to individual user preferences. This process, known as content curation, involves selecting, organizing, and presenting content in a way that is interesting to the user (Anderson, 2015). Personalization algorithms can lead to the creation of *filter bubbles*, where users are exposed to content that confirms their views (Pariser, 2011). According to Zuboff (2019), these algorithms contribute to creating homogeneous information environments, which in turn can reinforce an individual's identity by continuously adjusting content to their previous choices. Isolation from diverse viewpoints and information that contradicts one's beliefs can result in the reinforcement of existing attitudes, leading to prejudice and radicalization of views (Wolfowicz et al., 2021; Zakaria et al., 2018).

Dąbrowski et al. (2023) found that intellectual humility may play a vital role in mitigating the adverse effects of filter bubbles. Primarily because intellectually humble individuals are more conscious of filter bubble issues, display less bias towards information on social media, and have weaker group identification on these platforms. Unfortunately, despite being more aware of filter bubbles, intellectually humble individuals do not necessarily use more methods to counteract them. Breaking free from them requires critical thinking skills, diversifying information sources (e.g., engaging in dialogue with people with different views), and education about media and algorithms (Kumar & Shadbolt, 2018). This is not an easy process, as many companies treat personalization algorithms as trade secrets, meaning that the details of their operation are proprietary.

3.2 *Personal Online Profiles and the Challenge for Identity Coherence*

Research on the impact of personal profiles on identity formation predominantly focuses on social media platforms. Future generations primarily access these platforms via smartphones, which are carried ubiquitously, including in educational settings. The pervasive use of these devices has been associated with a notable increase in mental health issues among adolescents (Haidt, 2024). Smartphones function as "experience blockers," impeding engagement in real-world interactions and independent play, both of which are essential for healthy development. Moreover, studies involving students aged 12–16 have found a correlation between problematic smartphone use and feelings of loneliness (Przepiórka et al., 2024). Valkenburg and Peter (2008) further discovered that lonely adolescents are more inclined to engage in virtual identity experimentation compared to their non-lonely peers.

Individuals escaping from loneliness feed on virtual interaction with others (represented by avatars) and the feedback they receive from them. Effective management of multiple identities, as well as adjusting to the diverse norms and expectations of internet users should lead to identity coherence – that is, maintaining personal integrity despite the various and sometimes conflicting online roles (Luyckx et al., 2006; Luyckx et al., 2008). On the other hand, the lack of proper integration between online and offline identities can lead to feelings of disconnection or identity fragmentation (boyd, 2014). Research shows that positive effects on identity coherence are observed in individuals who prefer more surface-level, shallow online self-presentation (e.g., posting status updates that do not provide meaningful insights into the user's thoughts or feelings; Yang et al., 2017) and are more engaged in presenting their true self on social media rather than an idealized or false image (Michikyan, 2020). It was also found that the negative relationship between online inner-level self-presentation (e.g., a weak point they want to overcome, an ability they worry about) and identity-development process applies to individuals high in neuroticism (Kawamoto, 2021). The source of deviations from authentic self-presentation is the adaptation of online profile content to perceived trends. Social media profiles serve as a reference point for many people in constructing their social identity. Unfortunately, such comparisons negatively affect the self-esteem of many individuals (Steers et al., 2014).

Another motivation for adolescents to present themselves differently than in reality is the exploration of their own identity (Valkenburg et al., 2005). It was found that adolescents with a less coherent sense of self are more likely to engage in identity experiments on the internet (Ceyhan, 2014), and present their false self to a greater extent on Facebook (Michikyan et al., 2015). Users tend to build a better self-image by showing a positive side of their life and avoiding posting negative events, enhancing profile photos, lying about physical descriptors (e.g., height and weight), or presenting their personality traits in a more desirable way (Huang et al., 2021). Research shows that while presenting positive aspects of the self on online profiles can boost self-esteem (Gonzales & Hancock, 2011), false self-presentation is a risky behavior that can result in increased anxiety, depression, and stress (Duan et al., 2020). Furthermore, discrepancies between offline and online images can be noticed by peers. It turns out that when inconsistencies were observed, individuals were likely to make negative attributions about the authenticity and honesty of the person's self-presentation, which has negative social consequences (low trust and credibility; DeAndrea & Walther, 2011).

3.3 *The Relationship between Avatars, Online Activity and Identity Development*

Empirical research has established a significant relationship between the selection of avatars and online behavior, highlighting that the formation of identity in digital contexts is influenced by social interaction rather than occurring in isolation. For instance, users of the virtual world Second Life who chose avatars more attractive than their real selves exhibited increased confidence, sociability, risk-taking, and extroversion within the virtual environment, particularly if they were less confident and introverted in real life (Messinger et al., 2008).

Behaviors that reflect personal values play a crucial role in shaping an authentic identity, as individuals who act in alignment with their beliefs experience enhanced internal coherence and strengthened identity (Gentile, 2012). Research indicates that the customization and personalization of avatars foster greater identification with these virtual representations, leading to increased engagement in activities that require trust and cooperation (Pan & Steed, 2017) and enhancing the coherence between one's identity and actions within the virtual environment (Waltemate et al., 2018). For example, users who present themselves honestly and altruistically online are more likely to participate in pro-social crowdfunding efforts (Cox et al., 2018).

The feedback received from online activities – such as likes, comments, and shares – can either affirm or undermine an individual's self-presentation, thereby influencing subsequent behavior and self-perception. Positive feedback on social media posts related to pro-social behavior, for example, reinforces the likelihood of future altruistic actions (Cox et al., 2018). Research involving Singaporean teenage girls has shown that positive feedback in the form of likes and favorable comments enhances self-esteem, while negative feedback or lack of attention may induce feelings of inadequacy or self-doubt

(Chua & Chang, 2016). This supports the broader principle that affirmative opinions on social media can elevate self-esteem and reinforce aspects of identity that receive validation, whereas negative feedback may prompt self-reflection and adjustments in self-presentation (Walther et al., 2011).

3.4 *The Proteus Effect*

The Proteus Effect is a psychological phenomenon which may occur when individuals adjust their attitudes, traits and behaviors based on the characteristics of their digital presentation in the form of an avatar or in-game character. In the game context, there may be an adjustment between the gamer and a game character (see Szolin et al., 2023; Yee & Bailenson, 2007; Yee et al., 2009). Specifically, the change in gamers' attitudes, traits and behaviors can take place as a result of their virtual self-presentation in the gameplay through their game characters. The Proteus Effect can lead to changes in attitudes, traits and behaviour of the gamer both in and out of the game (Szolin et al., 2023). For example, a gamer with an attractive and confident game character can feel confident in interacting with other individuals both, in the gaming world as well as in the real world outside the game.

Gamers who are more immersed in the gaming world tend to demonstrate heightened the Proteus Effect behaviors (Stavropoulos et al., 2021). Additionally, the potential for multidimensional customization of a game character, which is commonly seen, e.g., in Massively Multiplayer Online Role-Playing Games (MMORPG), favors the emergence of the Proteus Effect (Sun et al., 2023; Szolin et al., 2023). This effect is enhanced when gamers combine their own traits with those of the game character, who represents a trait desirable by gamers and gamers' embodied presence (Praetorius & Görlich, 2020). However, when game character customization is not fully possible and the game character is imposed by the gameplay, gamers may sometimes manifest dissatisfaction related to their own characteristics and attributes, which may be perceived as worse than the game character's characteristics and attributes (see Sylvia et al., 2014). Overall, the Proteus Effect shows the possible dynamic interactions between individuals and their virtual presentations. Consequently, this effect allows to point out that the development of individual's identity and self can be linked to the interaction with an individual's own virtual presentation in the form of an avatar or game character.

3.5 *Game Characters in Dialogical Self*

Research into the extension of identity through game characters has been explored within the framework of dialogical self theory. In a preliminary study, Fortuna et al. (submitted) found that 83% of participants (n = 203) engaged in imaginary dialogues with in-game characters. A detailed analysis involving 69 individuals identified 158 distinct characters, predominantly from RPG and adventure games, with Geralt of Rivia from "The Witcher" series being the most frequently mentioned character.

The analysis of player interviews revealed that engaging in dialogue within games provides a variety of benefits, which can be broadly categorized into personal development and an enhanced gaming experience. Within the category of personal development, players described how dialoguing models their behavior (e.g., "A bit more self-confidence would be necessary. Such a character, for example, has all of that ..."), improves cognitive engagement by taking on new perspectives (e.g., "This experience cultivates in me the habit of considering others' viewpoints."; "I believe it facilitates a greater understanding of the emotions of those around me."), and develops parasocial relations with game characters, who offer emotional support and a sense of security (e.g., "I think it's because, for example, even during the worst times in life or something like that, I could just sit down, turn on my Nintendo, and I knew that he would be there ..."). Additionally, some players emphasized the emotional benefits of dialogue, such as processing and regulating emotions (e.g., "In my personal life, as I mentioned earlier, it allows me to step back from life's challenges. On difficult days, it helps me regain calm and maintain emotional stability."). The second major category of benefits relates to game experience improvement. Many players expressed that dialogue allows them to experience adventure in other worlds (e.g., "... to immerse oneself and be in a different world than the one we live in. And to escape from some kind of reality."). Moreover, dialogue contributed to greater immersion in the storyline, making gameplay feel more engaging and lifelike (e.g., "I believe that this enables me to immerse myself more fully in the game's narrative and comprehend the characters on a deeper level.").

In analysis based on Hermans and Hermans-Jansen's (1995) categorization of experiences and incorporating quantitative data from the same study, four types of game characters were identified (Puchalska-Wasyl et al., submitted). The first type, "Faithful Friend," is characterized by a sense of "strength and unity," representing a powerful and caring character whose close bond with the player provides a source of strength. The second type, "Ambivalent Parent," shares similarities with the "Faithful Friend" but is distinguished by the proportion of positive to negative feelings experienced in the relationship. This character resembles a parent who exhibits both pride and ambivalence, reflecting fluctuating emotions depending on the player's behavior. The third type, "Proud Rival," is defined by the experience of "autonomy and success," characterized by self-confidence and a sense of superiority over the player, with no emotional bond or closeness. This type corresponds to three out of four internal interlocutors identified in previous research (Puchalska-Wasyl, 2015, 2016). The fourth type, "Hesitant Doer," is similar to the "Proud Rival" in its focus on self-improvement but differs in experiencing ambivalence and doubt about the value of its actions, indicating a less robust sense of self.

In the context of Hermans' theory, each game character functions as an I-position within a person's dialogical self, possessing its own autonomous voice to comment on life events from its perspective. This interaction occurs not only during gameplay but also when the person occupies other I-positions, such as "I-son" or "I-student." The presence of game characters as I-positions allows for dialogue with other I-positions, contributing to the formation of a narratively structured self and identity. Our findings confirm that game characters do play a role in the dialogical self of players, although their precise impact on identity formation remains unclear. The effect is likely influenced by the type of game character, the level of engagement with the game, potential addiction, and the nature of other I-positions within the dialogical self. Further research is required to elucidate the extent of this influence and its implications for identity development.

4 A Look into the Future

What will be the nature of the identity for individuals like Laura and her peers, the so-called creators of the future? In contrast to earlier paradigms of identity formation, which emphasized the development of a stable inner core (Erickson, 1968), contemporary conditions of soft cyborgization provide unprecedented opportunities for identity experimentation and feedback acquisition. As individuals navigate their existence as "dividuals" and data contributors for cyberbusiness, they face challenges such as filter bubbles, intrusive social comparisons, rapidly evolving trends in self-presentation, and the allure of monetizing their online image.

It is possible that functioning in a layered reality and spontaneous, unregulated identity processes will lead to the emergence of something like a "hybrid identity" (or *h-self*). Such a phenomenon is observed in the context of postcolonialism, globalization, migration, and transculturalism analyses (Bhabha, 1994) and is discussed within the framework of the concept of the dialogical self (Hermans, 2004). A hybrid identity would be a synthesis of real and virtual elements, a new quality, consolidated by the "I". The role of stimulators is played by combining real characteristics (e.g., interests) with fictional ones (avatar and game character traits), mixing real and fictional roles (as in

RPGS), as well as assimilating diverse cultural content from the entire world represented on the Internet. A premise that inclines one to draw such futuristic visions is the observed phenomenon of incorporating game characters into the dialogical self.

Currently, in alignment with positive cyberpsychology principles (Fortuna, 2023), the technosphere can be viewed as a resource with the potential to enhance well-being through thoughtful self-development. Achieving a stable and coherent identity remains crucial for healthy personality development and mental health. However, effectively managing the technological environment necessitates addressing not only the question "Who am I?" but also "Who would I like/should I be?". This requires cultivating the concept of the "best self" – an individual who maximizes their strengths and realizes their full potential, aligned with their highest values, aspirations, and goals. The creators of the future will benefit from thoughtful guidance and a "mental compass" to navigate the complexities of multi-identity and achieve holistic well-being.

References

Acar, A. (2013). Culture and social media usage: Analysis of Japanese Twitter users. *International Journal of Electronic Commerce Studies*, *4*, 21–32. https://doi.org/10.7903/ijecs.989

Anderson, S. W. (2015). *Content curation: How to avoid information overload.* Corwin Press.

Archer, M. S. (2000). *Being human: The problem of agency.* Cambridge University Press.

Arfini, S., Botta Parandera, L., Gazzaniga, C. et al. (2021). Online identity crisis identity issues in online communities. *Minds & Machines*, *31*, 193–212. https://doi.org/10.1007/s11023-020-09542-7

Baumeister, R. F., & Tice, D. M. (1986). Four selves, two motives, and a substitute process self-regulation model. In R. F. Baumeister (Ed.), *Public self and private self* (pp. 63–74). New York, NY: Springer-Verlag. https://doi.org/10.1007/978-1-4613-9564-5_3

Bhabha, H. K. (1994). *The Location of Culture.* Routledge.

Boyd, D. (2014). *It's complicated: The social lives of networked teens.* Yale University Press.

Brougham, D., & Haar, J. (2018). Smart technology, Artificial Intelligence, robotics, and algorithms (STARA): Employees' perceptions of our future workplace. *Journal of Management & Organization*, *24*(2), 239–257. https://doi.org/10.1017/jmo.2016.55

Castronova, E. (2003). Theory of the Avatar. Available at SSRN: https://ssrn.com/abstract=385103 or http://dx.doi.org/10.2139/ssrn.385103

Ceyhan, E. (2014). Internet-based identity experiments in late adolescence. *Egitim ve Bilim, 39*(176), 249–258. https://doi.org/10.15390/EB.2014.1366

Chua, T. H. H., & Chang, L. (2016). Follow me and like my beautiful selfies: Singapore teenage girls' engagement in self-presentation and peer comparison on social media. *Computers in Human Behavior, 55*, 190–197. https://doi.org/10.1016/j.chb.2015.09.011

Cox, J., Nguyen, T., Thorpe, A., Ishizaka, A., Chakhar, S., & Meech, L. (2018). Being seen to care: The relationship between self-presentation and contributions to online pro-social crowdfunding campaigns. *Computers in Human Behavior, 83*, 45–55. https://doi.org/10.1016/j.chb.2018.01.014

Dąbrowski, G., Kutnik, J., & Bąk, W. (2023). Beyond the echo chamber: Intellectual humility and functioning in the context of filter bubble. Poster presented at the XV Congress of the Polish Society of Social Psychology (PSPS), Lublin, Poland, September 21–23.

DeAndrea, D. C., & Walther, J. B. (2011). Attributions for inconsistencies between online and offline self-presentations. *Communication Research, 38*(6), 805–825. https://doi.org/10.1177/0093650210385340

Duan, W., He, C., & Tang, X. (2020). Why browsing and posting on WeChat Moments? The relationships among fear of missing out, strategic self-presentation, and online social anxiety. *Cyberpsychology, Behavior, and Social Networking, 23*, 708–714. https://doi.org/10.1089/cyber.2019.0654

Erickson, E. H. (1968). *Identity: Youth and crisis*. Norton.

Fortuna, P. (2023). Positive cyberpsychology as a field of study of the well-being of people interacting with and via technology. *Frontiers in Psychology, 14*, Article 1053482. https://doi.org/10.3389/fpsyg.2023.1053482

Fortuna, P., Puchalska-Wasyl, M., Cudo, A., & Kaczmarczyk, Ł. (submitted). A new look at the relationship between the gamer and the game character: An exploratory study of internal dialogical activity. *Cyberpsychology, Behavior and Social Networking*.

Fox, J., & Rooney, M. C. (2015). The dark triad and trait self-objectification as predictors of men's use and self-presentation behaviors on social networking sites. *Personality and Individual Differences, 76*, 161–165. https://doi.org/10.1016/j.paid.2014.12.017

Friedenberg, J. (2020). *Humanity 2.0: What it means to be human past, present and future*. Cambridge University Press.

Gentile, M. C. (2012). *Giving voice to values*. Yale University Press.

Gonzales, A. L., & Hancock, J. T. (2011). Mirror, mirror on my Facebook wall: Effects of exposure to Facebook on self-esteem. *Cyberpsychology, Behavior, and Social Networking, 14*(1–2), 79–83. https://doi.org/10.1089/cyber.2009.0411

Haidt, J. (2024). *The anxious generation: How the great rewiring of childhood is causing an epidemic of mental illness*. Penguin Press.

Haraway, D. (1991). *Simians, cyborgs, and women: The reinvention of nature*. Routledge.

Hermans, H. J. M. (2001). The dialogical self: Toward a theory of personal and cultural positioning. *Culture and Psychology, 7*(3), 243–281. https://doi.org/10.1177/1354067X0173001

Hermans, H. J. M. (2002). The dialogical self as a society of mind. *Theory and Psychology, 12*(2), 147–160. https://doi.org/10.1177/0959354302122001

Hermans, H. J. M. (2003). The construction and reconstruction of a dialogical self. *Journal of Constructivist Psychology, 16*, 89–130. https://doi.org/10.1080/10720530390117902

Hermans, H. J. M. (2004). Introduction: The dialogical self in a global and digital age. *Identity, 4*(4), 297–320. https://doi.org/10.1207/s1532706xid0404_1

Hermans, H. J. M., & Hermans-Jansen, E. (2001). Dialogical processes and the development of the self. In J. Valsiner & K. Connolly (Eds.), *Handbook of developmental psychology* (pp. 534–559). Sage.

Hermans, H. J. M., & Hermans-Jansen, E. (1995). *Self-narratives: The construction of meaning in psychotherapy*. Guilford Press.

Higgins, E. T. (1987). Self-discrepancy: A theory relating self and affect. *Psychological Review, 94*(3), 319–340.

Huang, J., Kumar, S., & Hu, C. (2021). A literature review of online identity reconstruction. *Frontiers in Psychology, 12*, 696552. https://doi.org/10.3389/fpsyg.2021.696552

James, W. (1890). *The principles of psychology*. Henry Holt and Company.

Jin, S. A. (2012). The virtual malleable self and the virtual identity discrepancy model: Investigative frameworks for virtual possible selves and others in avatar-based identity construction and social interaction. *Computers in Human Behavior, 28*(6), 2160–2168.

Jupiter, A. (2016). The Human-cyborg continuum: Why AI is pointless and why we should all become cyborgs instead. https://medium.com/@AlexJupiter/the-human-cyborg-continuum-why-ai-is-pointless-and-why-we-should-all-become-cyborgs-instead-4de0c4bb476f

Kamieński, Ł. (2014). *The new brave soldier: The biotechnology revolution and 21st century war* (Nowy wspaniały żołnierz. Rewolucja biotechnologiczna i wojna w XXI wieku). Wydawnictwo Uniwersytetu Jagiellońskiego.

Kim, H. W., Zheng, J. R., & Gupta, S. (2011). Examining knowledge contribution from the perspective of an online identity in blogging communities. *Computers in Human Behavior, 27*, 1760–1770. https://doi.org/10.1016/j.chb.2011.03.003

Kumar, A., & Shadbolt, N. (2018). Challenging filter bubbles: An approach to increasing information diversity through collaborative filtering. *International Journal of Information Management*, *39*, 259–266. https://doi.org/10.1016/j.ijinfomgt.2017.12.008

Leménager, T., Gwodz, A., Richter, A., Reinhard, I., Kämmerer, N., Sell, M., & Mann, K. (2013). Self-concept deficits in massively multiplayer online role-playing games addiction. *European Addiction Research*, *19*(5), 227–234.

Łukaszewicz Alcaraz, A. (2020). *Are cyborgs persons? An Account of futurists ethics*. Palgrave Macmillan.

Luyckx, K., Goossens, L., & Soenens, B. (2006). A developmental contextual perspective on identity construction in emerging adulthood: Change dynamics in commitment formation and commitment evaluation. *Developmental Psychology*, *42*(2), 366–380. https://doi.org/10.1037/0012-1649.42.2.366

Luyckx, K., Soenens, B., Goossens, L., Beckx, K., & Wouters, S. (2008). Identity exploration and commitment in late adolescence: Correlates of perfectionism and mediating mechanisms on the pathway to well-being. *Journal of Social and Clinical Psychology*, *27*(4), 336–361. https://doi.org/10.1521/jscp.2008.27.4.336

Mazur, E., & Li, Y. (2016). Identity and self-presentation on social networking web sites: A comparison of online profiles of Chinese and American emerging adults. *Psychology of Popular Media Culture*, *5*, 101–118. https://doi.org/10.1037/ppm0000054

Mancini, T., Imperato, C., & Sibilla, F. (2019). Does avatar's character and emotional bond expose to gaming addiction? Two studies on virtual self-discrepancy, avatar identification and gaming addiction in massively multiplayer online role-playing game players. *Computers in Human Behavior*, *92*, 297–305.

Mancini, T., & Sibilla, F. (2017). Offline personality and avatar customisation. Discrepancy profiles and avatar identification in a sample of MMORPG players. *Computers in Human Behavior*, *69*, 275–283.

Marody, M. (2014). *Jednostka po nowoczesności: Perspektywa socjologiczna*. Wydawnictwo Naukowe Scholar.

Markus, H. R., & Kitayama, S. (1991). Culture and the self: Implications for cognition, emotion, and motivation. *Psychological Review*, *98*(2), 224–253.

Messinger, P. R., Ge, X., Stroulia, E., Lyons, K., Smirnov, K., & Bone, M. (2008). On the relationship between my avatar and myself. *Journal of Virtual Worlds Research*, *1* (2), 1–17.

McLuhan, M. (1964). *Understanding media: The extensions of man*. McGraw-Hill.

Michikyan, M., Dennis, J., & Subrahmanyam, K. (2015). Can you guess who I am? Real, ideal, and false self-presentation on Facebook among emerging adults. *Emerging Adulthood*, *3*(1), 55–64. https://doi.org/10.1177/2167696814532442

Michikyan, M. (2020). Linking online self-presentation to identity coherence, identity confusion, and social anxiety in emerging adulthood. *British Journal of Developmental Psychology, 38*, 543–565. https://doi.org/10.1111/bjdp.12337

Morf, C. C., & Mischel, W. (2012). The self as a psycho-social dynamic processing system: Toward a converging science of self-hood. In M. R. Leary, J. P. Tangney (Eds.) *Handbook of Self and Identity* (pp. 21–49). Guilford Press.

Oleś, P. (2012). Tożsamość osobista I społeczna – płynna czy określona. In W. Łukaszewski, D. Doliński, A. Fila-Jankowska et al. (Eds.), *Tożsamość. Trudne pytanie kim jestem* (p. 115–126). Wydawnictwo Smak Słowa.

Pan, Y., & Steed, A. (2017). The impact of self-avatars on trust and collaboration in shared virtual environments. *PLOS ONE*, *12*(12), e0189078. https://doi.org/10.1371/journal.pone.0189078

Pariser, E. (2011). *The filter bubble: What the internet is hiding from you.* Penguin Books.

Praetorius, A. S., & Görlich, D. (2020, September). How avatars influence user behavior: A review on the proteus effect in virtual environments and video games. In Proceedings of the 15th International Conference on the Foundations of Digital Games (pp. 1–9).

Prensky, M. (2001). Digital Natives, Digital Immigrants, Part 1. *On the Horizon*, *9*(5), 1–6. https://doi.org/10.1108/10748120110424816

Przepiórka, A., Blachnio, A., Kot, P., & Cudo, A. (2024). What is the role of motives for smartphone use in elementary school students? Problematic smartphone use, family satisfaction, loneliness, and academic performance. *The Journal of Early Adolescence*, 0(0). https://doi.org/10.1177/02724316241240113

Puchalska-Wasyl, M. M. (2015). Self-talk: conversation with oneself? On the types of internal interlocutors. *Journal of Psychology: Interdisciplinary and Applied*, *149*(5), *443–460*. https://doi.org/10.1080/00223980.2014.896772

Puchalska-Wasyl, M. M. (2016). Coalition and opposition in myself? On integrative and confrontational internal dialogs, their functions, and the types of inner interlocutors. *Journal of Constructivist Psychology*, *29*(2), 197–218. https://doi.org/10.1080/10720537.2015.1084601

Puchalska-Wasyl, M. M., Fortuna, P., Cudo, A., & Kaczmarczyk, Ł. (in preparation). Virtual game characters as our internal interlocutors: Their affective types and functions.

Ranzini, G., & Lutz, C. (2017). Love at first swipe? Explaining tinder self-presentation and motives. *Mobile Media & Communication*, *5*, 80–101. https://doi.org/10.1177/2050157916664559

Rosana, A., & Fauzi, I. (2024). The role of digital identity in the age of social media: Literature analysis on self-identity construction and online social interaction. *Join: Journal of Social Science*, *1*(4), 477–489. https://ejournal.mellbaou.com/index.php/join/index

Santrock, J. W. (2007). *Lifespan development*. McGraw-Hill Education.

Sendyka, R. (2015). *Od kultury „ja" do kultury „siebie". O zwrotnych formach w projektach tożsamościowych* [From the culture of "I" to the culture of "self": On reflexive forms in identity projects]. Universitas.

Schröter, F. & Thon, J. N. (2014). Video game characters: Theory and analysis. *DIEGESIS: Interdisciplinary E-journal for Narrative Research 3*(1). 40–77.

Sibilla, F., & Mancini, T. (2018). I am (not) my avatar: A review of the user-avatar relationships in massively multiplayer online worlds. *Cyberpsychology: Journal of Psychosocial Research on Cyberspace, 12*(3):4.

Soenens, B., & Vansteenkiste, M. (2011). When is identity congruent with the self? A self-determination theory perspective. In S. J. Schwartz, K. Luyckx, & V. L. Vignoles (Eds.), *Handbook of identity theory and research* (Vol. 3, pp. 381–402). Springer. https://doi.org/10.1007/978-1-4419-7988-9_17

Stavropoulos, V., Rennie, J., Morcos, M., Gomez, R., & Griffiths, M. D. (2021). Understanding the relationship between the Proteus effect, immersion, and gender among World of Warcraft players: An empirical survey study. *Behaviour & Information Technology, 40*(8), 821–836.

Steers, M. L. N., Wickham, R. E., & Acitelli, L. K. (2014). Seeing everyone else's highlight reels: How Facebook usage is linked to depressive symptoms. *Journal of Social and Clinical Psychology, 33*(8), 701–731. https://doi.org/10.1521/jscp.2014.33.8.701

Steinberg, L. (2013). *Adolescence*. McGraw-Hill Education.

Suler, J. R. (2016). *Psychology of the digital age: Humans become electric*. Cambridge University Press.

Suler, J. R. (2017). The dimensions of cyberpsychology architecture. In J. Gackenbach & J. Brown (Eds.), *Boundaries of self and reality online: Implications of digitally constructed realities* (pp. 1–26). Academic Press.

Sun, S., Kim, J. H., Lee, K. M., & Nan, D. (2023). Exploring the association between the Proteus effect and intention to play massive multiplayer online role-playing games (MMORPGs). *Internet Research, 34*(1), 58–78.

Sylvia, Z., King, T. K., & Morse, B. J. (2014). Virtual ideals: The effect of video game play on male body image. *Computers in Human Behavior, 37*(1), 183–188.

Szolin, K., Kuss, D. J., Nuyens, F. M., & Griffiths, M. D. (2023). Exploring the user-avatar relationship in videogames: A systematic review of the Proteus effect. *Human–Computer Interaction, 38*(5–6), 374–399.

Tegmark, M. (2017). *Life 3.0: Being human in the age of artificial intelligence*. Alfred A. Knopf.

Thon, J. N. (2019). Transmedia characters: Theory and analysis. *Frontiers of Narrative Studies, 5*(2), 176–199.

Valkenburg, P. M., & Peter, J. (2008). Adolescents' identity experiments on the internet: Consequences for social competence and self-concept unity. *Communication Research, 35*, 208–231. https://doi.org/10.1177/0093650207313164

Valkenburg, P. M., Schouten, A. P., & Peter, J. (2005). Adolescents' identity experiments on the internet. *New Media & Society*, *7*, 383–402. https://doi.org/10.1177/1461444805052282

Vignoles, V. L., Schwartz, S. J., & Luyckx, K. (2011). Introduction: Toward an integrative view of identity. In S. J. Schwartz, K. Luyckx, & V. L. Vignoles (Eds.), *Handbook of identity theory and research* (pp. 1–27). Springer Science + Business Media. https://doi.org/10.1007/978-1-4419-7988-9_1

Waltemate, T., Gall, D., Roth, D., Botsch, M., & Latoschik, M. E. (2018). The impact of avatar personalization and immersion on virtual body ownership, presence, and emotional response. *IEEE Transactions on Visualization and Computer Graphics*, *24*(4), 1643–1652. https://doi.org/10.1109/TVCG.2018.2794621

Walther, J. B., Van Der Heide, B., Hamel, L. M., & Shulman, H. C. (2011). Self-generated versus other-generated statements and impressions in computer-mediated communication. *Communication Research*, *36*(2), 229–253.

Ward, A. F., & Wegner, D. M. (2013). Mind-blanking: When the mind goes away. *Frontiers in Psychology*, *4*, 650. https://doi.org/10.3389/fpsyg.2013.00650

Williams, D. (2006). Virtual identity and gaming: The impact of avatar and virtual identity on player behavior. *Games and Culture*, *1*(4), 376–397. https://doi.org/10.1177/1555412006292914

Wolfowicz, M., Weisburd, D. L., & Hasisi, B. (2021). Examining the interactive effects of the filter bubble and the echo chamber on radicalization. *Journal of Experimental Criminology*, *19*(5). https://doi.org/10.1007/s11292-021-09471-0

Yang, C., Holden, S. M., & Carter, M. D. K. (2017). Emerging adults' social media self-presentation and identity development at college transition: Mindfulness as a moderator. *Journal of Applied Developmental Psychology*, *52*, 212–221. https://doi.org/10.1016/j.appdev.2017.08.006

Yee, N., & Bailenson, J. (2007). The Proteus effect: The effect of transformed self-representation on behavior. *Human Communication Research*, *33*(3), 271–290.

Yee, N., Bailenson, J. N., & Ducheneaut, N. (2009). The Proteus effect: Implications of transformed digital self-representation on online and offline behavior. *Communication Research*, *36*(2), 285–312.

Zakaria, T., Busro, B., & Furqon, S. (2018). Filter bubble effect and religiosity: Filter bubble effect implication in the formation of subjects and views of religiosity. *IOP Conference Series: Materials Science and Engineering*, *434*(1), 1–9.

Zuboff, S. (2019). *The age of surveillance capitalism: The fight for a human future at the new frontier of power*. Public Affairs.

CHAPTER 2

Unlocking the Creative Future: A Framework for Intuitive Foresight

Piotr Zielonka[*,1] *and Sławomir Jakiela*[*,2]

Abstract

People continuously make intuitive predictions as an adaptive mechanism for managing uncertainty. This study identifies three primary forms of such predictions: law-based predictions that are rooted in established rules; focused predictions that rely on observed patterns and habitual experiences; and visionary forecasts, which involve creative extrapolation into uncharted territory. While these cognitive strategies can be effective when informed by expertise, they remain vulnerable to biases. For example, a cognitive tendency to assume that current trends will continue, along with motivational biases such as wishful thinking, can distort predictions. Despite these limitations, intuitive forecasts provide a sense of control over an unpredictable future. Media experts often address this psychological need by delivering confident predictions that align with popular narratives, while artificial intelligence models similarly generate coherent and seemingly plausible responses even when faced with uncertainty.

Keywords

intuitive predictions – law-based predictions – focused predictions – visionary forecasts – overconfidence – media experts

•••

* Warsaw University of Life Sciences, Institute of Biology, Warsaw, Poland

1 https://orcid.org/0000-0003-1555-6231

2 https://orcid.org/0000-0003-1557-1650

> The future ain't what it used to be.
>
> YOGI BERRA

∴

In everyday life, people constantly predict future events – whether planning daily activities, managing finances, or making career decisions. Forecasts range from those based on established natural or statistical rules to more intuitive, less quantifiable judgments. This chapter explores the cognitive processes behind intuitive forecasting, aiming to develop a theoretical model of how these predictions are formed.

Prediction enables individuals to anticipate future events and shape behavior across diverse contexts, playing a crucial role in fields from business to the natural and social sciences. Economist Milton Friedman (1953) argued that the value of an economic theory lies not in the realism of its assumptions but in its ability to predict real-world outcomes; even models based on simplified or unrealistic assumptions remain useful if they demonstrate strong predictive power. However, while intuitive predictions are efficient and often automatic, they are vulnerable to cognitive biases, limited data, and unpredictable variables, which can prevent them from fully capturing the complexity of real-world scenarios. Despite these shortcomings, people rely on intuitive judgments as a practical method for decision-making when detailed analytical approaches are unavailable. Intuitive predictions are most accurate when they rely on just one or two clear clues. People do fairly well at judging near-term rain from local temperature and humidity (Wilks, 2011) or gauging illness from a single fever curve (Steyerberg, 2009). They struggle, however, with broad, complex events such as economic recessions (Hastie & Dawes, 2010). Too many details overwhelm short-term memory – limited to about seven items (Miller, 1956) – and that overload drives the errors.

This paper introduces a novel perspective on intuitive prediction by examining the mental processes that underpin experience-based forecasting. Although no new empirical data is presented, the framework builds on established cognitive psychology concepts and offers insights into how gut feelings shape predictions under uncertainty. In this context, intuition is defined as the process of making judgments or decisions without a deliberate, step-by-step analysis, relying instead on past experiences, pattern recognition, and mental shortcuts when complete information is lacking. Scientific research indicates that these forecasts are not random but reflect the brain's use of prior knowledge and familiar patterns, even if the underlying process remains partly implicit (Gigerenzer, 2007). It should be noted that forecasting is often subject to errors that are difficult to estimate. However, because people poorly tolerate uncertainty or ignorance about the future, they have always formulated a variety of predictions.

1 Dual-Process Theory of Cognitive Processing

Cognitive psychologists Keith Stanovich and Richard West (2000) developed the "two systems" framework to explain how the human brain processes information. According to their model, cognitive capabilities are organized into System 1 and System 2, which operate in fundamentally different ways to handle both swift reactions and analytical thought. This dual-process theory accounts for how the brain manages both evolutionary survival mechanisms and complex problem-solving tasks. Daniel Kahneman expanded on this dual-process theory in his book Thinking, Fast and Slow, further refining the distinction between System 1 and System 2. Kahneman emphasized how reliance on System 1 can lead to cognitive biases and errors, as it often operates through heuristics. His work built on the foundation established by Stanovich and West, illustrating the real-world implications of these two modes of thinking in decision-making and judgment (Kahneman, 2011).

System 1, also known as the automatic or intuitive system, operates rapidly, effortlessly, unconsciously, and autonomously. It enables individuals to process information and respond to situations almost instantaneously, often without awareness of the underlying mental processes. This system relies on patterns, learned associations, and heuristics – mental shortcuts developed through experience – to produce judgments and guide behavior. The evolutionary roots of System 1 lie in its ability to handle immediate survival needs, such as detecting threats or seizing opportunities, where speed is essential. For example, the ability to instinctively step back from a fast-moving object or recognize a friend in a crowded room exemplifies the efficiency of System 1. Its capacity for parallel processing allows it to handle multiple inputs simultaneously, such as navigating a familiar route while carrying on a conversation. Additionally, because it requires minimal cognitive resources, System 1 is constantly active, managing the routine tasks of daily life with ease (Evans, 2008).

System 2, by contrast, represents the deliberate and reflective mode of thinking. It is slower, more effortful, and fully conscious. System 1 works best with familiar and repetitive tasks, while System 2 handles new, complex, or unclear problems that need careful thinking and planning. System 2 is engaged when individuals need to analyze information critically, compare alternatives, or anticipate long-term outcomes. This deliberate mode of reasoning is indispensable for tasks such as solving mathematical equations or drafting a legal argument. Unlike System 1, which operates in parallel, System 2 works sequentially, focusing on one problem at a time. Its reliance on sustained attention and cognitive effort means that it is energy-intensive and cannot be maintained for extended periods without fatigue (Zielonka et al., 2024).

System 1 is known for generating predictions, drawing on implicit knowledge acquired through repeated exposure to similar situations. For example, drivers anticipate the movement of surrounding vehicles without conscious deliberation, and skilled tennis players quickly gauge a ball's trajectory based on their opponent's posture. Evidence from professions such as firefighting and medicine further illustrates this principle. Experienced firefighters detect hidden dangers from subtle environmental cues, and physicians recognize patterns in patient symptoms, allowing for rapid, accurate diagnoses. Such intuitive processing proves most effective in dynamic and uncertain settings, where experience-based judgments offer a clear advantage over slower, more analytical reasoning (Kahneman & Klein, 2009).

Intuitive processes can be understood in two key ways. Direct experience involves active, repeated engagement that leads to automaticity. For example, a pianist practices a complex piece over and over until their movements become fluid and almost instinctive (Schmidt & Lee, 2011). Similarly, a basketball player who drills free throws repeatedly eventually develops an automatic shooting motion that requires little conscious thought. Indirect learning, in contrast, occurs through observation, listening, and inference rather than hands-on practice. For instance, medical students develop an intuitive sense for diagnoses by observing experienced physicians at work, picking up on subtle cues and patterns in patient behavior and symptoms (Ericsson, 2006). Another example is a language learner who, through immersion in a native-speaking environment, begins to intuitively understand and use idiomatic expressions without formal study.

Intuitive processes, whether developed through direct practice or acquired indirectly through observation, lay the groundwork for understanding how individuals make predictions. This foundational role of intuition is central to decision-making theories in economics and psychology, where researchers examine how people assess risks and rewards. One influential approach in this field focuses on intuitive predictions, which rely on two key components that have been central to decision theory since the 17th century. This framework began with Pascal's work on expected value, evolved through Bernoulli's expected utility theory, and ultimately contributed to modern prospect theory (Kahneman & Tversky, 1979). The first component is the payoff, which refers to the value or consequence associated with each possible outcome of a decision. In simple terms, it measures the benefit, reward, or cost that results from a particular choice. For example, in a financial decision, the payoff might represent the profit made or the loss incurred based on the outcome. Payoffs can be quantified in monetary terms but may also include factors such as psychological satisfaction, social status, or emotional impact (Peterson, 2017). The second component is probability, which describes the estimated likelihood of potential outcomes. The interaction between payoffs and probabilities forms the foundation of decision theory. Pascal established expected value theory by mathematically combining probabilities with monetary outcomes (Hacking, 2006). Bernoulli's utility theory further demonstrated that the subjective value assigned to an outcome can differ from its objective monetary value (Bernoulli, 1738/1954). Later, Kahneman and Tversky's prospect theory highlighted systematic deviations from statistical optimality in the assessment of probability and value (Kahneman & Tversky, 1979).

Understanding intuitive predictions requires distinguishing between risk and uncertainty, two foundational concepts introduced by Knight (1921). These concepts clarify whether predictions can rely on measurable probabilities or must depend on judgment due to the lack of data. Risk describes situations where measurable probabilities can be derived from empirical data, such as manufacturing defect rates. Uncertainty, on the other hand, arises in situations where probability calculations are impossible due to the absence of precedent data. For example, the adoption rate of novel technology exemplifies uncertainty, as no historical data exists to estimate probability distributions.

We can identify distinct levels of challenges based on our ability to assess payoffs and probabilities. In the ideal case of certainty, the outcome has a probability of 1 and its payoff is known. Under risk, we can evaluate payoffs and calculate probabilities reliably. Under uncertainty, we can identify possible payoffs but cannot assign meaningful probabilities. With ambiguity, payoff evaluations remain possible, but probability assessments become unclear due to incomplete or conflicting information. Finally, under ignorance we cannot even identify possible outcomes, making both payoff and probability assessment impossible (Ellsberg, 2015).

Intuitive predictions thus operate across a spectrum based on our ability to assess these two fundamental components – from situations where both payoffs and probabilities are clear, through various states where one or both

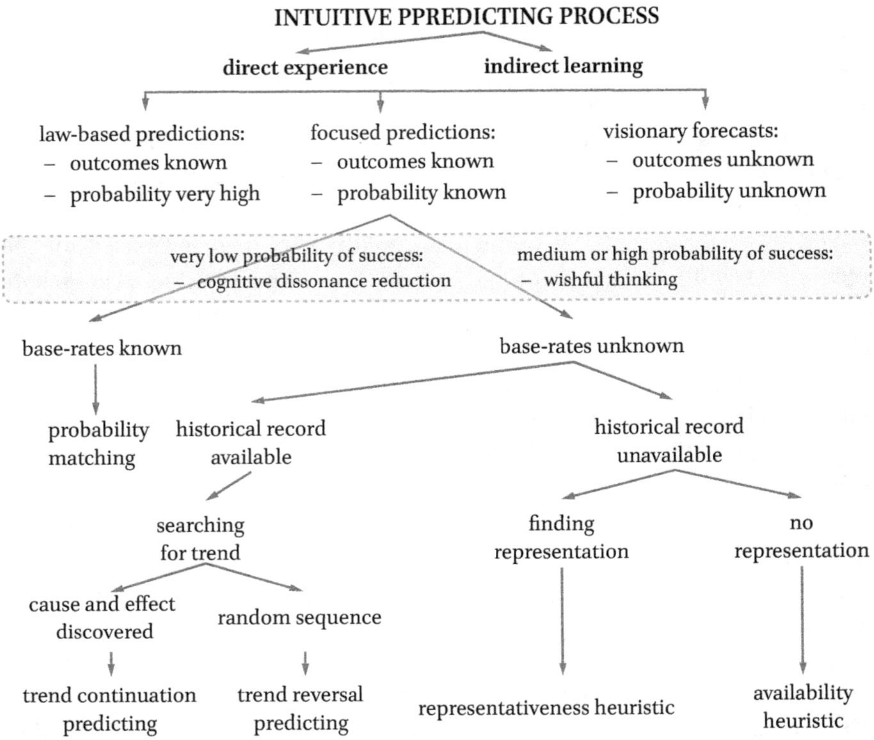

FIGURE 2.1 Scheme of intuitive forecasting.
SOURCE: OWN WORK

become increasingly difficult to evaluate, to complete ignorance where neither can be meaningfully assessed.

2 Three Types of Intuitive Predictions

Three categories of intuitive predictions can be distinguished: law-based predictions, focused predictions and visionary forecasts (Bar, 2009; Seif, 1981; Winther, 2008). Each defined by how it addresses probabilities and payoffs. The scheme of intuitive forecasting is illustrated in Figure 2.1.

2.1 *Law-Based Predictions*

Law-based predictions typically apply to situations characterized by high certainty, where both the probabilities and outcomes are well understood. For instance, Newton's laws of motion enable precise forecasts of how objects will behave under known forces, making outcomes highly predictable in controlled scenarios. In these cases, the governing principles are straightforward, making outcomes highly predictable. Law-based predictions extend beyond Knight's concept of risk because typically their outcomes may be nearly certain, with probabilities approaching 1. Examples include predicting that the sun will rise or that a hot drink will cool – events dictated by natural laws with near-absolute certainty. In these cases, making a prediction requires only recognizing that the situation follows a physical law, where the probability of occurrence is effectively 1.

However, even when the underlying physical laws are well understood, predicting complex, rare events remains challenging. Consider the twenty-kilometer-wide asteroid that struck Earth 66 million years ago. This impact set off a catastrophic sequence – an initial shockwave, massive wildfires, towering tsunamis, and prolonged darkness from debris blocking sunlight – which ultimately led to the collapse of ecosystems and the extinction of the dinosaurs. While the physical laws governing such an event are clear, forecasting when or where a similar occurrence might happen today is nearly impossible due to its complexity and rarity (Alvarez et al., 1980; Dolowy & Wroblewski, 2025). Thus, while law-based predictions work reliably in simpler, more controlled scenarios, their effectiveness diminishes when applied to highly complex and infrequent events.

2.2 *Focused Predictions*

Focused predictions seem the most frequent type of intuitive forecast. They emerge when individuals analyze available data, recognize patterns, and apply past experiences to anticipate specific outcomes. Unlike law-based predictions, which follow deterministic principles, focused predictions operate in areas where outcomes are uncertain but can still be estimated with a reasonable degree of confidence.

These predictions are widely used in contexts where potential payoffs can be assessed, even if probability estimates vary in reliability. They rely on a combination of empirical evidence and pattern recognition to estimate what is most likely to happen in situations involving risk and uncertainty.

For example, key societal issues often depend on clear, targeted predictions.

- Will governments provide universal basic income to counter economic instability?
- Will traditional retail stores disappear as digital commerce evolves, or will goods be distributed in new ways?
- Will AI-driven automation lead to mass unemployment, or will it transform the job market with new opportunities?

– Will printed books endure in a digital world, or will they become obsolete? Since focused predictions are the most common form of intuitive forecasting, it is essential to understand how individuals formulate them. The following sections will explore the key stages in developing focused predictions, examining the cognitive processes involved and the factors that influence their accuracy.

2.2.1 Relying on Base Rates

The first step in making focused predictions appears to be examining base rates. Base rates refer to the overall frequencies or probabilities of an event or characteristic within a population, serving as a baseline for comparing and interpreting new data. When base rate data is clearly presented and directly applicable, individuals are more likely to incorporate it into their predictions. For instance, if they know that 80% of applicants with a specific qualification are accepted into a program, they may use this information to estimate their own or others' chances.

When making repeated predictions with known base rates, individuals often engage in probability matching. This means they set their prediction probabilities to match the historical frequency of an event. For example, if an event has occurred 80% of the time, they might predict an 80% chance of it happening again. However, this strategy is generally less effective than consistently choosing the most frequent outcome, which maximizes the overall success rate. An example of probability matching can be observed in the behavior of technical analysts in the stock market. Although historical data show that stock indices tend to rise over time, this growth is uneven. Consequently, many investors attempt to outperform the market by identifying short-term patterns rather than adopting a simple buy-and-hold strategy, which involves holding investments over long periods to benefit from long-term market growth (cf. Corser et al., 2024).

Under time pressure or when faced with more complex problems, individuals may entirely overlook base rates. Furthermore, people recognize that in unstable or non-stationary environments, relying solely on base rates is insufficient. In such contexts, base probabilities lose their relevance as the underlying conditions are constantly changing. Instead, the historical record of event sequences that most closely matches the scenario being predicted becomes the primary determinant.

2.2.2 Pattern Seeking

When base rates are unavailable but historical records exist, people naturally look for patterns. Humans are remarkably adept at detecting patterns in their environment. Research shows that this ability emerges early in life. For instance, a study by Kirkham and colleagues (2002) demonstrated that 3.5-month-old infants could identify predictable patterns in a sequence of visual stimuli. By tracking the infants' eye movements, the researchers found that the infants anticipated the location of the next shape in the sequence before it appeared, indicating they had learned the pattern's structure.

The ability to recognize patterns evolved as a vital survival skill. Over time, this capacity became advantageous due to the asymmetry in the consequences of pattern detection errors. For example, mistaking a harmless rustling bush for a predator resulted in wasted energy but posed no significant threat. Conversely, failing to detect signs of an actual predator could have fatal consequences. This evolutionary dynamic led to a natural bias toward detecting patterns, even in cases where they might not exist (Haselton & Nettle, 2006).

Among patterns, trends represent the simplest form – characterized by a steady change in one direction over time. When observing a sequence of events, individuals typically require three to four similar occurrences before realizing that a trend exists. Each additional occurrence further strengthens this belief, and by the fifth to seventh occurrence, most individuals are confident that a trend is present (Kahneman & Tversky, 1972).

2.2.3 Recognizing a Trend

In nature, trends often persist due to the inherent advantages of stability and predictability in ecological systems – animals frequently follow familiar migration routes because these paths optimize resource availability and minimize risks during seasonal changes, ensuring survival and reproduction. Similarly, predators maintain established territories as they represent known sources of prey and shelter, reducing the energy expenditure and uncertainties associated with venturing into new areas. Plants also grow predictably in response to environmental conditions such as light, water, and soil nutrients, adapting their growth patterns to maximize photosynthesis and nutrient uptake (Zielonka et al., 2020). This expectation of continuity aligns with the Lindy Effect, a concept popularized by Taleb (2012). The term "Lindy Effect" originates from observations at Lindy's, a New York City deli, where writers and performers noted that the longer a Broadway show ran, the more likely it was to continue. The Lindy Effect applies to entities that do not naturally decay, such as ideas, books, traditions, or cultural practices, and suggests that the longer these entities have existed, the more likely they are to endure. For example, a book valued for fifty years is expected to remain relevant longer than one published only a year ago. The longevity of such entities often reflects their ability to withstand challenges – social, cultural, or intellectual – that might have eliminated weaker alternatives. Each additional year of survival reinforces their perceived durability, indicating that their persistence is not coincidental.

The story of Polycrates of Samos illustrates how human interpretations of randomness can lead to misjudgments. Polycrates, a ruler celebrated for his continuous success in governance, trade, and warfare, maintained an unbroken streak of victories. This persistent fortune troubled Amasis, the King of Egypt, who believed that a long sequence of wins could not continue indefinitely because randomness would eventually force a reversal. To avert impending misfortune, Amasis advised Polycrates to sacrifice something valuable. Polycrates complied by casting an emerald ring into the sea, yet the ring was later found inside a fish – a sign, in Amasis's view, that his streak was indeed unbreakable, prompting him to end their alliance. Ultimately, despite this apparent sign of enduring luck, Polycrates's extraordinary run ended in betrayal and death at the hands of the Persians (Herodotus, ca. 440 B.C.E./2003).

Modern research reflects similar misinterpretations of randomness. Studies show that when a process is labeled as random, people tend to expect patterns to fade and reversals to occur, driven by misconceptions about how randomness works and an unfounded belief in fairness (Tyszka et al., 2008). This bias manifests in high-stakes settings as well; for instance, research on asylum cases and parole hearings reveals that judges become less likely to rule favorably after a series of approvals, mistakenly assuming that outcomes must balance – even though each case should be judged independently (Chen et al., 2016). Both the ancient narrative of Polycrates and contemporary studies highlight how a mistaken belief in fairness within random processes can lead to significant biases and errors.

2.2.4 Applying Heuristics

When base rates and historical data are unavailable, or when individuals are highly confident in their personal knowledge of similar situations, they turn to heuristics – mental shortcuts that allow them to make quick judgments based on experience and intuition.

A common mental shortcut for making predictions is judging the likelihood of an event based on how closely it resembles a familiar pattern or category. This approach, known as the representativeness heuristic, relies on perceived similarities to past experiences. Instead of analyzing probabilities, individuals use mental templates of how events or outcomes "should" look, often leading to biased predictions.

In the case of random sequences, people are likely to predict that an alternating pattern of heads and tails in coin tosses is more representative of randomness than a sequence of consecutive heads, even though both are equally probable. This reflects a bias toward patterns that appear "typical" of randomness, despite the lack of statistical support for such judgments (Tversky & Kahneman, 1971). This heuristic also manifests in real-world scenarios. In medical diagnoses, doctors may predict the presence of a condition based on how closely a patient's symptoms match a prototypical case, sometimes overlooking less obvious but statistically more likely conditions. Similarly, in criminal profiling, law enforcement may focus on suspects who resemble preconceived ideas of an offender rather than relying on broader statistical evidence (Kahneman & Tversky, 1984).

When people cannot identify a clear pattern, they judge the likelihood of an event based on how easily they can recall similar examples. This is known as the availability heuristic. This works because events that are easy to remember tend to feel more common or probable. However, this approach can lead to errors when recent, vivid, or emotional memories disproportionately influence judgments. For example, after seeing news about a plane crash, someone might think flying is very dangerous, even though it's one of the safest ways to travel. Similarly, shark attacks might seem more common than they are because they're dramatic and get a lot of attention. This way of thinking often ignores actual data and focuses too much on what's easiest to recall.

2.3 *Visionary Forecasts*

Visionary forecasts arise in situations where even the potential outcomes are difficult to determine. Unlike law-based or focused predictions that rely on clear, established outcomes, these forecasts grapple with long-term uncertainties and often involve revolutionary shifts in technology, science, or society. In such contexts, defining what might happen is as challenging as predicting when it will occur.

Despite the critical role of scientific and technological advancements in shaping our future, public discourse on these topics is frequently dominated by politicians rather than by the experts who drive progress – scientists, engineers, and technologists. Yet it is their work that will ultimately determine the trajectory of technological development. One major challenge in visionary forecasting is the inherently unpredictable nature of scientific progress. The time between a breakthrough and its widespread adoption can span an entire generation, rendering long-term predictions highly unreliable as future discoveries and their applications remain uncertain. Consequently, many futuristic visions, particularly those popularized in science fiction, rarely unfold as originally imagined (Bennett, 2003; Dolowy & Wroblewski, 2025).

Many critical questions remain unanswered. Will strong AI surpass human intelligence? Will we reach the technological singularity, often referred to as "Life 3.0"? Will transhumanism become a reality? Could artificial consciousness be created? Will mind-uploading ever be possible? Challenges that were once the domain of speculative fiction may soon demand real-world answers. As technology advances, the need for informed, evidence-based forecasting becomes increasingly urgent – shaping not only our understanding of the future but also the choices we make today.

In forming visionary predictions, our minds rely on two complementary strategies, which can be employed separately or together. The first strategy involves detecting weak signals – subtle, early indicators of emerging trends in technology, society, or the economy that might otherwise go unnoticed. Although these signals are often faint and uncertain, they can provide valuable clues about future developments. The second strategy draws on analogies by comparing current advancements to historical events in order to anticipate potential outcomes. For example, analyzing how electricity or the internet reshaped society helps estimate the possible impact of new technologies (Inayatullah, 2008).

However, history shows that established ways of thinking – shaped by prevailing assumptions, widely accepted theories, and dominant technological models – can make it difficult to recognize groundbreaking innovations. When a particular framework of understanding becomes deeply ingrained, people tend to interpret new developments through that familiar lens, often overlooking or dismissing ideas that do not fit existing expectations. This resistance to change can delay the acceptance of transformative innovations, even when they ultimately redefine industries, economies, and societies. In 1943, Thomas Watson, then chairman of IBM, reportedly stated, "I think there is a world market for maybe five computers," reflecting the limited view of computers as specialized devices, unable to anticipate the personal computing revolution (Ceruzzi, 2012). Similarly, William Orton, president of Western Union, dismissed Alexander Graham Bell's telephone in 1876 as a "toy" with "too many shortcomings to be seriously considered as a means of communication," underestimating its future significance (Standage, 1998). In 1977, Kenneth H. Olsen, founder of Digital Equipment Corporation, remarked, "There is no reason anyone would want a computer in their home," failing to predict the widespread adoption of home computing (Ceruzzi, 2012).

Overcoming fixed paradigms requires an openness to uncertainty and a willingness to question established assumptions. Visionary predictions demand not only the ability to detect weak signals and draw meaningful analogies but also the flexibility to imagine possibilities beyond conventional thinking. This includes recognizing that emerging trends may not follow linear paths and that disruptive innovations often appear insignificant or impractical in their early stages.

3 Cognitive Dissonance Reduction and Wishful Thinking

Both focused predictions and visionary forecasts may be influenced by our personal motivations. When we try to predict an outcome, we often favor conclusions that match what we want to happen or avoid outcomes we fear. In simple terms, our inner motivations "contaminate" our predictions, causing us to see the future in a way that supports our personal hopes and beliefs rather than relying solely on objective facts.

Motivated prediction produces two distinct effects based on the perceived likelihood of undesired outcomes. When a desired result appears highly unlikely or even impossible – essentially when the undesired outcome seems nearly certain – individuals adjust their predictions to match this likelihood. This shift is a form of cognitive dissonance reduction (Festinger, 1957), where people modify their opinions and preferences to bridge the gap between what they want and what seems inevitable. This phenomenon, known as the sour grapes bias, involves reinterpreting the undesirable outcome as acceptable or even inevitable, thereby reducing the emotional strain from conflicting expectations. In contrast, wishful thinking arises when the probability of a desired outcome appears higher. In such cases, individuals transform their predictions to reflect an increased perceived likelihood of positive outcomes or a decreased likelihood of negative ones. This adjustment involves an optimistic bias, where people reinterpret evidence to align with their hopes, often underestimating the weight of opposing information. As a result, predictions lean toward unwarranted optimism, with insufficient scrutiny of contradictory evidence. For example, in competitive environments, individuals may expect favorable results despite minimal indicators of success, as their desire for a positive outcome shapes their expectations and interpretations of the situation. A notable illustration is the courtroom, where both prosecutors and defense lawyers routinely overestimate their chances of winning; research shows that their combined confidence frequently exceeds 100 %, underscoring the sway of wishful thinking over judgment and forecasting (Loewenstein et al., 1993). More broadly, people tend to forecast the future more favorably than they assess the present – a tendency that underpins economic growth. If they consistently expected tomorrow to be worse than today, the willingness to lend, invest, and extend credit would quickly vanish, stalling the economy.

Individuals often overestimate their chances of experiencing positive events and underestimate their likelihood of encountering negative ones – a pattern known as unrealistic optimism (Weinstein, 1980). For example, college students in their studies frequently rated their chances of career success as higher than average while considering their risk of health problems, such as heart disease, to be lower than that of their peers. The optimism bias influences judgments across various domains, such as financial planning, and relationships. The planning fallacy, studied by Buehler et al. (1994), provides a clear example of these biases in action. This phenomenon occurs when individuals underestimate task requirements, often driven by the desire to see projects completed quickly or easily.

4 Media Expert Predictions: A Modern Version of Ancient Practices

For centuries, people have turned to individuals who claimed to foresee the future. Ancient methods of prediction – such as shamanism, prophecy, oracles, astrology, dream interpretation, necromancy, and the reading of omens – each offered a distinct approach while sharing a common goal: to find meaning in uncertainty and provide guidance. Although modern science dismisses these practices as superstition, their appeal endures.

Shamans were among the first people to claim they could foresee the future. Many ancient cultures believed that shamans could talk with spirits and receive messages about what was coming. Using rituals, drumming, fasting, or hallucinogenic substances, shamans entered altered states where they claimed to see visions of future events.

Prophets, on the other hand, claimed to receive direct messages from a deity. They delivered warnings, moral lessons, and guidance for both leaders and society. In traditions that stressed one supreme deity, prophets spoke with great authority, condemning injustices and urging people to follow divine laws.

Oracles served as intermediaries who communicated divine messages through formal rituals, usually with the help of priests. In cultures with many gods, such as those in Greece and Rome, rulers and citizens sought their advice before making important decisions. A famous example is the priestess at Delphi, who would enter a trance-like state and give cryptic messages open to many interpretations.

Astrology took a more systematic approach by studying the movements of the stars, planets, and the moon. Ancient observers believed that these celestial patterns were linked to the will of the gods and could predict events like natural disasters or shifts in power. Over time, scholars also used astrology to help diagnose illnesses and understand changes in society.

Dreams were seen as messages from the divine that revealed hidden truths or future events. Experts in many cultures interpreted dreams, believing they provided clues about personal destinies or even the fate of nations.

Necromancy, the practice of communicating with the dead, was another method of seeking future insights. Many believed that the spirits of the deceased held valuable knowledge, and special rituals were performed to summon them for guidance. This practice was closely related to dream interpretation, as both were seen as ways to access hidden realms.

Omens, taken from natural events like unusual animal behavior or rare celestial occurrences, were also used to predict the future. People carefully recorded these signs and linked them to specific outcomes, guiding decisions in politics, war, and daily life.

Finally, some civilizations attempted a more structured approach by studying recurring patterns in time. They believed that events followed natural cycles and that history repeated itself. This belief led to the development of detailed calendar systems that tracked celestial movements and seasonal changes, helping them anticipate events such as floods or the rise and fall of leaders.

This method of prediction was not confined to the ancient world. Today, economic and political analysts follow a similar logic, examining historical patterns to forecast future developments. By analyzing economic cycles, political shifts, and market trends, they attempt to predict crises, recessions, and geopolitical conflicts. Though modern forecasting relies on data-driven models rather than divine revelations, the fundamental principle remains the same: insights from the past provide a framework for anticipating what lies ahead (Van Creveld, 2020).

Despite scientific advancements, the human desire for foresight remains unchanged. Experts regularly appear in the media, offering predictions on global affairs, yet research suggests that many rely more on intuition than rigorous analysis. While their language is more sophisticated than that of ancient seers, the challenge persists: predicting the future is inherently uncertain, and even the most methodical approaches cannot fully eliminate the element of unpredictability.

Tetlock (2005) conducted a comprehensive 12-year study analyzing over 27,000 forecasts from more than 200 experts across domains such as politics, economics, and military affairs. The study focused on predictions related to major geopolitical and economic events, including the fate of the Soviet Union, the trajectory of South Africa, and the establishment of the European Monetary Union. Experts were also asked to assess their own competence, make specific probabilistic predictions, and later evaluate the accuracy of their forecasts. The results showed that, on average, expert predictions were only slightly more accurate than chance. Despite this, experts often exhibited significant overconfidence, frequently estimating their accuracy at around 80%, when in reality it was closer to 40%.

This raises the question: if experts in fields like political science or economics are often no more accurate than non-experts, why are their predictions so widely trusted? The answer lies in people's discomfort with uncertainty. Predictions, even flawed ones, provide a sense of control and reassurance in the face of an unpredictable future. Experts in the media meet this psychological need by delivering forecasts with confidence, often framing their predictions to resonate with popular narratives or making bold claims to capture attention. This combination of authority and confidence makes their predictions seem more credible, even when their accuracy is limited.

Tyszka and Zielonka (2002) examined how the characteristics of prediction environments and methodologies influence forecasting confidence. They highlighted that some domains, such as weather forecasting, operate within relatively stable and predictable systems governed by physical laws. This predictability enables forecasters to systematically refine their methods through repeated feedback and analysis. When errors occur, they are often attributed to the inherent uncertainties of atmospheric systems or limitations in predictive models. This structured feedback loop encourages learning and gradual improvement, resulting in more accurate forecasts over time. In contrast, financial analysts operate in a highly unpredictable domain dominated by random fluctuations and complex human behavior. Due to the lack of stable relationships in financial data, their predictive accuracy is often poor, regardless of expertise. Tyszka and Zielonka (2002) noted that financial analysts tend to exhibit elevated levels of overconfidence. When their predictions fail, they frequently externalize blame, attributing inaccuracies to external factors such as market manipulation, political events, or irrational market behavior. This externalization of failure limits opportunities for reflection and learning, reinforcing overconfidence and leading to persistent inaccuracies in future forecasts. Experts in fields such as politics, economics, and military affairs often exhibit a similar attitude, favoring definitive answers over acknowledging gaps in knowledge. Social pressures further encourage this tendency by rewarding confident responses rather than admissions of uncertainty. Additionally, the human cognitive system instinctively fills in missing information with plausible assumptions, thereby creating complete narratives even when the underlying data is incomplete or inaccurate.

Interestingly, artificial intelligence (AI) systems exhibit a similar behavior. Trained through reinforcement learning, these systems often produce plausible responses rather than admitting uncertainty. In AI, this is known as "hallucination," where the system generates coherent but sometimes inaccurate or fabricated information when faced with ambiguous or insufficient data. Like humans, AI fills in gaps in understanding because of discomfort with uncertainty. This shared tendency to favor narrative coherence over accuracy reveals an inherent bias in both human and artificial information processing. In humans, it can lead to false memories, overconfidence, or explanations that simply confirm existing beliefs, while in AI it stems from design choices that prioritize fluency and contextual relevance over accuracy.

5 Discussion

People continuously form intuitive forecasts, often without realizing it, that shape their expectations about the future across various fields. These predictions can be divided into two main types. The first, law-based predictions, are grounded in established natural principles. The second, focused predictions, relies on the assumption that current trends – in areas like technology, society, or the economy – will continue. In this case, individuals base their expectations on patterns observed in past experiences. When explicit precedents are lacking, heuristics such as representativeness and availability shape predictions, leading individuals to rely on perceived similarities or recent experiences. However, the dominant cognitive tendency remains the expectation of trend continuity. This reflects an implicit cause-and-effect understanding of events, distinguishing structured, predictable patterns from random outcomes. However, in cases perceived as random, people exhibit the gambler's fallacy, erroneously expecting reversals rather than recognizing statistical independence.

Not all intuitive predictions involve well-defined probabilities or clear trend patterns. Visionary forecasting occurs when future outcomes are highly uncertain, and even potential possibilities remain unclear. In such cases, two primary cognitive strategies are employed. The first is identifying weak signals – subtle, early indicators of change. These signals may initially appear insignificant but can reveal emerging trends that become more apparent over time. Sensitivity to such cues allows individuals to anticipate shifts before they reach broader recognition. The second strategy is drawing analogies, where historical parallels inform expectations about future developments. By comparing present situations to past events, individuals construct frameworks that help estimate potential trajectories, even in the absence of precise probabilities. This structured reasoning provides a reference for forecasting under uncertainty.

Beyond basic cognitive processes, motivational biases strongly influence intuitive forecasts. Our desires and fears shape our expectations, causing us to favor outcomes that align with our hopes while downplaying those we wish to avoid. This bias takes two forms. When facing a potential negative outcome, we adjust our predictions to make it seem more likely, which helps reduce cognitive dissonance. Conversely, when a positive outcome appears less likely, wishful thinking can lead to overly optimistic forecasts that ignore contradictory evidence.

Even expert predictions in fields such as political science, economics, and military strategy frequently rely on intuition rather than systematic reasoning. Research suggests that expert forecasts often exhibit overconfidence, as definitive predictions, even when flawed, provide an illusion of control in uncertain environments.

This tendency toward confident but unreliable predictions is also observed in AI systems. Both human experts and AI models generate coherent, plausible responses – even when uncertain – rather than acknowledging gaps in knowledge. In AI, this results in hallucinations (false but confidently stated outputs), while in humans, it manifests as false memories or overstated certainty. This similarity suggests a shared bias in both biological and artificial information-processing systems: a preference for narrative consistency over factual accuracy.

The frequent occurrence of black swan events – high-impact, unpredictable occurrences – illustrates the limits of all forecasting methods, including intuitive predictions. This challenge stems from the inherent unpredictability of events shaped by human behavior, political dynamics, and social change. Even forecasts of physical systems like climate or geological activity are fraught with uncertainty. As the number of variables increases and predictions extend further into the future, errors accumulate and unforeseen influences become more likely.

A key limitation of intuitive predictions is that they, like all forecasts, rely on past and present observations, yet the future remains unobservable. Even the most rigorous models may be built on assumptions that are influenced by cognitive and emotional biases, a problem that persists in algorithmic forecasting since these models inevitably mirror the judgments of their human creators.

Forecasting is further complicated by imprecise language. Predictions rarely assert that something "will" or "will not" happen, instead using terms like "probability," "likelihood," or "possibility." Such terminology, including numerical probabilities, can be interpreted differently depending on context, leading to miscommunication. Additionally, without clearly defined timeframes, failed predictions can be indefinitely postponed – explaining the persistence of rescheduled doomsday scenarios and vague warnings about future crises (Dolowy & Wroblewski, 2025).

Finally, forecasts are not passive observations; they can influence the very future they attempt to predict. Once a potential outcome becomes widely known, it can trigger reactions that accelerate, prevent, or reshape it in unexpected ways. In this sense, revealing a possible future alters its trajectory, making it different from what it would have been had it remained unknown.

References

Alvarez, W., Alvarez, L. W., Asaro, F., & Michel, H. V. (1980). Extraterrestrial cause for the Cretaceous-Tertiary extinction. *Science, 208*(4448), 1095–1108. https://doi.org/10.1126/science.208.4448.1095

Bar, M. (2009). The proactive brain: Memory for predictions. *Philosophical Transactions of the Royal Society B: Biological Sciences, 364*(1521), 1235–1243. https://doi.org/10.1098/rstb.2008.0310

Bennett, W. L. (2003). *The personalization of politics: Political identity, public opinion, and news media.* Cambridge University Press.

Bernoulli, D. (1738/1954). Exposition of a new theory on the measurement of risk. *Econometrica, 22*(1), 23–36.

Ellsberg, D. (2015). *Risk, ambiguity and decision.* Routledge.

Buehler, R., Griffin, D., & Ross, M. (1994). Exploring the "planning fallacy": Why people underestimate their task completion times. *Journal of Personality and Social Psychology, 67*(3), 366–381. https://doi.org/10.1037/0022-3514.67.3.366

Ceruzzi, P. E. (2012). *Computing: A concise history.* MIT Press.

Chen, D. L., Moskowitz, T. J., & Shue, K. (2016). Decision-making under the gambler's fallacy: Evidence from asylum judges, loan officers, and baseball umpires. *The Quarterly Journal of Economics, 131*(3), 1181–1242. https://doi.org/10.1093/qje/qjw017

Corser, R., Voss Jr, R. P., & Jasper, J. D. (2024). Do errors on classic decision biases happen fast or slow? Numeracy and decision time predict probability matching, sample size neglect, and ratio bias. *Journal of Numerical Cognition, 10,* e12473. https://doi.org/10.5964/jnc.12473

Dolowy, K., & Wroblewski, A. (2025). *Why are we helpless?* Unpublished manuscript.

Ericsson, K. A. (2006). *The Cambridge handbook of expertise and expert performance.* Cambridge University Press.

Evans, J. S. B. T. (2008). Dual-processing accounts of reasoning, judgment, and social cognition. *Annual Review of Psychology, 59*, 255–278. https://doi.org/10.1146/annurev.psych.59.103006.093629

Festinger, L. (1957). *A theory of cognitive dissonance.* Stanford University Press.

Friedman, M. (1953). *Essays in positive economics.* University of Chicago Press.

Gigerenzer, G. (2007). *Gut feelings: The intelligence of the unconscious.* Viking.

Hacking, I. (2006). *The emergence of probability* (2nd ed.). Cambridge University Press.

Haselton, M. G., & Nettle, D. (2006). The paranoid optimist: An integrative evolutionary model of cognitive biases. *Personality and Social Psychology Review, 10*(1), 47–66. https://doi.org/10.1207/s15327957pspr1001_3

Hastie, R., & Dawes, R. M. (2010). *Rational choice in an uncertain world: The psychology of judgment and decision making.* Sage.

Herodotus (ca. 440 B.C.E./2003). *The histories* (A. D. Godley, Trans.). Harvard University Press.

Inayatullah, S. (2008). Six pillars: Futures thinking for transformative change. *Foresight, 10*(2),15–29. https://doi.org/10.1108/14636680810863340

Kahneman, D. (2011). *Thinking, fast and slow.* Farrar, Straus and Giroux.

Kahneman, D., & Klein, G. (2009). Conditions for intuitive expertise: A failure to disagree. *American Psychologist, 64*(6), 515–526. https://doi.org/10.1037/a0016755

Kahneman, D., & Tversky, A. (1972). Subjective probability: A judgment of representativeness. *Cognitive Psychology, 3*(3), 430–454. https://doi.org/10.1016/0010-0285(72)90016-3

Kahneman, D., & Tversky, A. (1979). Prospect theory: An analysis of decision under risk. *Econometrica, 47*(2), 263–291.

Kahneman, D., & Tversky, A. (1984). Choices, values, and frames. *American Psychologist, 39*(4), 341–350. https://doi.org/10.1037/0003-066X.39.4.341

Kirkham, N. Z., Slemmer, J. A., & Johnson, S. P. (2002). Visual statistical learning in infancy: Evidence for a domain-general learning mechanism. *Cognition, 83*(2), B35–B42. https://doi.org/10.1016/S0010-0277(02)00004-5

Knight, F. H. (1921). *Risk, uncertainty and profit.* Houghton Mifflin.

Loewenstein, G., Issacharoff, S., Camerer, C., & Babcock, L. (1993). Self-serving assessments of fairness and pretrial bargaining. *Journal of Legal Studies, 22*(1), 135–159. https://doi.org/10.1086/468160

Miller, G. A. (1956). The magical number seven, plus or minus two: Some limits on our capacity for processing information. *Psychological Review*, 63(2), 81–97. https://doi.org/10.1037/h0043158

Peterson, M. (2017). *An introduction to decision theory* (2nd ed.). Cambridge University Press.

Schmidt, R. A., & Lee, T. D. (2011). *Motor control and learning: A behavioral emphasis* (5th ed.). Human Kinetics.

Seif, E. (1981). Futures education for the gifted. *Roeper Review, 4*(2), 24–25. https://doi.org/10.1080/02783198109552581

Standage, T. (1998). *The Victorian Internet: The remarkable story of the telegraph and the nineteenth century's online pioneers*. Walker & Company.

Stanovich, K. E., & West, R. F. (2000). Individual differences in reasoning: Implications for the rationality debate? *Behavioral and Brain Sciences, 23*(5), 645–665. https://doi.org/10.1017/S0140525X00003435

Steyerberg, E. W. (2009). *Clinical prediction models*. Springer.

Taleb, N. N. (2012). *Antifragile: Things that gain from disorder*. Random House.

Tetlock, P. E. (2005). *Expert political judgment: How good is it? How can we know?* Princeton University Press.

Tversky, A., & Kahneman, D. (1971). Belief in the law of small numbers. *Psychological Bulletin, 76*(2), 105–110. https://doi.org/10.1037/h0031322

Tyszka, T., & Zielonka, P. (2002). Expert judgments: Financial analysts versus weather forecasters. *Journal of Psychology and Financial Markets, 3*(3), 152–160. https://doi.org/10.1207/S15327760JPFM0303_03

Tyszka, T., Zielonka, P., Sawicki, P., & Dacey, R. (2008). Perception of randomness and predicting uncertain events. *Thinking and Reasoning, 14*(1), 45–69. https://doi.org/10.1080/13546780701677669

Van Creveld, M. (2020). *Seeing into the future: A short history of prediction*. Reaktion Books.

Weinstein, N. D. (1980). Unrealistic optimism about future life events. *Journal of Personality and Social Psychology, 39*(5), 806–820. https://doi.org/10.1037/0022-3514.39.5.806

Wilks, D. S. (2011). *Statistical methods in the atmospheric sciences* (3rd ed.). Academic Press.

Winther, R. G. (2008). Systemic Darwinism. *Proceedings of the National Academy of Sciences of the United States of America, 105*(33), 11833–11838. https://doi.org/10.1073/pnas.0711445105

Zielonka, P., Białaszek, W., Biedrzycki, P., & Dzik, B. (2020). Don't fight the tape! Technical analysis momentum and contrarian signals as common cognitive biases. *Central European Management Journal, 28*(2), 98–110. https://doi.org/10.7206/cemj.2658-0845.24

Zielonka, P., Szymanek, K., Dzik, B., Jakieła, S., & Białek, M. (2024). The history of dual-process thinking. Orbis Idearum. *European Journal of the History of Ideas, 12*(1). https://doi.org/10.26106/9yrc-7k78

CHAPTER 3

Creativity, Reproduction, or Co-creativity? The Concept of Friendly Generative Artificial Intelligence

Michał Kalisz[*,1] *and Maksymilian Kulicki*[*,2]

Abstract

The rapid development of generative artificial intelligence (GAI) raises the question about the nature of the creative process: do AI models truly create or merely reproduce? The aim of this article is to analyze the creative potential of GAI. The text undertakes an analysis of the achievements of GAI in the process of generating and processing text, images, sound and video, considering the question of originality and intentionality. The general technical foundations of generative models are also presented. The article introduces the concept of positive generative AI, rooted in principles of positive cyberpsychology, which emphasizes designing AI systems that support psychological, social, and cognitive dimensions of human functioning, respecting fundamental needs such as autonomy, competence, and relatedness. The concept of "human-AI co-creativity" and "wellbeing-informed design" are explored as frameworks for enhancing rather than replacing human creativity. The need for responsible and conscious shaping of technology to enrich human creativity rather than limit or replace it is emphasized. The article calls for further interdisciplinary research and dialogue between creators, researchers and decision-makers to maximize benefits and minimize risks associated with the development of GAI.

Keywords

creativity – generative artificial intelligence – authorship – artificial intelligence – friendly generative artificial intelligence

* The John Paul II Catholic University of Lublin, Institute of Philosophy, Lublin, Poland
1 https://orcid.org/0000-0003-1955-1884
2 IDEAS NCBR, Institute of Fundamental Technological Research, Polish Academy of Sciences, Warsaw, Poland, https://orcid.org/0000-0001-7138-9592

Generative artificial intelligence (GAI) represents one of the most dynamic achievements in modern technology, evoking both admiration and concerns among researchers, creators, and art audiences. Through the application of advanced machine learning models and neural networks, artificial intelligence (AI) is capable of generating texts, images, music, and other forms of creative expression.

GAI refers to a class of AI technologies that use deep learning models to create content resembling human-generated material. This technology encompasses various outputs, including text, images, audio, and video, and works by responding to complex prompts provided by users (Kanbach, 2023).

The development of GAI raises fundamental dilemmas related to the concept of creativity. Traditionally, creativity has been viewed as the ability to create something new and unique, embedded in cultural and emotional contexts. In the case of AI, the question arises whether its "creativity" stems from true innovation or is merely an advanced form of recombination of existing patterns.

The purpose of this text is to collect and analyze current achievements and technologies used by GAI. Through a review of the latest models and their applications, we will attempt to outline a comprehensive picture of this dynamically developing area of research. We will focus on both the theoretical foundations of GAI and practical examples of its use in various fields – from natural language processing, image and sound generation to film material, analyzing its applications and impact on various aspects of creativity. In addition, the text outlines a proposal for the concept of positive GAI as a new paradigm for designing AI systems that focuses on identifying and strengthening mechanisms supporting human well-being in their interactions with and through generative technologies.

In the context of GAI's latest achievements, a fundamental question arises regarding the nature of its operation: can we truly speak of authentic creation, or merely advanced imitation? The analysis undertaken aims not only to determine the potential of GAI technology, but also to take a critical look at its limitations and challenges for the future of human expression. This text also aims to initiate a broader discussion on the impact of GAI on the future of creativity in the era of AI technology development.

The development of GAI presents society with complex challenges regarding intellectual property and creative originality. Generative models, trained on huge datasets acquired through automatic content harvesting from the internet, may unknowingly duplicate fragments of existing works. The problem is exacerbated by the fact that the creators of the largest models do not publicly disclose their training sets, making it difficult to assess potential copyright infringement.

Studies have shown that language models like GPT-3 can literally reproduce phrases and paragraphs from training data (Carlini et al., 2021), and image models such as DALL-E or Stable Diffusion can reproduce distinctive artistic styles and motifs (Guadamuz, 2017). The ongoing class action lawsuit in the USA between artists and creators of popular generative models could be groundbreaking for the future of the industry (Robertson, 2024).

An additional complication is introduced by the use of transfer learning (Pan & Yang, 2009). Models initially trained on general datasets and then fine-tuned for specific applications can lead to knowledge "leakage" between domains in ways that are difficult to trace (Yosinski et al., 2014).

In response to these controversies, initiatives are emerging that use only licensed training data, such as Adobe Firefly (Lardinois, 2023), or rely solely on public domain materials, like the Public Diffusion project (Exline, 2024). However, strict application of copyright laws creates the risk of technology monopolization by large corporations, which alone possess the means to acquire extensive, licensed datasets.

The authorship status of AI-generated content also remains ambiguous. In the United States, the U.S. Copyright Office recognizes the possibility of legal protection for AI content only on the condition of significant human contribution (United States Copyright Office, 2025), while in China, a precedent-setting ruling granted copyright for an image to the author of a text prompt (Tan et al., 2024).

Solving these problems requires developing international standards for transparency and accountability in the process of training and using generative models. These standards should take into account both the protection of rights of creators whose works are used in the learning process and the interests of end users (Fjeld et al., 2020).

1 Types of Generative AI

The development of generative models is based on advanced neural network models, particularly transformer networks (Vaswani et al., 2017), generative adversarial networks (Goodfellow et al., 2014), and diffusion models (Sohl-Dickstein et al., 2015). In the context of AI models, several key categories can be distinguished that reflect the diversity of applications and techniques used in this field. This paper will discuss language models, image-generating models, sound and video models, taking into account their characteristics, appli-

AI; Grok – X.AI Corp.; DeepSeek – Hangzhou DeepSeek Artificial Intelligence Co., Ltd.; Bielik – Polish LLM, a community initiative within the SpeakLeash project.

Despite their successes, the implementation of large language models raises significant challenges. A key issue is bias – models may unintentionally perpetuate prejudices present in training data (Kadan et al., 2023). Therefore, there is increasing emphasis on ethical evaluation and responsible use of these technologies (Rasekh & Eisenberg, 2022). Another challenge is interpreting and explaining decisions made by LLMs. Due to their complexity and non-linearity, these models function as "black boxes," making it difficult to understand the foundations of their operation (Belinkov & Glass, 2019).

Language models are finding increasingly broader applications in creative fields, demonstrating abilities to generate various textual forms, from poetry to prose, and also showing impressive capabilities in imitating the style of well-known authors. A groundbreaking study published in Nature (Porter et al., 2024) found that readers not only have difficulty distinguishing AI-written poems from human poetry but actually prefer the former. In the experiment, participants rated AI poems as more rhythmic and beautiful, achieving identification accuracy below random chance (46.6%). Paradoxically, the simplicity and accessibility of AI-generated poems were perceived as features of human authorship, while the complexity of human poetry was interpreted as a sign of artificial origin.

An innovative application of LLMs are platforms such as Character AI (Character Technologies, 2024), which enable creating and interacting with virtual characters by defining their personality, character, and communication style. Chatbots can assume the roles of historical figures or fictional characters, finding applications in entertainment and creative processes. This technology also opens new possibilities in computer game design, where language models can power virtual characters capable of conducting open dialogues with players, going beyond traditional predefined conversation paths.

1.2 *Architectures and Models Related to Image Processing and Generation*

Image generation is one of the most impressive areas of GAI. In recent years, significant progress has been made in creating models capable of generating photorealistic images, artistic graphics, and animations based on textual descriptions or other images (Ramesh et al., 2022; Saharia et al., 2022; Rombach et al., 2022). In the context of art, these models can be used to create new works interpreted as contemporary forms of artistic expression (Wójtowicz, 2020; Zawojski, 2019).

Two key architectures used in generative image models are GAN (Generative Adversarial Networks) (Goodfellow et al., 2014) and diffusion models (Ho et al., 2020). A GAN consists of two competing neural networks: a generator and a discriminator. The generator attempts to create realistic images, while the discriminator tries to distinguish real images from generated ones. Although GAN models such as StyleGAN (Karras et al., 2019) and BigGAN (Brock et al., 2018) introduced groundbreaking capabilities for controlling generated images through manipulation in latent space, their development encountered limitations related to scaling and training stability.

The currently dominant architecture is diffusion models, in which the generation process begins with random noise that is gradually transformed into a coherent image through a series of denoising steps, guided by a textual description or another image (Ho et al., 2020). Models such as DALL-E (Ramesh et al., 2021), Midjourney, or Stable Diffusion (Rombach et al., 2022) achieve impressive results both in terms of the visual quality of generated images and the precision in interpreting complex textual descriptions.

A significant advancement in controlling image generation is ControlNet technology, which allows precise guidance of the generation process through the use of reference images (Zhang et al., 2023). This system enables the preservation of specific visual features, such as pose, contours, or semantic segmentation, when transforming one image into another. ControlNet is particularly useful in transforming conceptual sketches into photorealistic images.

Generative image models find wide applications in various fields – from computer graphics and special effects (Suwajanakorn et al., 2017), through fashion design (Chen et al., 2024) and interior design (Chaillou, 2020), to medical (Yi et al., 2019) and scientific applications (Ye et al., 2024).

1.3 *Architectures and Models Related to Audio Processing and Generation*

AI has made significant progress in generating realistic sounds, enabling the creation of original musical compositions, synthetic speech, and sound effects based on textual descriptions or audio samples.

The first significant achievements in sound generation were based on convolutional networks (CNNs), exemplified by the WaveNet model (Oord et al., 2016) developed by DeepMind. This model introduced the ability to directly model sound waves in the time domain, making it possible to generate naturally sounding speech and music. Another significant step in the development of this field was the application of transformer architecture (Vaswani et al., 2017), used in OpenAI's Jukebox model to generate coherent, multi-minute musical compositions with vocals.

The latest generation of music systems, represented by MusicLM, Audio-Craft, and Suno AI, offers advanced control over the creative process. These models allow precise specification of musical parameters such as tempo, tonality, and instrumentation style. They can also compose music to a given song text, taking into account textual cues regarding genre, mood, or instrumentation.

A separate, specialized area of sound generation is human voice synthesis. Systems such as ElevenLabs offer comprehensive voice processing and generation capabilities, integrating text and audio analysis. They can not only transform text into naturally sounding speech but also analyze voice samples to extract characteristic features such as timbre, accent, and articulation method. Based on these features, they create a digital voice model that can be used to generate new utterances. Advanced algorithms allow for maintaining the naturalness and expressiveness of speech, taking into account context and emotional coloring of the text. This technology promises to revolutionize the dubbing industry, offering the possibility of creating multilingual versions of films while preserving the original expressiveness of actors, and also opens new possibilities in the development of personalized voice assistants. At the same time, the development of this technology raises concerns about the possibility of creating convincing voice deepfakes that could be used for misinformation or fraud.

Generative sound models also find applications in noise reduction (Pascual et al., 2017), improving sound quality (Biswas & Jia, 2020), and creating sound effects for games and films (Donahue et al., 2018). Research shows an ambiguous attitude of the younger generation toward AI-generated music (Kowalski, 2024), which may affect its future adoption in the music industry.

1.4 *Architectures and Models Related to Video Processing and Generation*

Video and film generation is among the most demanding and complex areas of GAI. It combines not only the generation of convincing images but also maintaining temporal consistency, motion fluidity, and sound synchronization (Skorokhodov et al., 2021). Despite these challenges, significant progress has been made in this area in recent years, and generative video models are finding more applications in the entertainment industry, advertising, and education (Tulyakov et al., 2018; Wang et al., 2018).

Early approaches to video generation relied on convolutional (CNN) and recurrent (RNN) networks. Architectures such as VideoVAE and SAVP used convolutional networks to encode and decode individual frames and recurrent networks to model temporal relationships between frames (Denton et al.,

2018). The next development stage was models based on transformer architecture, adapting attention mechanisms to the video domain, enabling the generation of longer and more complex sequences (Weissenborn et al., 2020). An important innovation is the Sound2Sight model, which enables generating synchronized video sequences based on an audio track (Shlizerman et al., 2018). A breakthrough in video is represented by the latest large-scale transformer models such as Sora (OpenAI) and Veo-3 (Google DeepMind), which enable creating coherent, realistic video sequences several tens of seconds long based on textual descriptions. Chinese video models, including Vidu and Kling, also demonstrate impressive capabilities in this area.

Generating coherent video sequences requires AI models to do much more than just create individual frames. The model must "understand" the principles of physics and natural movement patterns, model three-dimensional space visible from different perspectives, and maintain consistency of objects and characters over time.

Contemporary models offer various methods for generating video materials. Although textual description remains the basic method, models such as Sora also enable "animating" individual images, extending existing clips, or creating variants of similar sequences with the same content. This flexibility allows for various applications – from creating entirely new visual materials to modifying and extending existing recordings.

A separate, specialized area is modeling people in video materials. Advanced AI models can reproduce and manipulate facial expressions, enabling the transfer of expressions between different people or synchronizing mouth movement with speech sound (Fried et al., 2019). These technologies find applications in film production, avatar creation, or videoconferencing systems, although they also raise questions about potential misuse in the context of deepfakes.

Video generation requires significantly more computing power than other forms of GAI, due to the need to maintain temporal and spatial consistency and model complex relationships between successive frames. At the same time, it represents the pinnacle achievement in the field of GAI, combining the ability to generate images, model motion, and understand three-dimensional space.

2 Friendly Generative Artificial Intelligence, Its Challenges and Dilemmas

GAI, as a breakthrough technology with growing impact on human experiences, requires a perspective that considers not only potential threats but also opportunities for enhancing human well-being. Positive GAI, which should be rooted in the principles of positive cyberpsychology (Fortuna, 2023), represents an attempt to answer the question of how to design and use generative AI models in ways that support the psychological, social, and cognitive dimensions of human functioning.

Positive GAI should be designed and created with consideration for fundamental human psychological needs such as autonomy, competence, and relatedness, which according to self-determination theory (Ryan & Deci, 2000) form the basis of intrinsic motivation and psychological well-being. GAI systems should enhance users' sense of agency by offering transparent insight into the content generation process and the ability to control parameters, supporting conscious collaboration rather than replacing human creativity. Research suggests that technologies supporting autonomy contribute to increased user satisfaction and psychological well-being (Peters et al., 2018).

In the domain of creativity, positive GAI should enhance human creativity in line with the idea of "human-AI co-creativity" (Kantosalo & Toivonen, 2016). A fundamental aspect is also designing GAI with human well-being in mind from the very beginning of the creative process, consistent with the concept of "wellbeing-informed design" (Desmet & Pohlmeyer, 2013). This means integrating knowledge about psychological needs into the design process and assessing the impact on well-being at various stages of development.

Developing the concept of positive GAI also involves a number of challenges, such as creating a methodology for systematically evaluating the impact of GAI systems on various dimensions of well-being, balancing automation and human agency, and reflecting on ethical boundaries and responsibility, including the boundaries between support and manipulation.

Proper development of the positive GAI concept can contribute to achieving the desired balance, offering a more complete picture of human functioning in a technological environment enriched with GAI.

The application of GAI in the fields of art and media leads to social transformations. Generative tools democratize the creative process, giving a wider range of users the ability to create sophisticated visual and textual content (Mazzone & Elgammal, 2019). At the same time, this raises concerns about potential job losses for artists, graphic designers, journalists, and other creators (Manyika et al., 2017).

A particular challenge is the issue of trust and credibility of AI-generated content. The possibilities for their detection vary significantly depending on the medium. Text, due to the restrictive and rule-bound nature of language, offers few signals allowing for reliable source identification. Even patterns characteristic of AI in vocabulary choice or sentence construction are relatively easy to mask. The situation is different for visual content – diffusion models generating images and videos leave characteristic traces in the pixel structure, creating recognizable patterns and artifacts that can be subject to automatic detection.

In response to these challenges, hidden signature technology (SynthID) is being developed (Dathari et al., 2024), allowing for automatic identification of AI-generated content without affecting its quality or aesthetics. However, this is a solution limited to models that choose to implement it. Although social media platforms, including Instagram, already require marking AI content, the industry is still searching for universal standards for their identification.

Another significant problem is the tendency toward uniformity and homogenization of messages when many creators rely on the same models and datasets (Hertzmann, 2018). Algorithms can also perpetuate and strengthen existing stereotypes present in training data, leading to the reproduction of harmful social patterns.

Economic and ethical issues are also significant. The widespread availability of AI-generated content can undermine the foundations of artistic and media activity (Elgammal, 2019). It is necessary to develop new business models and legal regulations that will ensure fair compensation for creators while utilizing the potential of new technologies (Anantrasirichai & Bull, 2021).

The development of AI in art and media also prompts fundamental reflection on the nature of creativity and the role of humans in the creative process. Questions arise about the criteria for evaluating the artistic value of works generated by algorithms (Colton & Wiggins, 2012) and about the boundaries between human and machine creativity. The answers to these questions will shape how we perceive and value creativity in the age of AI.

Finding a balance between the democratization of creativity and protecting the rights and interests of professional creators becomes crucial. This requires thoughtful policy on the development and use of AI technology, taking into account both its transformative potential and the associated social, economic, and ethical challenges.

In analyzing the contemporary development of GAI, it is necessary to systematically identify both normative postulates aimed at optimizing its applications and the fundamental dilemmas generated by its implementation in the socio-cultural context. Key aspects of both these dimensions are presented below, summarizing the above considerations and providing a starting point for in-depth reflection on the future of positive GAI technology and its relationship with humans. Finally, the following normative postulates for implementing GAI can be identified:

- Implementation of positive GAI principles. Designing GAI in a way rooted in the tenets of positive cyberpsychology, supporting mental, social, and cognitive dimensions of human functioning.
- Consideration of fundamental psychological needs. Creating GAI systems with respect for the needs of autonomy, competence, and relatedness, in accordance with self-determination theory.
- Strengthening users' sense of agency. Providing transparent insight into the content generation process and the ability to control parameters, fostering conscious collaboration rather than replacing human creativity.
- Promotion of human-AI co-creativity. Developing generative AI as a tool enhancing human creativity, in line with the idea of "human-AI co-creativity."
- Implementation of well-being-oriented design. Integrating knowledge about psychological needs into the GAI creation process and systematically assessing the impact on users' well-being, in accordance with the "wellbeing-informed design" concept.
- Development of methodologies for assessing GAI's impact on well-being. Establishing systems for evaluating the impact of generative AI on various dimensions of human well-being.
- Development of generative content identification technologies. Improving solutions like SynthID enabling automatic identification of content source without affecting its quality or aesthetics.

The following epistemological and axiological challenges related to GAI can also be identified:

- Balancing automation and human agency. The need to maintain a balance between automation potential and the need to preserve human control and sense of agency.
- Defining ethical boundaries between support and manipulation. The difficulty in establishing the boundary between using AI to support people and potentially manipulating their behaviors and decisions.
- Changes in employment structure in the creative sector. Concerns about job losses for artists, graphic designers, journalists, and other content creators.
- Verification of AI-generated content credibility. Varied possibilities for detecting generative content depending on the medium, with particular attention to the difficulty in identifying texts.
- Homogenization of cultural messages. The risk of uniformity and standardization of content when many creators use the same models and datasets.
- Reproduction of stereotypes and prejudices. The threat of perpetuating and reinforcing harmful social patterns present in training data.

- Transformation of the economic foundations of creative activity. The need to develop new business models and legal regulations ensuring fair compensation for creators in an era of widespread availability of AI-generated content.
- Redefining criteria for artistic value. The need to establish new criteria for evaluating the artistic value of algorithm-generated works.
- Universalization of AI content marking standards. The challenge related to developing and implementing universal standards for identifying and marking content generated by AI.
- Balancing between democratization of creativity and protection of creators' rights. Finding equilibrium between increasing the availability of creative tools and safeguarding the interests of professional creators.

3 Summary

When considering the nature of GAI, we face a fundamental question: is it a manifestation of authentic creativity, or merely an advanced form of reproduction? Generative models are capable of creating new, original content that goes beyond simple imitation, but their operation is limited by the framework of training data, which calls into question their creative autonomy.

The development of generative AI prompts reflection on the future of creativity. Key issues include:

- Changing the definition of creativity and authorship. AI may shift the emphasis from the creative process to the result, questioning the role of artistic intention and expression.
- New forms of collaboration. Creators can use AI as a tool to explore new ideas and possibilities, creating hybrid works at the intersection of human and machine.
- Evolution of the artist's role. The development of GAI fundamentally changes our understanding of the creative process. Key challenges include redefining the role of the artist, who increasingly becomes a moderator and director of generative processes (Elgammal, 2019), and the evolution of the very concept of artistic creation (McCormack et al., 2019). Artists will need to adapt to new conditions by developing skills in selecting, moderating, and directing generative processes.
- Impact on artistic education. Art education will need to incorporate AI as a creative tool, emphasizing its critical and ethical use (Mazzone & Elgammal, 2019). At the same time, it is necessary to develop new business models and regulations to protect creators' interests (Miller, 2019).

– Questions about the value of art. The proliferation of AI-generated works may lead to a redefinition of the artistic and market value of art.

The future of GAI technology will be shaped by several key trends: development of multimodal models combining different forms of data (text, image, sound) to create richer experiences; refinement of control and fine-tuning of generated content; research on explainable and interpretable AI; development of methods for detecting and counteracting unwanted effects; and creation of interfaces facilitating human interaction with generative models.

Further development of GAI requires interdisciplinary collaboration among artists, researchers, and decision-makers. Only such an approach will allow shaping this technology in a way that enriches rather than limits human creativity, while addressing the ethical, legal, and social challenges associated with it.

References

Anantrasirichai, N., & Bull, D. (2021). Artificial intelligence in the creative industries: A review. *Artificial Intelligence Review, 54*(4), 2221–2233. https://doi.org/10.1007/s10462-021-10039-7

Arnab, A., Dehghani, M., Heigold, G., Sun, C., Lučić, M., & Schmid, C. (2021). ViViT: A video vision transformer. arXiv. https://doi.org/10.48550/arXiv.2103.15691

Awad, E., Dsouza, S., Bonnefon, J. F., Shariff, A., & Rahwan, I. (2020). Crowdsourcing moral machines. *Communications of the ACM, 63*(3), 48–55. https://doi.org/10.1145/3339904

Balaji, Y., Min, M. R., Bai, B., Chellappa, R., & Graf, H. P. (2019). Conditional GAN with discriminative filter generation for text-to-video synthesis. arXiv. https://doi.org/10.48550/arXiv.1907.10597

Belinkov, Y., & Glass, J. (2019). Analysis methods in neural language processing: A survey. *Transactions of the Association for Computational Linguistics, 7*, 49–72. https://doi.org/10.1162/tacl_a_00254

Bendel, O. (2019). The synthetization of human voices. *AI & Society, 34*(4), 835–841. https://doi.org/10.1007/s00146-017-0748-x

Biswas, A., & Jia, D. (2020). Audio codec enhancement with generative adversarial networks. In *ICASSP 2020–2020 IEEE International Conference on Acoustics, Speech and Signal Processing* (ICASSP) (pp. 356–360). IEEE. http://doi.org/10.1109/ICASSP40776.2020.9053113

Boden, M. A. (2004). *The creative mind: Myths and mechanisms.* Routledge.

Boden, M. A. (2014). Creativity and artificial intelligence: A contradiction in terms? In E. S. Paul & S. B. Kaufman (Eds.), *The philosophy of creativity: New essays* (pp.

224–244). Oxford University Press. https://doi.org/10.1093/acprof:oso/9780199836963.003.0012

Botha, E., & Reyneke, M. (2013). To share or not to share: The role of content and emotion in viral marketing. *Journal of Public Affairs*, *13*(2), 160–171. https://doi.org/10.1002/pa.1471

Brock, A., Donahue, J., & Simonyan, K. (2018). Large scale GAN training for high fidelity natural image synthesis. arXiv. https://doi.org/10.48550/arXiv.1809.11096

Brown, T., Mann, B., Ryder, N., Subbiah, M., Kaplan, J. D., Dhariwal, P., et al., (2020). Language models are few-shot learners. *Advances in Neural Information Processing Systems*, *33*, 1877–1901. https://doi.org/10.5555/3495724.3495883

Carlini, N., Ippolito, D., Jagielski, M., Lee, K., Tramer, F., & Zhang, C. (2021). Quantifying memorization across neural language models. arXiv. https://doi.org/10.48550/arXiv.2202.07646

Chaillou, S. (2020). AI+ architecture: Towards a new approach. *Architectural Intelligence*, 223.

Chan, C., Ginosar, S., Zhou, T., & Efros, A. A. (2019). Everybody dance now. In *Proceedings of the IEEE/CVF International Conference on Computer Vision* (pp. 5933–5942). https://doi.org/10.1109/ICCV.2019.00919

Character Technologies, Inc. (2024). *Character.ai*. https://character.ai

Chen, L., Zhang, Y., Han, J., Sun, L., Childs, P., & Wang, B. (2024). A foundation model enhanced approach for generative design in combinational creativity. *Journal of Engineering Design*, 35(11), 1394–1420. https://doi.org/10.1080/09544828.2024.2333622

Chen, M., Tworek, J., Jun, H., Yuan, Q., Pinto, H. P. O., Kaplan, J., Edwards, H., Burda, Y., et al. (2021). Evaluating large language models trained on code. arXiv. https://doi.org/10.48550/arXiv.2107.03374

Chesney, R., & Citron, D. K. (2020). Deep fakes: A looming challenge for privacy, democracy, and national security. In *The Internet of Bodies* (pp. 141–155). Routledge. https://doi.org/10.1109/ICCV.2019.00603

Chowdhery, A., Narang, S., Devlin, J., Bosma, M., Mishra, G., Roberts, A., Barham, P., et al. (2022). PaLM: Scaling language modeling with Pathways. arXiv. https://doi.org/10.48550/arXiv.2204.02311

Colton, S., & Wiggins, G. A. (2012). Computational creativity: The final frontier? *ECAI*, *12*, 21–26. https://doi.org/10.3233/978-1-61499-098-7-21

Dathathri, S., See, A., Ghaisas, S., Hanna, A., Chaudhary, A., Bai, J., Chen, E., Thakkar, M., et al. (2024). Scalable watermarking for identifying large language model outputs. *Nature*, *634*, 818–823. https://doi.org/10.1038/s41586-024-08025-4

Deahl, D. (2019). FTC says the tech behind audio deepfakes is getting better. *The Verge*. https://www.theverge.com/2019/1/29/18202602/ftc-audio-deepfakes-getting-better-ai

Denton, E., & Fergus, R. (2018). Stochastic video generation with a learned prior. In *International Conference on Machine Learning* (pp. 1174–1183). PMLR. Retrieved from https://proceedings.mlr.press/v80/denton18a.html

Desmet, P. M. A., & Pohlmeyer, A. E. (2013). Positive design: An introduction to design for subjective well-being. *International Journal of Design*, *7*(3), 5–19.

Devlin, J., Chang, M. W., Lee, K., & Toutanova, K. (2018). BERT: Pre-training of deep bidirectional transformers for language understanding. arXiv. https://doi.org/10.48550/arXiv.1810.04805

Dhariwal, P., Jun, H., Payne, C., Kim, J. W., Radford, A., & Sutskever, I. (2020). Jukebox: A generative model for music. arXiv. https://doi.org/10.48550/arXiv.2005.00341

Donahue, C., McAuley, J., & Puckette, M. (2018). Adversarial audio synthesis. arXiv. https://doi.org/10.48550/arXiv.1802.04208

Elgammal, A. (2017). Generating "art" by learning about styles and deviating from style norms. arXiv. https://doi.org/10.48550/arXiv.1706.07068

Elgammal, A. (2019). AI is blurring the definition of artist. *American Scientist*, *107*(1), 18–21. https://doi.org/10.1511/2019.107.1.18

Engel, J., Agrawal, K. K., Chen, S., Gulrajani, I., Donahue, C., & Roberts, A. (2019). GANsynth: Adversarial neural audio synthesis. arXiv. https://doi.org/10.48550/arXiv.1902.08710

Epstein, S. L. (2015). Wanted: Collaborative intelligence. *Artificial Intelligence*, *221*, 36–45.

Exline, L. (2024). *A fireside chat with the creators of Public Diffusion*. Substack. https://spawning.substack.com/p/a-fireside-chat-with-the-creators

Fjeld, J., Achten, N., Hilligoss, H., Nagy, A., & Srikumar, M. (2020). *Principled artificial intelligence: Mapping consensus in ethical and rights-based approaches to principles for AI*. Berkman Klein Center Research Publication, http://doi.org/10.2139/ssrn.3518482

Fortuna, P. (2023). Positive cyberpsychology as a field of study of the well-being of people interacting with and via technology. *Frontiers in Psychology*, *14*:1053482 https://doi.org/10.3389/fpsyg.2023.1053482

Fried, O., Tewari, A., Zollhöfer, M., Finkelstein, A., Shechtman, E., Goldman, D. B., Genova, K., Jin, Z., Theobalt, C., & Agrawala, M. (2019). Text-based editing of talking-head video. *ACM Transactions on Graphics* (*TOG*), *38*(4), 1–14. https://doi.org/10.1145/3306346.3323028

Goodfellow, I., Pouget-Abadie, J., Mirza, M., Xu, B., Warde-Farley, D., Ozair, S., Courville, A., & Bengio, Y. (2014). Generative adversarial nets. *Advances in Neural Information Processing Systems*, *27*. http://doi.org/10.1145/3422622

Guadamuz, A. (2017). Do androids dream of electric copyright? Comparative analysis of originality in artificial intelligence generated works. *Intellectual Property Quarterly*, 2, 169–186. http://doi.org/10.1093/oso/9780198870944.003.0008

Gupta, S., Sharaff, A., & Nagwani, N. K. (2023). Graph ranked clustering based biomedical text summarization using top k similarity. *Computer Systems Science and Engineering*, *45*(3), 2333–2349. http://doi.org/10.32604/csse.2023.030385

He, J., Lehrmann, A., Marino, J., Mori, G., & Sigal, L. (2018). Probabilistic video generation using holistic attribute control. In Proceedings of the European Conference on Computer Vision (ECCV) (pp. 452–467). https://doi.org/10.48550/arXiv.1803.08085

He, Z., Zuo, W., Kan, M., Shan, S., & Chen, X. (2019). AttGAN: Facial attribute editing by only changing what you want. *IEEE Transactions on Image Processing*, *28*(11), 5464–5478.

Hertzmann, A. (2018). Can computers create art? *Arts*, *7*(2), 18. http://doi.org/10.3390/arts7020018

Ho, J., Jain, A., & Abbeel, P. (2020). Denoising diffusion probabilistic models. *Advances in Neural Information Processing Systems*, *33*, 6840–6851. https://doi.org/10.48550/arXiv.2006.11239

Hu, R., Xu, H., Rohrbach, M., Feng, J., Saenko, K., & Darrell, T. (2016). Natural language object retrieval. In Proceedings of the IEEE Conference on Computer Vision and Pattern Recognition (pp. 4555–4564). https://doi.org/10.1109/CVPR.2016.493

Jacovi, A., & Goldberg, Y. (2020). Towards faithfully interpretable NLP systems: How should we define and evaluate faithfulness? arXiv. https://doi.org/10.48550/arXiv.2004.03685

Kadan, A., Deepak, P., Bhadra, S., Gangan, M. P., & L, L. V. (2023). Blacks is to anger as whites is to joy? Understanding latent affective bias in large pre-trained neural language models. arXiv. https://doi.org/10.48550/arXiv.2301.09003

Kanbach, D. (2023). The GenAI is out of the bottle: Generative artificial intelligence from a business model innovation perspective. *Review of Managerial Science*, *18*(4), 1189–1220. http://doi.org/10.1007/s11846-023-00696-z

Kantosalo, A., & Toivonen, H. (2016). Modes for creative human-computer collaboration: Alternating and task-divided co-creativity. In *Proceedings of the Seventh International Conference on Computational Creativity* (pp. 77–84). http://computationalcreativity.net/iccc2016/wp-content/uploads/2016/01/Modes-for-Creative-Human-Computer-Collaboration.pdf

Kaplan, J., McCandlish, S., Henighan, T., Brown, T. B., Chess, B., Child, R., Gray, S., Radford, A., Wu, J., & Amodei, D. (2020). Scaling laws for neural language models. arXiv. https://doi.org/10.48550/arXiv.2001.08361

Karras, T., Laine, S., & Aila, T. (2019). A style-based generator architecture for generative adversarial networks. In Proceedings of the IEEE/CVF Conference on Computer Vision and Pattern Recognition (pp. 4401–4410). https://doi.org/10.1109/CVPR.2019.00453

Korporowicz, L. (2023). Sztucznej mądrości nie będzie. *Perspektywy Kultury*, *42*(3), 117–130.

Kowalski, M. (2024). Muzyka generowana przez sztuczną inteligencję – ocena przedstawicieli pokolenia z. Com.press, 7(1), 6–21. https://doi.org/10.51480/compress.2024.7-1.703

Lardinois, F. (2023). *Adobe brings Firefly to the enterprise.* TechCrunch. https://techcrunch.com/2023/06/08/adobe-brings-firefly-to-the-enterprise/

Manovich, L. (2019). Defining AI arts: Three proposals. *Leonardo, 52*(3), 237–238.

Manyika, J., Lund, S., Chui, M., Bughin, J., Woetzel, J., Batra, P., Ko, R., & Sanghvi, S. (2017). *Jobs lost, jobs gained: Workforce transitions in a time of automation.* McKinsey Global Institute.

Mazzone, M., & Elgammal, A. (2019). Art, creativity, and the potential of artificial intelligence. *Arts, 8*(1), 26. https://doi.org/10.3390/arts8010026

McCormack, J., Gifford, T., & Hutchings, P. (2019). Autonomy, authenticity, authorship and intention in computer generated art. In International Conference on Computational Intelligence in Music, Sound, Art and Design (pp. 35–50). Springer. https://doi.org/10.48550/arXiv.1903.02166

Midjourney. (2024). https://www.midjourney.com/

Miller, A. I. (2019). *The artist in the machine: The world of AI-powered creativity.* MIT Press.

Nguyen, T. T., Nguyen, C. M., Nguyen, D. T., Nguyen, D. T., & Nahavandi, S. (2019). Deep learning for deepfakes creation and detection. arXiv. https://doi.org/10.48550/arXiv.1909.11573

Oord, A. V. D., Dieleman, S., Zen, H., Simonyan, K., Vinyals, O., Graves, A., Kalchbrenner, N., Senior, A., & Kavukcuoglu, K. (2016). WaveNet: A generative model for raw audio. arXiv. https://doi.org/10.48550/arXiv.1609.03499

Oord, A. V. D., Li, Y., & Vinyals, O. (2018). Representation learning with contrastive predictive coding. arXiv. https://doi.org/10.48550/arXiv.1807.03748

Pan, S. J., & Yang, Q. (2009). A survey on transfer learning. *IEEE Transactions on Knowledge and Data Engineering*, 22(10), 1345–1359. https://doi.org/10.1109/TKDE.2009.191

Pascual, S., Bonafonte, A., & Serra, J. (2017). SEGAN: Speech enhancement generative adversarial network. arXiv. https://doi.org/10.48550/arXiv.1703.09452

Pearlman, R. (2018). Recognizing artificial intelligence (AI) as authors and inventors under US intellectual property law. *Richmond Journal of Law & Technology, 24*(2), 2.

Peters, D., Calvo, R. A., & Ryan, R. M. (2018). Designing for motivation, engagement and wellbeing in digital experience. *Frontiers in Psychology, 9*, 797. https://doi.org/10.3389/fpsyg.2018.00797

Pietrzykowski, A. (2023). Wykorzystanie sztucznej inteligencji w ocenie prac pisemnych: idea, stan aktualny, ryzyka, perspektywy. *Scripta Neophilologica Posnaniensia, 23*, 121–132. https://doi.org/10.14746/snp.2023.23.09

Porter, B., & Machery, E. (2024). AI-generated poetry is indistinguishable from human-written poetry and is rated more favorably. *Scientific Reports, 14*, 26133. http://doi.org/10.1038/s41598-024-76900-1

Przygoda, W. (2024). Sztuczna inteligencja a duszpasterstwo. Obietnice – zagrożenia – wyzwania. *Społeczeństwo, 34*(1), 51–65. http://doi.org/10.58324/s.378

Purwins, H., Li, B., Virtanen, T., Schlüter, J., Chang, S. Y., & Sainath, T. (2019). Deep learning for audio signal processing. *IEEE Journal of Selected Topics in Signal Processing, 13*(2), 206–219.

Rae, J. W., Borgeaud, S., Cai, T., Millican, K., Hoffmann, J., Song, F., Aslanides, J., Henderson, S., Ring, R., et al., (2021). Scaling language models: Methods, analysis & insights from training gopher. arXiv. https://doi.org/10.48550/arXiv.2112.11446

Raffel, C., Shazeer, N., Roberts, A., Lee, K., Narang, S., Matena, M., Zhou, Y., Li, W., & Liu, P. J. (2020). Exploring the limits of transfer learning with a unified text-to-text transformer. *Journal of Machine Learning Research, 21*(140), 1–67.

Raiaan, M. A. K., Mukta, M. S. H., Fatema, K., Fahad, N. M., Sakib, S., Mim, M. M. J., Hoq, A., Naha, M., & Azam, S. (2024). A review on large language models: Architectures, applications, taxonomies, open issues and challenges. *IEEE Access, 12*, 26839–26874. http://doi.org/10.1109/ACCESS.2024.3365742

Ramesh, A., Dhariwal, P., Nichol, A., Chu, C., & Chen, M. (2022). Hierarchical text-conditional image generation with CLIP latents. arXiv. https://doi.org/10.48550/arXiv.2204.06125

Ramesh, A., Pavlov, M., Goh, G., Gray, S., Voss, C., Radford, A., Chen, M., & Sutskever, I. (2021). Zero-shot text-to-image generation. arXiv. https://doi.org/10.48550/arXiv.2102.12092

Rasekh, A., & Eisenberg, I. W. (2022). Democratizing ethical assessment of natural language generation models. arXiv. https://doi.org/10.48550/arXiv.2207.10576

Robertson, A. (2024). Artists' lawsuit against Stability AI and Midjourney gets more punch. *The Verge*. https://www.theverge.com/2024/8/13/24219520/stability-midjourney-artist-lawsuit-copyright-trademark-claims-approved

Rombach, R., Blattmann, A., Lorenz, D., Esser, P., & Ommer, B. (2022). High-resolution image synthesis with latent diffusion models. In Proceedings of the IEEE/CVF Conference on Computer Vision and Pattern Recognition (pp. 10684–10695). https://doi.org/10.48550/arXiv.2112.10752

Runco, M. A., & Jaeger, G. J. (2012). The standard definition of creativity. *Creativity Research Journal*, 24(1), 92–96. http://doi.org/10.1080/10400419.2012.650092

Ryan, R. M., & Deci, E. L. (2000). Self-determination theory and the facilitation of intrinsic motivation, social development, and well-being. *American Psychologist, 55*(1), 68–78. https://psycnet.apa.org/doi/10.1037/0003-066X.55.1.68

Saharia, C., Chan, W., Saxena, S., Li, L., Whang, J., Denton, E., Ghasemipour, S. K. S., Ayan, B. K., Mahdavi, S. S., Lopes, R. G., Salimans, T., Ho, J., Fleet, D. J., & Norouzi,

M. (2022). Photorealistic text-to-image diffusion models with deep language understanding. arXiv. https://doi.org/10.48550/arXiv.2205.11487

Shlizerman, E., Dery, L., Schoen, H., & Kemelmacher-Shlizerman, I. (2018). Audio to body dynamics. In Proceedings of the IEEE Conference on Computer Vision and Pattern Recognition (pp. 7574–7583). https://doi.org/10.1109/CVPR.2018.00790

Skorokhodov, I., Tulyakov, S., & Elhoseiny, M. (2021). StyleGAN-V: A continuous video generator with the price, image quality and perks of StyleGAN2. arXiv. https://doi.org/10.48550/arXiv.2112.14683

Sohl-Dickstein, J., Weiss, E. A., Maheswaranathan, N., & Ganguli, S. (2015). Deep unsupervised learning using nonequilibrium thermodynamics. arXiv. https://doi.org/10.48550/arXiv.1503.03585

Sopek, M. (2021). Metafory sztucznej inteligencji. *Metafory ucieleśnione*, 73–98. http://doi.org/10.52097/acapress.9788362475810.73-98

Suwajanakorn, S., Seitz, S. M., & Kemelmacher-Shlizerman, I. (2017). Synthesizing Obama: Learning lip sync from audio. *ACM Transactions on Graphics* (*TOG*), *36*(4), 1–13. https://doi.org/10.1145/3072959.3073640

Szopa, R. (2024). Filozofia sztucznej inteligencji – podstawowe koncepcje i problemy. *Społeczeństwo*, *34*(1), 78–90. http://doi.org/10.58324/s.380

Tan, L.-K., Lau, J., & Wong, H. (2024). China: A landmark court ruling on copyright protection for AI-generated works. *Baker McKenzie Global Litigation News*. https://globallitigationnews.bakermckenzie.com/2024/05/08/china-a-landmark-court-ruling-on-copyright-protection-for-ai-generated-works/

Tanaka, M., Taura, K., Hanawa, T., & Torisawa, K. (2021). Automatic graph partitioning for very large-scale deep learning. arXiv. https://doi.org/10.48550/arXiv.2103.16063

Thies, J., Zollhofer, M., Stamminger, M., Theobalt, C., & Nießner, M. (2016). Face2face: Real-time face capture and reenactment of RGB videos. In *Proceedings of the IEEE Conference on Computer Vision and Pattern Recognition* (pp. 2387–2395). http://doi.org/10.1109/CVPR.2016.262

Thoppilan, R., De Freitas, D., Hall, J., Shazeer, N., Kulshreshtha, A., Cheng, H.-T., Jin, A., Bos, T., Baker, L., et al. (2022). LaMDA: Language Models for Dialog Applications. arXiv. https://doi.org/10.48550/arXiv.2201.08239

Topsakal, O., & Akıncı, T. Ç. (2023). Creating large language model applications utilizing langchain: A primer on developing LLM apps fast. *International Conference on Applied Engineering and Natural Sciences*, *1*(1), 1050–1056. http://doi.org/10.59287/icaens.1127

Tulyakov, S., Liu, M. Y., Yang, X., & Kautz, J. (2018). MoCoGAN: Decomposing motion and content for video generation. In Proceedings of the *IEEE Conference on Computer Vision and Pattern Recognition* (pp. 1526–1535). https://doi.org/10.1109/CVPR.2018.00165

United States Copyright Office. (2025). *Copyright and Artificial Intelligence Part 2: Copyrightability*. https://www.copyright.gov/ai/Copyright-and-Artificial-Intelligence-Part-2-Copyrightability-Report.pdf

Vaswani, A., Shazeer, N., Parmar, N., Uszkoreit, J., Jones, L., Gomez, A. N., Kaiser, Ł., & Polosukhin, I. (2017). Attention is all you need. *Advances in Neural Information Processing Systems, 30*. http://doi.org/10.48550/arXiv.1706.03762

Veale, M., & Zuiderveen Borgesius, F. (2021). Demystifying the Draft EU Artificial Intelligence Act. *Computer Law Review International, 22*(4), 97–112. https://doi.org/10.9785/cri-2021-220402

Wang, A., Singh, A., Michael, J., Hill, F., Levy, O., & Bowman, S. R. (2019). GLUE: A multi-task benchmark and analysis platform for natural language understanding. Paper presented at 7th International Conference on Learning Representations, ICLR 2019, New Orleans, United States. https://doi.org/10.18653/v1/W18-5446

Wang, T. C., Liu, M. Y., Zhu, J. Y., Liu, G., Tao, A., Kautz, J., & Catanzaro, B. (2018). Video-to-video synthesis. arXiv. https://doi.org/10.48550/arXiv.1808.06601

Wang, T. C., Liu, M. Y., Zhu, J. Y., Tao, A., Kautz, J., & Catanzaro, B. (2018). High-resolution image synthesis and semantic manipulation with conditional GANs. In *Proceedings of the IEEE Conference on Computer Vision and Pattern Recognition* (pp. 8798–8807). http://doi.org/10.1109/CVPR.2018.00917

Wei, J., Wang, X., Schuurmans, D., Bosma, M., Chi, E., Le, Q., & Zhou, D. (2022). Chain of thought prompting elicits reasoning in large language models. arXiv. https://doi.org/10.48550/arXiv.2201.11903

Weissenborn, D., Täckström, O., & Uszkoreit, J. (2020). Scaling autoregressive video models. arXiv. https://doi.org/10.48550/arXiv.1906.02634

Westerlund, M. (2019). The emergence of deepfake technology: A review. *Technology Innovation Management Review, 9*(11), 39–52.

White House. (2023). *Executive Order on the Safe, Secure, and Trustworthy Development and Use of Artificial Intelligence*. The White House.

Wójtowicz, E. (2020). O nas bez nas. Postantropocentryczne kinematografie stref wykluczenia. *Kwartalnik Filmowy*, (110), 6–23. http://doi.org/10.36744/kf.339

Wu, C., Huang, L., Zhang, Q., Li, B., Ji, L., Yang, F., Sapiro, G., & Xie, W. (2021). GODIVA: Generating open-domain videos from natural descriptions. arXiv. https://doi.org/10.48550/arXiv.2104.14806

Xu, T., Zhang, P., Huang, Q., Zhang, H., Gan, Z., Huang, X., & He, X. (2018). AttnGAN: Fine-grained text to image generation with attentional generative adversarial networks. In *Proceedings of the IEEE Conference on Computer Vision and Pattern Recognition* (pp. 1316–1324). https://doi.org/10.48550/arXiv.1711.10485

Xue, L., Constant, N., Roberts, A., Kale, M., Al-Rfou, R., Siddhant, A., Barua, A., & Raffel, C. (2021). mT5: A massively multilingual pre-trained text-to-text transformer. *NAACL 2021*, 483–498. https://doi.org/10.18653/v1/2021.naacl-main.41

Yan, W., Zhang, Y., Abbeel, P., & Srinivas, A. (2021). VideoGPT: Video generation using VQ-VAE and transformers. arXiv. https://doi.org/10.48550/arXiv.2104.10157

Ye, Y., Hao, J., Hou, Y., Wang, Z., Xiao, S., Luo, Y., & Zeng, W. (2024). Generative AI for visualization: State of the art and future directions. *Visual Informatics*, 8, 1–14. https://doi.org/10.1016/j.visinf.2024.04.003

Yi, X., Walia, E., & Babyn, P. (2019). Generative adversarial network in medical imaging: A review. *Medical Image Analysis, 58*, 101552. http://doi.org/10.1016/j.media.2019.101552

Yosinski, J., Clune, J., Bengio, Y., & Lipson, H. (2014). How transferable are features in deep neural networks? *Advances in Neural Information Processing Systems, 27*.

Zawojski, P. (2019). Maszynom (inteligentnym) wbrew? O sztuce w czasach sztucznej inteligencji. *Kwartalnik Filmowy*, (104), 84–93.

Zhang, L., Rao, A., & Agrawala, M. (2023). Adding conditional control to text-to-image diffusion models. *Proceedings of the IEEE/CVF Conference on Computer Vision and Pattern Recognition* (*CVPR*), 9263–9273. https://doi.org/10.48550/arXiv.2302.05543

CHAPTER 4

A Journey through Wonder: The Creative Power of Epistemic Emotions

Anna Dutkowska[1] *and Michael Brady*[2]

Abstract

This paper explores the transformative role of epistemic emotions – such as curiosity, wonder, and intellectual awe – in driving creativity and intellectual discovery. Grounded in cognitive science, philosophy, and evolutionary biology, the study highlights the unique interplay of these emotions with human creativity while also tracing their evolutionary roots in non-human animals. Epistemic emotions serve as catalysts for exploration, problem-solving, and learning, extending beyond survival mechanisms to inspire philosophical and artistic pursuits. By examining the functions and adaptive significance of epistemic emotions, this research underscores their importance in fostering human culture, innovation, and well-being. The paper further investigates the potential of digital technologies in stimulating and enhancing epistemic emotions. While artificial systems, such as those utilizing reinforcement learning, lack the phenomenal consciousness required for genuine emotional experiences, they are capable of simulating curiosity and fostering enriching learning environments. These insights underline new opportunities for unleashing creative potential in the era of the digital revolution.

Keywords

epistemic emotions – creativity – evolutionary continuity – cognitive curiosity – epistemic awe

Imagine a young Isaac Newton sitting under a tree, lost in thought. Suddenly, an apple falls, striking the ground near him. What could have been a mundane

1 The John Paul II Catholic University of Lublin, Institute of Philosophy, Lublin, Poland https://orcid.org/0000-0002-6302-3651

2 University of Glasgow, School of Humanities, Philosophy, Glasgow, Scotland, https://orcid.org/0000-0001-5826-7136

moment became extraordinary – not because of the falling apple itself, but because of the epistemic emotions it evoked. Curiosity and wonder surged within Newton, prompting him to ask why the apple fell straight down instead of moving sideways or upwards. This question, fueled by his sense of awe, puzzlement and determination to explore the unknown, eventually led to groundbreaking insights into gravity and the laws of motion. This story, whether historical or anecdotal, epitomizes the transformative power of epistemic emotions – those unique emotional states that drive humans to question, explore, and innovate. Curiosity, wonder, and intellectual awe are not merely fleeting feelings; they are profound motivators of creativity and intellectual discovery (Vogl et al., 2020).

Creativity is a multidimensional phenomenon that intersects with emotions, cognition, and context. Central to this process is the role of epistemic emotions – emotions that emerge from cognitive engagements with knowledge, uncertainty, and discovery. These emotions could be the catalysts for deep exploration and problem-solving. They motivate individuals to learn and adapt, prompting profound engagement with novel ideas and abstract questions. Unlike general emotional states, epistemic emotions are intricately tied to processes such as critical thinking, knowledge acquisition, and cognitive flexibility. In humans, these emotions can transcend mere practical problem-solving, inspiring pursuits that are philosophical, artistic, and existential in nature (de Sousa, 2009).

This article explores the complex role of epistemic emotions in fostering creativity across both human and non-human species. While curiosity and surprise help animals adapt and survive by driving exploration of their environments, humans leverage these same emotions to fuel intellectual and creative pursuits. By examining the evolutionary and cognitive aspects of epistemic emotions, this study reveals a continuum of knowledge-seeking behaviors that bridges instinctual survival mechanisms in animals and the abstract, often transcendent, intellectual endeavors of humans.

The significance of this topic lies in its ability to bridge disciplines such as cognitive science, evolutionary biology, and philosophy. Understanding how epistemic emotions function offers insights into the mechanisms that drive exploration, creativity, and innovation. It illuminates the evolutionary roots of human intellectual pursuits while showcasing the unique ways humans harness these emotions to create art, philosophy, and science (Ivcevic & Hoffmann, 2024). This exploration also highlights the role of epistemic emotions in advancing human culture and intellectual progress, revealing what makes human creativity uniquely complex and transformative. The broader implications of this investigation extend into multiple fields, including artificial intelligence (AI), education, and creativity studies. By unpacking the mechanisms through which epistemic emotions drive exploration and innovation, this research informs the development of learning environments that inspire curiosity and foster creative problem-solving (Muis et al., 2018). It also underscores the potential of AI systems to emulate exploratory behavior, enabling them to act as tools for amplifying human creativity. Finally, this study emphasizes the potentially transformative role of epistemic emotions in human well-being. By driving moments of transcendence and connection, these emotions foster a profound sense of purpose and satisfaction that enhances personal growth and collective progress (Fredrickson, 2004).

1 Defining Epistemic Emotions and Their Role in Knowledge Exploration

Epistemic emotions can be defined as affective mental states that are inherently tied to our cognitive processes, especially those involving knowledge acquisition, problem-solving, and exploration. Unlike other emotional experiences, epistemic emotions are directly related to one's own mental states, thoughts, and perceptions, influencing how we interpret, evaluate, and assimilate information (de Sousa, 2009). These emotions arise from an evaluation focused on the alignment or discrepancy between new information and existing beliefs or knowledge. For instance, they emerge when there is cognitive dissonance caused by unexpected information that challenges prior knowledge or assumptions. This cognitive inconsistency can interrupt ongoing mental processes and redirect attention to address the inconsistency, facilitating learning and adaptation (Muis et al., 2018; Vogl et al., 2019).

In the class of epistemic emotions, we can distinguish surprise, curiosity, interest, uncertainty (Carruthers, 2017; Scarantino & de Sousa, 2018), confusion, wonder (Nerantzaki & Efklides, 2019), a sense of correctness, appreciation (An, 2022), and even hope or fear when they contribute to evaluative attitudes (Kozak, 2018). Some authors, in their studies on epistemic emotions, also identify epistemic feelings, including the feeling of knowing, feeling of doubt, feeling of certainty, feeling of familiarity, feeling of forgetting (de Sousa, 2009; Arango-Muñoz & Michaelian, 2014), and the tip of the tongue feeling (Meylan, 2014). Each of these emotions serves distinct functions that enhance cognitive performance: they drive exploration, promote critical evaluation of new evidence, and influence how individuals acquire and adjust their beliefs. Moreover, these emotions play a significant role in conceptual changes and the development of strategies that enhance cognitive efficiency (Vogl et al., 2020).

The role of epistemic emotions goes beyond merely reacting to information. They serve as essential heuristic tools, are capable of optimizing decision-making processes by balancing the speed and accuracy of cognitive tasks, while also reducing the cost of information processing. This function is particularly relevant for learning and adapting to new environments, highlighting their survival value (Vogl et al., 2020). Moreover, epistemic emotions can be classified by their specificity to cognitive experiences. Unlike general moods or character traits, epistemic emotions have both an intentional component, being directed towards a specific object or event, and an evaluative component, wherein they assess the appropriateness or correctness of a cognitive response. For example, curiosity is an emotion that not only drives an individual towards acquiring new information but also signals the presence of an unexplored gap in knowledge that needs to be addressed (Scarantino & de Sousa, 2018).

Psychological (Muis et al., 2015; Muis et al., 2018; Rosman & Mayer, 2018; Nerantzaki & Efklides, 2019;) and philosophical (de Sousa, 2009; Morton, 2010; Kozak, 2018) literature on epistemic emotions typically restricts the discussion to the human species, assuming that these highly refined emotions are predominantly found in humans and play a significant role in the accurate assimilation of beliefs that may later serve specific purposes (Morton, 2010). However, cross-species emotion research in the field of epistemic emotions explore emotions like surprise (Courville et al., 2006; Barto et al., 2013), curiosity (Pisula, 2009; Byrne, 2013), and uncertainty (Smith & Washburn, 2005; Smith et al., 2010; Le Pelley, 2012; Beran et al., 2016) in animals, which can be challenging to capture using purely descriptive methods (de Waal, 2011).

2 Epistemic Emotions Across Species

Experimental studies on epistemic emotions (Muis et al., 2015; Muis et al., 2018; Nerantzaki & Efklides, 2019; Rosman & Mayer, 2018; Vogl et al., 2019; 2020) lack a cross-species comparative perspective. Contemporary researchers exploring the occurrence and nature of animal emotions increasingly highlight the importance of considering how emotional states influence day-to-day decision-making in relation to needs, intentions, and desires, noting that these states are intricately interwoven with emotions and play a crucial role in organizing behavior. Research on non-human animal emotions is far from new (Bekoff, 2007; Watanabe & Kuczaj, 2013 ; de Waal, 2017, 2019). However, these studies typically lack a comprehensive analysis of epistemic emotions as a distinct category, focusing primarily on general behavioral and neurological indicators of emotion.

At first glance, this focus may seem unproblematic, given that the category of epistemic emotions is typically defined in ways that seem exclusive to humans. Research in primatology and cognitive ethology suggest that epistemic emotions are not exclusive to humans. Scientistsin these fields, examining the behaviors of other species, frequently report animal behaviors that suggest a wide range of emotions, including some that are typically classified as epistemic emotions, even though animal behavior researchers do not explicitly use this terminology. Studies indicate that non-human animals may experience epistemic emotions like curiosity, surprise, and uncertainty, which support their ability to navigate and adapt to their environments. This suggests that epistemic emotions are not exclusively human and may not require complex language or advanced metacognition, but rather serve fundamental adaptive functions in animals' exploration and learning. The presence of these emotions in different animals challenges traditional views and supports an evolutionary continuity of epistemic emotions, showing that they play a crucial role in cognitive processes across species (Dutkowska, 2023).

Non-human animals also exhibit behaviors driven by curiosity and surprise, which are essential for their survival and adaptation. Primates, birds, and other intelligent species often engage in exploratory behaviors that indicate a desire to understand their environment, suggesting the presence of rudimentary epistemic emotions. Bermúdez (2003) describes these forms of exploration as protothoughts: basic cognitive processes that enable non-linguistic creatures to interact effectively with novel stimuli and solve problems without the use of language. From an evolutionary perspective, epistemic emotions have adaptive value as they help organisms to deal with the unknown. Curiosity and surprise encourage exploration, leading to a better understanding of the environment and enabling individuals to make informed decisions. In animals, curiosity-driven behaviors, such as the exploration of new objects or unfamiliar areas, are crucial for acquiring the knowledge needed to survive and thrive in dynamic environments. For example, the surprise experienced by a primate when encountering an unfamiliar food source may lead to further exploration and learning about its properties – whether it is safe, nutritious, or useful in other ways (Dutkowska, 2019). These epistemic behaviors demonstrate what researchers might argue are evolutionary roots of knowledge-seeking activities, providing insight into the continuity between non-human animal cognition and human intellectual pursuits.

Animal creativity can be defined as the capacity for novel and adaptive behavior that emerges in response to environmental challenges. This creativity, often observed in the context of play, is more than mere survival adaptation; it reflects an animal's potential for cognitive and behavioral flexibility. Through various types of play – such as object manipulation, social play, and locomotor activities – animals engage in exploratory behaviors that encourage the development of innovative solutions to new situations. Creative behavior, observed across a range of species, serves as an adaptive mechanism, allowing animals to explore and exploit new resources, improve problem-solving, and enhance survival odds. Creativity in animals is often linked to behavioral plasticity and a willingness to engage with novel stimuli, which may lead to innovations like tool use, social learning, or unique foraging methods. For example, primates exhibit creative problem-solving through tool use and food processing techniques, while birds may engage in complex song learning and innovative feeding behaviors. These actions are driven by intrinsic motivations, such as curiosity or neophilia (attraction to new stimuli), and social contexts that encourage the spread of learned behaviors within a group. Such creative capabilities illustrate the evolutionary benefits of cognitive flexibility, where creativity in animals functions as a "behavioral mutation" that allows individual and species-level adaptation to changing environments (Kaufman & Kaufman, 2015).

In animals, epistemic emotions like curiosity, surprise, and uncertainty play a critical role in fostering creativity, especially through behaviors associated with play and exploration. These emotions drive animals to engage with novel or unfamiliar stimuli, motivating them to explore their environment in ways that may lead to innovative solutions or adaptive behaviors. Curiosity, for instance, prompts animals to investigate new objects or scenarios, laying the groundwork for creative problem-solving by broadening their experience and enhancing their adaptability to new challenges. Surprise, often resulting from unexpected outcomes, encourages animals to re-evaluate their approaches and learn from novel interactions, which can foster flexibility in behavior. Uncertainty, similarly, pushes animals to continue exploring until they achieve a satisfactory understanding or solution, a process that reinforces persistence and resilience. In essence, epistemic emotions fuel an ongoing engagement with the environment that supports the development of creative behaviors and traits essential for survival. This interaction between emotional and cognitive responses allows animals to approach problem-solving dynamically, adjusting strategies based on new insights gained through these exploratory actions.

3 Epistemic Emotions in Human Creativity and Innovation

Human creativity involves generating new and useful ideas, products, or processes that are valued within a social or cultural context. This capacity extends beyond mere novelty, requiring that the creative output is both original and appropriate to its domain of application. Creativity is seen not only as an individual cognitive process but also as deeply rooted in collaborative and organizational structures. Sawyer and Henriksen (2024) believe it is embedded within sociocultural systems where new ideas emerge through complex social interactions, exchanges, and incremental improvements on previous knowledge. According to them, innovation involves the effective implementation or commercialization of creative ideas within an organizational context. While creativity centers on generating novel ideas, innovation emphasizes transforming these ideas into practical applications and embedding them within existing systems and markets. Together, creativity and innovation drive progress by continuously evolving and building upon a foundation of shared knowledge and collaborative effort, allowing for the cumulative advancement of society's cultural, scientific, and technological achievements.

Ivcevic and Hoffmann (2017) explore the intricate interplay between emotions and creativity, emphasizing how both temporary emotional states and stable personality traits shape creative processes. For instance, positive emotions often lead to broader thinking and greater openness, enabling creators to explore diverse ideas. On the other hand, negative emotions can foster persistence and attention, a critical factor in overcoming challenging tasks. Research highlights that while positive affect enhances flexibility and the generation of original ideas, transitioning from a negative to a positive mood can significantly amplify creative output. Additionally, they emphasize the importance of emotion regulation in navigating emotions that arise during the creative process, such as frustration from creative blocks or the excitement sparked by the development of new ideas. Effective emotion regulation, like reframing frustration as a motivational tool, supports sustained engagement with creative tasks. For example, individuals who can shift from a negative to a positive mood while working tend to report higher creativity in their output. This aligns with findings that the process of "affective shift" is often more beneficial than the presence of a single positive or negative mood alone. Furthermore, the concept of "emotional creativity", or the ability to experience and combine emotions in unique ways, significantly enhances creative expression, especially in artistic domains. Emotionally creative individuals may, for instance, integrate complex emotions like joy and sadness in artwork, creating more profound and evocative pieces that resonate with audiences.

Understanding and leveraging these nuanced relationships between emotions, traits, and emotion regulation abilities can provide insights into optimizing creativity across different fields.

Human creativity stands out as uniquely complex due to its interplay between cognitive flexibility, emotional depth, and cultural influence. Human creativity is characterized not only by the ability to produce novel and useful ideas but also by a social and collaborative context that fosters innovation. Unlike animal creativity, which primarily serves immediate survival needs, human creativity often transcends practical purposes, engaging with abstract concepts and aiming for cultural, scientific, or artistic breakthroughs. This is partly driven by epistemic emotions – such as curiosity, surprise, and wonder – which propel humans to question the unknown and explore abstract domains (Sawyer & Henriksen, 2024). Furthermore, the emotional dimension of human creativity is particularly profound. Emotions like curiosity and uncertainty are not merely reactions but essential motivators for exploratory behavior and problem-solving. Human creativity is also bolstered by advanced emotional regulation abilities, which enable individuals to sustain motivation and resilience in the face of creative challenges. These capacities allow for complex, intentional engagement with ideas and concepts, often guided by personal and societal values. These elements – cognitive, emotional, and social – contribute to a uniquely human creative process that integrates both individual expression and collective knowledge, leading to achievements that shape cultural and intellectual landscapes (Ivcevic & Hoffmann, 2017).

Awe holds a particularly significant role in human creativity and innovation. Often described as a complex emotional response to vast or profound stimuli, awe arises when individuals encounter something that challenges their understanding or evokes a sense of grandeur and interconnectedness (Keltner & Haidt, 2003). This emotion is deeply tied to the creative process because it opens individuals to new perspectives and motivates them to explore abstract and existential dimensions of their experiences. Awe can catalyze shifts in thinking, encouraging creators to break free from conventional frameworks and seek inspiration from the sublime. The unique cognitive and emotional impact of awe has been highlighted in studies emphasizing its ability to expand one's mental models and foster integrative thinking. Shiota, Keltner, and Mossman (2007) found that experiences of awe often lead to greater cognitive openness and curiosity, enabling individuals to assimilate diverse ideas and develop innovative solutions. This connection between awe and cognitive flexibility underscores its importance in artistic, scientific, and philosophical pursuits. For example, many groundbreaking discoveries in science – such as Darwin's theory of evolution – have been inspired by awe-inspiring encounters with nature's complexity and diversity.

Moreover, awe facilitates creativity by fostering a sense of humility and interconnectedness, which shifts the focus away from the self and towards broader, universal concerns. This emotional shift can inspire individuals to engage in collaborative and altruistic creative efforts, as awe reduces egocentric bias and promotes a sense of collective purpose (Piff et al., 2015). In artistic contexts, this might manifest as the creation of works that resonate deeply with shared human experiences, evoking a sense of connection and meaning. For instance, awe-inspiring landscapes often serve as muses for visual artists, leading to works that transcend mere representation and evoke profound emotional responses in audiences. The relationship between awe and innovation extends beyond individual creativity to organizational and societal contexts. Awe can inspire teams and organizations to think beyond immediate goals and adopt visionary approaches. Researchers have suggested that this emotion can act as a catalyst for transformative innovation, as it encourages individuals and groups to tackle ambitious, paradigm-shifting challenges (Chirico & Yaden, 2018). This potential makes awe a valuable tool in fostering environments where creativity and collaboration thrive, particularly in interdisciplinary or cutting-edge fields. Finally, the role of awe in enhancing well-being further strengthens its connection to creativity. Fredrickson's (2001) broaden-and-build theory of positive emotions posits that awe, like other positive emotions, can build enduring psychological resources by fostering resilience, inspiration, and a sense of purpose. These benefits enhance individuals' capacity to engage with complex problems and maintain motivation in the face of creative challenges. Thus, awe not only enriches the creative process but also sustains the emotional and cognitive resources necessary for long-term innovation and growth.

4 Stimulating Curiosity through Digital Technologies

Epistemic emotions, particularly curiosity, play a crucial role in driving human cognition and creativity. These emotions motivate individuals to explore, question, and learn, making them essential for intellectual growth. The digital age has brought unprecedented opportunities to harness and stimulate these emotions through advanced technologies, such as AI and VR. While these tools cannot replicate the subjective depth of human epistemic emotions, they can foster environments that encourage exploration and discovery.

AI-driven systems have been developed to emulate certain aspects of curiosity to improve learning and problem-solving processes. For example, curiosity-driven algorithms in reinforcement learning prioritize exploration by assigning higher weights to less predictable or unvisited states within a dataset. This approach enables AI to uncover novel solutions and optimize performance (Tinio, 2013; Chirico et al., 2016). Such systems mimic the outward behaviors of curiosity, guiding users toward knowledge gaps and encouraging deeper engagement with complex problems. In educational contexts, adaptive learning platforms powered by AI use algorithms to identify moments of confusion or uncertainty in students. By tailoring feedback and offering customized guidance, these systems create conditions that spark curiosity and facilitate learning. Despite their effectiveness, these tools lack phenomenal consciousness – the subjective experience that underpins genuine curiosity (Nagel, 1974). As a result, they act as facilitators rather than intrinsic sources of epistemic emotions.

Virtual reality has emerged as one of the most powerful tools for stimulating curiosity and wonder. By immersing users in dynamic and interactive simulations, VR creates unique opportunities for individuals to explore novel, vast, or complex environments. For instance, VR applications that simulate cosmic phenomena or archaeological discoveries enable users to experience awe and curiosity by engaging directly with representations of otherwise inaccessible realms (Chirico et al., 2016; Liu et al., 2021). Interactive educational tools in VR further enhance curiosity by allowing users to manipulate virtual objects, solve puzzles, or uncover hidden information. For example, virtual "dig sites" in archaeology-based games let users discover artifacts and experientially learn about ancient civilizations. These applications challenge cognitive boundaries and evoke intellectual engagement, making them valuable tools for fostering creativity and learning.

Despite their promise, digital technologies face inherent limitations in replicating the full depth of epistemic emotions. The lack of phenomenal consciousness in AI systems means their contribution to curiosity is indirect, relying on human perception and interpretation of their outputs (Searle, 1980; Boden & Dartnall, 1994). Similarly, the effectiveness of VR experiences hinges on users' active engagement and willingness to immerse themselves in the simulated environment. While AI systems have been developed to detect and respond to emotional cues in human interactions, such as recognizing confusion or curiosity through facial expressions and vocal tones, these systems operate on pattern recognition rather than true emotional understanding (Dalziel, Schaffer, & Martin, 2024). For example, adaptive learning platforms use algorithms to identify when students are uncertain or struggling with a concept. By analyzing response times, errors, and engagement levels, these systems provide tailored interventions, such as hints or alternative explanations, that mimic the supportive role of a human teacher. While effective in enhancing learning outcomes, these interactions represent programmed responses rather than genuine emotional insight (Pelánek, 2024).

Some researchers propose that AI might eventually approximate cognitive states through advanced affective computing models. These systems would rely on deep neural networks to simulate emotional states based on context and feedback, creating the illusion of curiosity or doubt. However, even in these advanced scenarios, AI lacks the self-awareness and intentionality that characterize true epistemic emotions. For instance, an AI system may "act curious" by prioritizing the exploration of new data points, but it does so without the intrinsic drive or existential motivations that fuel human curiosity (Younis, Mohsen, Houssein, & Ibrahim). Moreover, the capacity for epistemic emotions in humans is deeply tied to their subjective experience and higher-order cognition. Emotions like wonder or intellectual awe often emerge from a sense of connectedness to broader existential or philosophical questions – dimensions that AI, as a purely computational entity, cannot access. While AI may facilitate the exploration of epistemic emotions in humans, such as by generating awe-inspiring art or ideas, its role remains that of a tool rather than an agent capable of independent emotional experience.

Digital technologies, particularly AI and VR, have shown immense potential in stimulating curiosity and fostering learning. While these systems cannot replicate the subjective depth of human epistemic emotions, they can create environments that inspire exploration and intellectual engagement. By leveraging these tools responsibly, we can expand the horizons of human creativity, making curiosity a driving force in both individual growth and collective innovation. This synergy between technology and human curiosity highlights the transformative possibilities of the digital age.

5 Conclusions

The exploration of epistemic emotions reveals their profound role in shaping human creativity, knowledge acquisition, and cultural innovation. These emotions are not merely reactive states but essential drivers of exploration and problem-solving. They bridge the gap between instinctual survival mechanisms observed in animals and the transcendent intellectual pursuits unique to humans. Epistemic emotions serve as a vital link between cognition and emotion, enabling humans to transcend immediate practical concerns and engage with abstract, existential, and philosophical ideas. Their influence extends across diverse domains, fueling not only artistic and scientific achievements but also broader societal advancements. The nuanced interplay between these emotions and creativity illustrates how they inspire not only individual growth but also collective progress. This understanding is critical for designing educational environments and AI systems that harness the potential of epistemic emotions to foster innovation and discovery.

While AI and VR platforms can emulate some functional aspects of epistemic emotions, they lack the phenomenal consciousness and intrinsic intentionality that characterize true emotional experiences. As a result, AI systems remain tools rather than agents capable of independently driving exploration or innovation. Nevertheless, these technologies can play a supportive role, amplifying human creativity and intellectual curiosity. Epistemic emotions are central to the human experience, driving our quest for knowledge and inspiring creativity that reshapes our understanding of the world. Their study not only enhances theoretical perspectives across disciplines but also holds practical implications for fostering environments that maximize human potential. By continuing to investigate the complexities of these emotions, we can deepen our appreciation of what makes human creativity and intellectual achievements uniquely extraordinary.

References

An, D. (2022). Appreciation as an epistemic emotion. *Ethical Theory and Moral Practice*, 1–16. https://doi.org/10.1007/s10677-021-10265-6

Andrews, K., & Beck, J. (Eds.). (2017). *The Routledge handbook of philosophy of animal minds*. Routledge.

Arango-Muñoz, S. (2014). The nature of epistemic feelings. *Philosophical Psychology*, 27(2), 193–211. https://doi.org/10.1080/09515089.2012.732002

Arango-Muñoz, S., & Michaelian, K. (2014). Epistemic feelings, epistemic emotions: Review and introduction to the focus section. *Philosophical Inquiries*, 2, 97–122. https://doi.org/10.4454/philinq.v2i1.79

Barto, A., Mirolli, M., & Baldassarre, G. (2013). Novelty or surprise? *Frontiers in Psychology*, *4*, 907. https://doi.org/10.3389/fpsyg.2013.00907

Bekoff, M. (2007). *The emotional lives of animals: A leading scientist explores animal joy, sorrow, and empathy and why they matter*. New World Library.

Beran, M., Perdue, B., Church, B., & Smith, J. D. (2016). Capuchin monkeys (Cebus apella) modulate their use of an uncertainty response depending on risk. *Journal of Experimental Psychology: Animal Learning and Cognition*, *42*, 32–43. https://doi.org/10.1037/xan0000080

Bermúdez, J. L. (2003). *Thinking without words*. Oxford University Press.

Bermúdez, J. L. (2006). Animal reasoning and proto-logic. In S. Hurley & M. Nudds (Eds.), *Rational animals?* (pp. 127–138). Oxford University Press.

Boden, M. A., & Dartnall, T. (1994). *Artificial intelligence and creativity: An interdisciplinary approach*. Springer Netherlands.

Byrne, R. W. (2013). Animal curiosity. *Current Biology*, *23*, R469–R470. https://doi.org/10.1016/j.cub.2013.02.058

Candiotto, L. (2019). Epistemic emotions: The case of wonder. *Journal of Philosophy Aurora*, *31*, 848–863. https://doi.org/10.7213/1980-5934.31.054.DS11

Carruthers, P. (1998). Animal subjectivity. *Psyche*, *4*. Retrieved from http://journalpsyche.org/files/0xaa52.pdf

Carruthers, P. (2005). *Consciousness: Essays from a higher-order perspective*. Oxford University Press.

Carruthers, P. (2017). Are epistemic emotions metacognitive? *Philosophical Psychology*, *30*(1–2), 58–78. https://doi.org/10.1080/09515089.2016.1262536

Chirico, A., & Yaden, D. B. (2018). Awe: A self-transcendent and sometimes transformative emotion. *Frontiers in Psychology*, *9*, 2357. https://doi.org/10.3389/fpsyg.2018.02357

Chirico, A., Yaden, D. B., Riva, G., & Gaggioli, A. (2016). The potential of virtual reality for the investigation of awe. *Frontiers in Psychology*, *7*. https://doi.org/10.3389/fpsyg.2016.01766

Courville, A. C., Daw, N. D., & Touretzky, D. S. (2006). Bayesian theories of conditioning in a changing world. *Trends in Cognitive Sciences*, *10*(7), 294–300. https://doi.org/10.1016/j.tics.2006.05.004

Csikszentmihalyi, M. (1996). *Creativity: Flow and the psychology of discovery and invention*. HarperCollins.

de Sousa, R. (2009). Epistemic feelings. *Mind and Matter*, *7*(2), 139–161.

de Waal, F. (2011). What is an animal emotion? *Annals of the New York Academy of Sciences*, *1224*, 191–206. https://doi.org/10.1111/j.1749-6632.2010.05912.x

de Waal, F. (2017). *Are we smart enough to know how smart animals are?* W. W. Norton & Company.

de Waal, F. (2019). *Mama's last hug: Animal emotions and what they tell us about ourselves*. W. W. Norton & Company.

Davidson, D. (1982). Rational animals. *Dialectica*, *36*(4), 317–327. https://doi.org/10.1111/j.1746-8361.1982.tb01546.x

Davidson, D. (2004). *Problems of rationality*. Clarendon Press.

Dalziel, M. V., Schaffer, K., & Martin, N. (2024). Navigating AI in Social Work and Beyond: A Multidisciplinary Review. *arXiv*. https://doi.org/10.48550/arXiv.2411.07245

Dummett, M. (1993). *The origins of analytical philosophy*. Duckworth.

Dunlosky, J., & Metcalfe, J. (2009). *Metacognition*. Sage.

Dutkowska, A. (2021). Filogeneza umysłu: w poszukiwaniu wskaźników myślenia. In Z. Wróblewski & A. Gut (Eds.), *Próby kognitywistyczne* (pp. 27–54). Wydawnictwo KUL.

du Sautoy, M. (2019). *The Creativity code: How AI is learning to write, paint and think*. Fourth Estate.

Dutkowska, A. (2023). Emocje epistemiczne – czym są i czy przysługują wyłącznie ludziom? *Analiza i Egzystencja*, *64*, 5–23. https://doi.org/10.18276/aie.2023.64-01

Fredrickson, B. L. (2001). The role of positive emotions in positive psychology: The broaden-and-build theory of positive emotions. *American Psychologist*, *56*(3), 218–226. https://doi.org/10.1037/0003-066X.56.3.218

Fredrickson, B. L. (2004). The broaden-and-build theory of positive emotions. *Philosophical Transactions of the Royal Society B: Biological Sciences*, *359*(1449), 1367–1377. https://doi.org/10.1098/rstb.2004.1512

Gigerenzer, G. (2015). *Simply rational*. Oxford University Press.

Gopnik, A. (1998). Explanation as orgasm. *Minds and Machines*, *8*, 101–118. https://doi.org/10.1023/A:1008290415597

Gut, A. (2009). *O relacji między myślą a językiem*. Towarzystwo Naukowe KUL.

Hookway, C. (1998). Doubt: Affective states and the regulation of inquiry. *Canadian Journal of Philosophy*, *24*, 203–226. https://doi.org/10.1080/00455091.1998.10717500

Hookway, C. (2002). Emotions and epistemic evaluation. In P. Carruthers (Ed.), *The cognitive basis of science* (pp. 251–262). Cambridge University Press.

Hookway, C. (2003). Affective states and epistemic immediacy. *Metaphilosophy*, *34* (1–2), 78–96. https://doi.org/10.1111/1467-9973.00261

Hookway, C. (2008). Epistemic immediacy, doubt and anxiety: On the role of emotions in epistemic evaluation. In G. Brun, U. Doğuoğlu, & D. Kuenzle (Eds.), *Epistemology and emotions* (pp. 51–66). Routledge.

Ivcevic, Z., & Hoffmann, J. (2017). Emotions and creativity: From states to traits and emotion abilities. In G. J. Feist, R. Reiter-Palmon, & J. C. Kaufman (Eds.), *The Cambridge Handbook of Creativity and Personality Research* (pp. 187-213). Cambridge University Press.

Kaufman, A. B., & Kaufman, J. C. (2015). *Animal Creativity and Innovation*. Elsevier, Academic Press.

Keltner, D., & Haidt, J. (2003). Approaching awe, a moral, spiritual, and aesthetic emotion. *Cognition and Emotion*, *17*(2), 297–314. https://doi.org/10.1080/02699930302297

Kouider, S., Long, B., Le Stanc, L., Charron, S., Fievet, A.-C., Barbosa, L. S., & Gelskov, S. V. (2015). Neural dynamics of prediction and surprise in infants. *Nature Communications, 6*, 8537. https://doi.org/10.1038/ncomms9537

Kozak, P. (2018). Emocje epistemiczne i normatywność albo o tym jak pokochać teorię znaczenia. *Studia Philosophiae Christianae, 54*(1), 121–140. https://doi.org/10.21697/2018.54.1.15

Le Pelley, M. E. (2012). Metacognitive monkeys or associative animals? Simple reinforcement learning explains uncertainty in nonhuman animals. *Journal of Experimental Psychology: Learning, Memory, and Cognition, 38*(3), 686–708. https://doi.org/10.1037/a0026478

Lechniak, M. (2011). *Przekonania i zmiana przekonań*. Wydawnictwo KUL.

Liu, Y., Liu, Y., Kim, J., & Wang, L. (2021). RelicVR: Archaeology-based virtual reality games for experiential learning. *International Journal of Human-Computer Studies, 152*, 102660. https://doi.org/10.1016/j.ijhcs.2021.102660

McDowell, J. (1994). *Mind and world*. Harvard University Press.

Meylan, A. (2014). Epistemic emotions: A natural kind? *Philosophical Inquiries, 2*(1), 173–190. https://doi.org/10.4454/philinq.v2i1.83

Miller, A. I. (2019). *The artist in the machine: The world of AI-powered creativity*. MIT Press.

Morton, A. (2010). Epistemic emotions. In P. Goldie (Ed.), *The Oxford handbook of philosophy of emotion* (pp. 385–400). Oxford University Press.

Muis, K. R., Psaradellis, C., Chevrier, M., & Singh, C. A. (2015). The role of epistemic cognition and epistemic emotions in learning from conflicting information. *Instructional Science, 43*(5), 595–617. https://doi.org/10.1007/s11251-015-9355-6

Muis, K. R., Chevrier, M., & Singh, C. A. (2018). The role of epistemic emotions in personal epistemology and self-regulated learning. *Educational Psychologist, 53*(3), 165–184. https://doi.org/10.1080/00461520.2017.1421465

Nagel, T. (1974). What is it like to be a bat? *The Philosophical Review, 83*(4), 435–450. https://doi.org/10.2307/2183914

Nerantzaki, K., & Efklides, A. (2019). Epistemic emotions: Interrelationships and changes during task processing. *Hellenic Journal of Psychology, 16*, 177–199.

Pelánek, R. (2024). Adaptive learning is hard: Challenges, nuances, and trade-offs in modeling. *International Journal of Artificial Intelligence in Education*, 34(1), 1–28. https://doi.org/10.1007/s40593-024-00400-6

Piff, P. K., Dietze, P., Feinberg, M., Stancato, D. M., & Keltner, D. (2015). Awe, the small self, and prosocial behavior. *Journal of Personality and Social Psychology, 108*(6), 883–899. https://doi.org/10.1037/pspi0000018

Pisula, W. (2009). *Curiosity and information seeking in animal and human behavior*. Brown Walker Press.

Proust, J. (2014). *The philosophy of metacognition*. Oxford University Press.

Rosman, T., & Mayer, A.-K. (2018). Epistemic beliefs as predictors of epistemic emotions: Extending a theoretical model. *British Journal of Educational Psychology, 88* (3), 410–427. https://doi.org/10.1111/bjep.12191

Sawyer, R. K., & Henriksen, D. (2024). *Explaining creativity: The Science of Human Innovation* (3rd ed.). Oxford University Press.

Scarantino, A., & de Sousa, R. (2018). Emotions. In *E. N. Zalta (Ed.), The Stanford Encyclopedia of Philosophy.* Retrieved from https://plato.stanford.edu/archives/win2018/entries/emotion

Schaffer, V., Huckstepp, T., & Kannis-Dymand, L. (2024). Awe: A systematic review within a cognitive behavioural framework and proposed cognitive behavioural model of awe. *International Journal of Applied Positive Psychology, 9*(1), 101–136. https://doi.org/10.1007/s41042-023-00116-3

Schetz, A. (2011). O tak zwanym problemie prostych umysłów. *Diametros, 30*, 41–60. https://doi.org/10.13153/diam.30.2011.455

Searle, J. R. (1980). Minds, brains, and programs. *Behavioral and Brain Sciences, 3*(3), 417–424. https://doi.org/10.1017/S0140525X00005756

Shiota, M. N., Keltner, D., & Mossman, A. (2007). The nature of awe: Elicitors, appraisals, and effects on self-concept. *Cognition and Emotion, 21*(5), 944–963. https://doi.org/10.1080/02699930600923668

Smith, J. D., & Washburn, D. A. (2005). Uncertainty monitoring and metacognition by animals. *Current Directions in Psychological Science, 14*(1), 19–24. https://doi.org/10.1111/j.0963-7214.2005.00327.x

Smith, J. D., Couchman, J. J., & Beran, M. J. (2010). The cognitive architecture of uncertainty monitoring: A comparative perspective. *Animal Behavior and Cognition, 6*(4), 367–386.

Sutton, R. S., & Barto, A. G. (1998). *Reinforcement learning: An introduction.* MIT Press.

Terpe, S. (2016). Epistemic feelings in moral experiences and moral dynamics of everyday life. *Digithum, 18*, 5–12. https://doi.org/10.7238/d.v0i18.2874

Tinio, P. P. L. (2013). From artistic creation to aesthetic reception: The mirror model of art. *Psychology of Aesthetics, Creativity, and the Arts, 7*(3), 265–275. https://doi.org/10.1037/a0030872

Vogl, E., Pekrun, R., Murayama, K., Loderer, K., & Schubert, S. (2019). Surprise, curiosity, and confusion promote knowledge exploration: Evidence for robust effects of epistemic emotions. *Frontiers in Psychology*, 10, 2474. https://doi.org/10.3389/fpsyg.2019.02474

Vogl, E., Pekrun, R., Murayama, K., Loderer, K., & Schubert, S. (2020). Epistemic emotions and learning: Exploring the relations between students' epistemic emotions and their motivation, cognitive resources, and achievement. In K. H. Knoop & L. W. Webb (Eds.), *Emotions in learning: Theory, research, and practice* (pp. 45–65). Springer.

Watanabe, S., & Kuczaj, S. A. (Eds.). (2013). *Emotions of animals and humans: Comparative perspectives*. Springer Science + Business Media. https://doi.org/10.1007/978-4-431-54123-3

Younis, E. M. G., Mohsen, S., Houssein, E. H., & Ibrahim, O. A. (2024). Machine learning for human emotion recognition: a comprehensive review. *Neural Computing and Applications*, 36, 8901–8947. https://doi.org/10.1007/s00521-024-09426-2

CHAPTER 5

Imagination-Oriented Design: Why and How to Create Objects and Environments with Imaginative Affordances?

Monika Dunin-Kozicka[1]

Abstract

Although typically the design of objects and environments is focused on the bodily actions that may be afforded, here I am considering the possibilities of developing a design framework that is more aimed at affording imaginative actions to those who come into contact with design, and that recognizes all their overt-physical and covert-psychical possible reactions to the world. Particularly, within the Imagination-Oriented Design (IOD), we can aim at (1) objects that are, regardless of their material properties, designed, i.e., devised, to afford the imagination, as well as (2) objects that are specifically designed in terms of their material properties, i.e., created, so as to afford imaginings to their perceivers. Regarding the latter, we may consider what specific features of objects will make these objects readily imagine-*x*-able, and, tentatively, I propose several types of such objects. Based on this, we-creators can design whole environments (both real and virtual) that afford imagination, that is, those that are either filled with imagine-*x*-able objects, or that are themselves imagine-*x*-able. This is just the theoretical launch of the Imagination-Oriented Design, and many possible refinements and extensions of the analysis presented here, as well as its practical applications, are yet to come.

Keywords

design – imagination – imaginative affordances – objects – environments – Imagination-Oriented Design

1 The John Paul II Catholic University of Lublin, Institute of Philosophy, Lublin, Poland, https://orcid.org/0000-0003-3163-4869

Objects and environments are typically designed to afford specific bodily actions to their users and explorers. Chairs are constructed for sitting, pencils for writing and sketching, skateboards for riding on and easy carrying with. Playgrounds are designed for playing, parks for walking and resting, shopping malls for efficient movement and shopping. Things and places we perceive in the world are there to enable certain physical actions to us.

As expressed by proponents of the enactive approach to cognition, perception is *for* action, or it is action-oriented (Varela et al., 1991). That is, perception serves goals of bodily action and is shaped by it. This idea that I perceive things in terms of what *I can do* with them – although it has only recently gained popularity thanks to enactivists – goes back a long way to Husserl (1989), and the notion that I experience the world in a prereflective action-guided way, and not through reflective intellectual observation, was already expressed by Merleau-Ponty (2012) in his *Phenomenology of Perception*. It was precisely these ideas, originating from leading philosopher-phenomenologists, that underlay the concept of affordances being widely applied in the field of design today (Norman, 1990). Affordances are possibilities for bodily action – such as pulling the door handle, grabbing the teapot – presented by one's surroundings or by objects in one's surroundings. Gibson (1979), who coined the term, prominently noted that affordances are to be directly perceived in the world. That is, we perceive things as actionable in an outright, prereflective manner.

Thus, the fact that objects and environments are designed by default to afford certain bodily actions to their users and explorers does not come out of nowhere. In light of the aforementioned theories, and in accordance with how we typically relate to the world phenomenologically, we, the users, perceive things as affording such actions to us.[2] That the design of things and places is bodily-action-centered because we are bodily-action-centered. Or at least we supposedly are.

Still, to some people in some circumstances chairs may be *affording imagining* that someone (like an old friend) is sitting on them, skateboards – imagining being a winner in Street League Skateboarding, and parks – imagining sitting and relaxing on a bench (when actually one is in a hurry to get to somewhere else). That is, objects and environments may afford mental

2 The fact that our perception, or at least some selected perceptual systems, serve the purpose of physical action has also been demonstrated in many empirical studies, (e.g., Aglioti et al., 1995; Milner & Goodale, 2008).

actions, such as imaginings – not just bodily actions[3] – to those who encounter them. Assuming this is the case (and I will argue that it is), just as we design objects and environments to afford bodily actions to their perceivers, we can also design things and environments to afford imaginative actions to us. While the former approach to design is dominant, the latter has not – to my knowledge – yet been openly articulated.

Thus, in this chapter I will consider the possibilities of design that is primarily mental-action-centered, or, precisely, to lay the foundations for the theory and practice of the Imagination-Oriented Design (IOD). Drawing on McClelland's (2020) mental affordance hypothesis, as well as the concept of imaginative affordances presented by McClelland and Dunin-Kozicka (2024), I would like to point out that: (1) regardless of their specific physical parameters, objects and environments can be designed, i.e., devised, to afford imagination; (2) objects and environments can be designed, i.e., created, with respect to their specific physical parameters so as to afford the imagination. As for the first design, let's call it designing-as-devising, I am drawing here on the observation that any object can theoretically afford any imagining. Our task as designers would then be to deliberately point to some imaginative affordance of a given thing (even a thing that has already been created so as to afford certain bodily affordances) so that people who come across that thing can perceive that imaginative affordance. For example, we can design, i.e., devise, a specific bench in the park to afford imagining to passer-by that a famous writer once sat on it. As for the second design, let's call it designing-as-creating, I am assuming that certain specific physical properties of objects can contribute to the perception of their imaginative affordances (as is the case with bodily affordances of objects). Our task as designers would then be to create things with respect to their material properties so as to increase the chances of perceiving their imaginative affordances. For example, we can design, i.e., create, a new object with a sound coming out of it that resembles

3 Some might argue here that imaginative actions cannot be sharply separated from bodily actions, because in the process of imagining a particular bodily action, certain motor patterns are potentiated that would have been potentiated if the action were overt (Bruineberg & van den Herik, 2021). Nevertheless, when we talk about affording imagining we do not only talk about affording imagining a bodily action but also imagining any other thing (like imagining an object). Still, some may argue that imaginative actions are bodily actions because they engage neural structures (e.g., motor areas of the brain) that are, after all, bodily or physical structures. However, while performing overt bodily actions we also engage some neural structures, but these actions are still additionally expressed in some overt form that is observable to others. In this article, therefore, I use our commonsense distinction between bodily (physical) and mental (psychical) actions.

the sound of an animal – so that we perceive the object and imagine a creature that could make such a sound. Both design in the sense of devising and design in the sense of creating will be described in detail below.

But why should we be concerned with Imagination-Oriented Design in the first place? Apart from the fact that no one has done it explicitly so far, this new approach to design recognizes us, experiencing things, not only as those who act bodily, but also as those who act mentally, including imaginatively. Perception *is* for action, and it *is* action oriented – but the actions we take are not merely bodily. With the involvement of various things and environments, we not only sit, skateboard, shop or walk in the park, but also imagine, remember, anticipate, reflect, etc. Why would not we then be more intentional about designing things that would (also) afford the latter?

Below I will introduce the IOD in the following steps. First, in Section 1, I will briefly describe the concept of imaginative affordances. Next, in Section 2, I will present some guidelines for designing objects with imaginative affordances, considering designing-as-devising and designing-as-creating successively. In Section 3, I will mention the possibilities of creating environments that afford imagination to those who explore them. In doing all this, I will also consider the prospects for further development of the IOD, which I believe will benefit both those of us who want to design for all human potential and those of us who want to experience the world more fully.

1 What Are Imaginative Affordances?

Just as bodily affordances – as affordances are classically understood – are opportunities for bodily actions perceived in one's environment or objects in one's environment, mental affordances would be opportunities for mental actions that environments and objects (but also certain situations) present to us. According to McClelland's (2020) "mental affordance hypothesis", the latter holds true on the same terms as the former. Since we can assign the status of mental actions to some of our mental events such as attending or counting (e.g., on the basis of their being controllable), and since affordances are, in general, environmental opportunities for actions, there should also be opportunities for mental actions that we perceive in the environment. A clover plant affords not only picking it but also counting its leaves; a smartphone affords not only scrolling it but also paying attention to it when a notification pops up; a playground affords not only playing and exploring but also pretending to be explorers of a new planet.

In reference to the above, imaginative affordances are possibilities for acts of imagination that certain environments, situations, or objects present to us. As McClelland and Dunin-Kozicka (2024) put it: "An object or situation *x* affords imagining for a subject S iff *x* makes it possible for S to perform a specific imaginative action φ" (p. 5). For example, a gift box may afford visualizing what is inside to its recipient; a calendar may afford imagining what might happen in the future to someone; a green block can afford pretending it is a frog to children while playing. As can be seen, various kinds of imaginative actions (i.e., generating a sensory image; supposing or mentally time traveling; pretending, as well as others) can be afforded – the concept of imagination is broad and encompasses all of these activities, and even more. In their entry in the *Stanford Encyclopedia of Philosophy*, Liao and Gendler (2020) describe this concept as follows:

> To imagine is to represent without aiming at things as they actually, presently, and subjectively are. One can use imagination to represent possibilities other than the actual, to represent times other than the present, and to represent perspectives other than one's own.[4]
>
> LIAO & GENDLER, 2020

From this definition it follows that imagination, in the most general sense, is about engaging with what is non-actual (with things that are not actually here or now, or that are not related to me in a way). In this Imagination-Oriented Design proposal, it is this most general sense of imagination that is at issue.

Phenomenologically speaking, many of our everyday experiences lead us to claim that perception is not only for bodily action, but also for mental action, including imaginative one. That is, one can speak of a specific phenomenology of imaginative affordances. As McClelland and Dunin-Kozicka (2024) propose, imaginative affordances are to be likely experienced when: (1) *S* mentally rehearses or visualizes their bodily action with an object and/or in the environment before actually performing that action (just as it happens in chess, when a specific arrangement of pieces on the chessboard affords simulating to the player which piece to move next and how, and does not necessarily afford grabbing the piece in the first place); (2) *S* cannot perform the desired bodily action with the object so the object affords imaginatively performing it, as when one cannot eat a certain food or is addicted to a substance but cannot

4 Liao and Gendler use the notion of representation in their definition, but in this chapter I will stay neutral on the question of whether imagination should be defined in representational terms.

use it (chocolate may afford imagining eating it to a person who is on a diet); (3) *S* has a rich history of interactions with a given type of object, environment or situation, and therefore when they perceive it they imagine entering into these interactions (e.g., a pianist seeing a piano imagines playing her favorite composition on it; a coffee lover seeing a coffee shop imagines drinking espresso); (4) *S* perceives certain incomplete objects or situations, such as Gestalt unfinished figures, and so these objects afford actions of "imaginative closure" to *S*; and, lastly, (5) *S* is mind-wandering, and thus their mind is guided by any random affordances for mental action *S* perceives in their environment (e.g., while mind-wandering *S* smells flowers and then imagines being in their garden as a part of their mind-wandering). Most likely, each of us has had experiences similar to these or some of these. Such experiences could form our evidence that perception is not only bodily-action-oriented; it may be imagination-oriented (or other-mental-action-oriented) as well.

As with bodily affordances, imaginative affordances may also be described as relations between the properties of the environment or object and the abilities (or dispositions, or effectivities) of those who come into contact with those objects and environments (Chemero, 2003, 2009).[5] Thus, if we actually perceive an affordance depends not only on certain features of the environment (e.g., a cup that is tall, allowing one to put tulips in it; a heavy box that is closed, allowing one to imagine what is inside) but also on our actual dispositions, such as our bodily and imaginative skills,[6] as well as our knowledge, memories, intentions, desires emotions,[7] etc. As Clark (2016) put it, our perception of the world is "constantly conditioned by our own 'action repertoire' … in interaction with our needs, projects, and opportunities" (p. 180). Whether I see the cup as graspable will depend both on its physical properties and on my motor skills and my current needs (e.g., to drink tea); whether I see the closed box as imagine-what-is-inside-able will depend both on its being closed and on my actual interest, curiosity, as well as my imaginative skills and propensities. Therefore, when designing things that will afford one's imagination, we should take into account the contributions of both the perceiver and the thing being perceived.

5 However, affordances can also be defined primarily as properties of objects (see, e.g., Turvey, 1992).

6 The issue of specific imaginative skills and how to improve them (see Kind, 2020, 2022) – which might lead to easier perception of imaginative affordances in the world – is worthy of additional in-depth discussion, but will not concern me here.

7 See the Chapter 4 of this book written by Dutkowska and Michael on epistemic emotions.

2 Designing Objects with Imaginative Affordances

In general, any object may afford imagination, and it may afford limitless imaginative actions to us. All objects perceived by us can be imaginatively altered by changing their size, shape, color, texture, location, etc., or they can be modified in any other way through visualization. When I see this candle burning in front of me, I can imagine it without a flame (so this candle affords this imagining to me); I can also mentally enlarge the size of my coffee mug so that when turned upside down it could serve me as a seat. What is more, any object we perceive can afford imagining other objects, or imagining various doings, backgrounds, events or situations. After all, I can imagine that a fish (a coffeefish!) swims out of my cup of coffee, and hands appear above the burning candle as someone wants to warm them. When analyzing this, McClelland and Dunin-Kozicka (2024) notice that the very perceptibility of properties of objects make them affording imagination to us; or, in other words, anything that is perceivable is also imagine-able. In the same vein they claim that

> … physical objects are universally *imagine-of-able* (as they can be the main objects for our imaginings), *imagine-x-able* (as they can lead to imagine some other objects), as well as *imagine-that-able* or *imagine-what-if-able* (as they can trigger imagining certain possible scenarios), or even *imagine-φ-ing-able* (as they can provoke imagining doing certain things with them).
>
> MCCLELLAND & DUNIN-KOZICKA, 2024, p. 8.

In a sense, then, we can say that there is an abundance of imaginative affordances in objects and environments. Why should we specifically design things affording our imagination when, wherever we look, everything can already afford it?

Yet, although hypothetically any object can trigger our imagination in any way, at any time and under any circumstances, practically this is not the case. Why is this? Firstly, our actual imaginative and other dispositions may not contribute to our perception of imaginative affordances. For example, our imaginative skills may be weak, or our current needs may be different from engaging in imaginative activities, or we may not be aware that some objects have been designed to afford our imagination in a specific way. Secondly, given objects or environments may be physically designed primarily to afford bodily actions, or they may lack the physical properties that are conducive to affording our imagination. For example, doors are designed primarily to be opened and closed – door designers typically do not consider what physical properties doors might have that would afford the imagination of those who interact with them.

In what follows I will show how, as designers, we can both influence (at least to some extent) the dispositions of people coming into contact with the objects we design, and shape these objects in terms of their material properties. Accordingly, I will demonstrate that (1) regardless of their physical parameters, objects can be designed, i.e., devised, to afford imagination – our task as designers would then be to purposefully point to some imaginative affordance of a thing so that people who come across that thing are *aware* of its imaginative affordance and can react to it more readily; (2) objects can be designed, i.e., created, with respect to their specific physical parameters so as to afford one's imagination. Through following the IOD's guidelines, we should increase the likelihood of triggering the imagination of those who come into contact with our designs.

2.1 *Objects Devised to Afford Imagination*

As noted at the very beginning, design is by default bodily-action-oriented. Designers and craftsmen typically care about making their objects usable: ensuring that the physical properties of objects contribute to their affording exactly the action targeted during the design process. Noteworthily, in his iconic *The design of everyday things*, Norman (1990) lists "Affordance" as one of the important design principles. As per him, to afford means to give a clue – that is, to be easily recognizable, already at the perceptual level, as an object for *this* (and not other) particular use. Norman demonstrates this repeatedly with well- and poorly-designed doors: a poorly-designed door is one that affords pushing when it is meant to be pulled, and pulling when it is meant to be pushed.

As can be inferred from the above, one essential element of object creation is the creator's intention or idea regarding the use of their object. Indeed, "to design" is often understood as "to devise", "to intend", "to target" – so to devise the object to be used in a certain way. Things are designed, that is, devised, to cause specific behaviors. Taking this into account, Costall (1995) proposes to speak of affordances as social in nature: people cause other people to use objects in certain ways. First, these people are the designers themselves, who assign specific functions to the objects they create – so even if we do not immediately perceive the affordance of a product, we can read on its instructions that it is for this purpose and not another, and only then notice this affordance. Second, these people are those whom we see actually using the objects: through observation, we learn about the affordances of a given object (so, for example, children are unlikely to discover the *targeted* affordances of a spoon on their own, but learn to use a spoon from their caregivers). In this vein, Costall (2012) also proposes that some affordances are "canonical"; that is, they are "established, widely agreed use-meanings of things" (p. 92). Canonically, a bench is to sit on, a glass is to drink from it, and a spoon is to eat liquid food with it. In a sense, then, canonical affordances are those action possibilities that we perceive in things by default, since those things are socially meant to, or devised to, afford given actions. Talking in terms of our dispositions, we are more aware of canonical affordances than of other object affordances.

From the above, we can now draw a beneficial conclusion towards Imagination-Oriented Design: things can be designed – that is, devised or targeted – to afford imaginative actions to us. In other words, people can intentionally make objects to afford imaginings to other people, or they can make others aware of some imaginative affordances of objects by telling, teaching, and encouraging them to perform certain imaginings with and over these objects. Thus, although we observe the superiority of the bodily-action-centered design, so that typically things are intentionally designed to afford physical action to us, we can make a different, purposeful move to treat some things as imagine-of-able, imagine-*x*-able, imagine-what-if-able, etc. This should not be difficult, since, as I have earlier shown, objects can potentially afford us countless imaginative actions: we can modify any objects in any way in our imagination simply by virtue of their being perceptible to us. It follows that we can actually devise objects to be imagination-affording *without them having any specific physical properties that would align with any specific imaginings.* Simply by (socially) targeting things to afford imagination – and making people aware of this – can we bring about that they actually do.

To illustrate this, assume a case of, let's call it, the School of Imagination (for now just a thought experiment, but a fully feasible one!). Let us suppose that somewhere there is the school where students are primarily taught to be good imaginers. There are numerous objects scattered throughout the school, specific teaching aids, which are intended to serve the educational goals of the school. Among these objects there are multi-colored buttons, the sight of which should immediately engage the student in the imaginative activities appropriately labeled for these objects. Students could be taught from an early age in their education that seeing these buttons should trigger their imagination in a certain way. Assume, then, that a yellow button is devised to trigger imagining a chicken, a red button to imagine a poppy flower, a white button to imagine a floating cloud, and so on and so forth. These are all simple buttons, nothing fancy and nothing which – apart from their colors – has any particular reference to chickens, clouds or poppy flowers. In other words, the physical properties of these buttons do not closely align with the imaginings they are devised to afford. And yet, one of the students' tasks is to imagine some specific things in as much detail as possible whenever they see any of these buttons in the School environment. Noticing a yellow button, they can, for example, imagine a chicken head in the button, or a whole chicken standing on it, or a chicken jumping, dancing, or even rising into the air and flying out of a nearby window while singing some Beatles song (it can be assumed that older students will more likely engage in highly complex mental activities than younger ones).

Now, considering such an imaginary scenario, we are inclined to think that those students who are already familiar with the task and accustomed to performing it regularly would perceive the imaginative affordances of the yellow buttons in a similar automatic way as they would perceive the bodily affordances of cups, spoons and chairs. Such yellow buttons would be imagine-chicken-able to these students, just as cups are graspable and chairs are sittable to them. Highly advanced students of the School would likely feel a strong urge to imagine a chicken whenever they came across yellow buttons, and they might experience such imaginative urges whenever they saw (or heard, or touched, or smelled) any other such intentionally designed educational props located throughout the school. In other words, their awareness of the imaginative affordances of some objects would increase as a result of learning and practice.

We can easily transfer the scenario from the imaginary School of Imagination to the real world – and not only in the sense that we could actually launch such an educational facility. After all, we can deliberately assign various imaginative actions to any objects in our environment. Even in our closest surroundings we can design, in the sense of devise, some things (e.g., a long-forgotten figurine of the Eiffel Tower, a souvenir from a vacation) to prompt imaginings to us (e.g., enlarging the Eiffel Tower in our imagination, imaginatively changing its color, visualizing a tiny self standing under the figurine, etc.). This allows us to become more aware of certain imaginative affordances of the things that are within our reach. Furthermore, in any open space we can place objects with intended imaginative affordances, or assign such affordances to objects already existing in the space. For example, in a city park, a single tree might be chosen to appeal to the imagination of passersby; in a playground, a special object might be placed (it could be located high enough to be out of reach) that would be meant to trigger imaginative actions of those playing. We just need to take care to place and disseminate appropriate instructions or guidelines about the imaginative affordances the object possesses (in the same way, for that matter, that we instruct people on how to physically use objects). As might be guessed, the possibilities for intentionally devising objects to afford imaginings to those who come into contact with them – thus making people (more) aware of these opportunities – are endless, and the feasibility of such design is relatively easy. All we need is our intent to do that.

2.2 *Objects Created So as to Afford Imagination*

Now, how to construct things in terms of their specific physical parameters such that these parameters can increase the likelihood of those things affording our imagination? At first glance, the task of pointing out such properties in things seems more tricky than pointing out properties in things that likely afford specific bodily actions. If a cup has a working handle (large enough) and is itself of the right size (not too big, not miniature), it is "graspable" to a suitably disposed person. If a pedestrian path is even and not very bumpy, it is "walkable" to people, including those using wheelchairs. If we place a sheet of metal at around arm height (rather than placing a doorknob) on the side of the door that has to be pushed, we will increase the likelihood of one's perception of the doors' "pushability". But how to construct doors that would likely be "imagine-*x*-able" to us (or at least some of us)?

Recalling the definition of imagination (see Section 1) to imagine, generally, is to mentally engage with what is non-actual. In all its possible manifestations – i.e., in the generation of sensory imagery, in supposition and counterfactual (what-if) imagination, in pretense, and in others – imagination somehow concerns itself with the realm of the non-actual. Therefore, in order to design objects that afford imagination, we may physically construct objects that have some parameters of "non-actuality" in them, that is, objects that are not (yet) known or defined, not (yet) acted upon, not (yet) connected, not (yet) transferred or rotated, not (yet) completed, or not perceptually unambiguous and thus not (yet) seen in all their possible manifestations. In a way, then, objects affording imagination would be non-actual themselves in some respects, so that they may enable certain things yet to be and/or happen. But in addition, we may construct objects that in some ways enable supposing, that is, thinking about possibilities, or "what-if" imagining (without necessarily generating any sensory imagery) – these objects themselves need not to be non-actual in the above sense, but they can lead to imagining, that is supposing, that certain non-actual scenarios or things are the case. Below, I will describe in more detail several types of objects that can be designed so as to afford various imaginings to us. I will also try to provide some inspiration for what such objects (or projects related to them) could look like in practice.

2.2.1 Bizarre Objects

What comes to mind first are objects that are completely new, unexpected, unknown, unnamed and undefined – undefined not only in terms of what they are, but also in terms of what can be done with them. Assuming that our perception is primarily for bodily action (as Gibson, 1979, Varela et al., 1991, and many others assume), if the object is so unusual, unfamiliar, or experienced so strange that it does not afford any bodily actions to us, the likelihood of its affording mental actions to us should increase. After all, it can trigger us both to wonder what it actually is as well as imagine what we could actually do with it. If you have ever encountered such a bizarre thing in your environment, you are probably familiar with this experience.

Earlier I asked what physical features of doors might contribute to their imaginative affordances. Certainly, typical doors do not belong to the class of curious objects – we see doors and know what they are and what to do with them (although sometimes, because of their poor bodily affordances, we pull on them when they need to be pushed). And yet, we can imagine something like odd doors – ones we haven't seen before. These might be tiny doors (like those in *Alice in Wonderland*) or gigantic doors (giving entrance to a place we have never visited). An unusually sized door could not afford us the bodily action of opening it. It is, however, quite possible that it would afford us imagining how to open it (e.g., by placing a ladder under the handle of a gigantic door) and to imagine what might be behind it (something tiny or enormous).

One might say that contemporary art galleries are places full of strange, uncanny objects. This may actually be one of the reasons why it is commonly believed that art stimulates our imagination. In fact, in our own research (Dunin-Kozicka et al., 2025) we have shown that those immersed in the exhibitions of the contemporary virtual art gallery (i.e., the Museum of Other Realities; https://www.museumor.com/) – which were filled with peculiar objects – are more creative or imaginative, perceiving more novel affordances in real-world objects than people who were not immersed or who had no contact with such a gallery at all. Others have also theoretically considered how exposure to art involves imagination to a greater extent than exposure to ordinary objects (Essom-Stenz & Roald, 2023). Having extraordinary perceptual experiences, as happens when dealing with art, spurs our imagination.

And yet, within the IOD, we can create a variety of new, bizarre objects and place them in different places not necessarily related to art: in parks, universities, playgrounds, and even shopping malls. And once these objects become familiar to those who see them regularly (which is inevitable), they can be exchanged for other new objects. There could even be an infrastructure created across cities or countries to exchange bizarre objects (if generating them were more problematic than relocating them). All I want to say is that contact with unknown, bizzare objects[8] is possible anywhere and for anyone. Imagination-Oriented Design could take this into account.

2.2.2 Mutable Objects

Another category of objects would be those that may be physically altered in many ways – that is re-shaped, re-combined or combined with other objects, rotated, transferred to other places, etc. – and therefore those that can still be "actualized" in some of their many potential forms. In this sense, they are not yet actualized, but they can never be finally actualized, because there is no single form (or target form) that we can stop at. Their nature is constant change, constant possibility of actualization. Someone who perceives such objects can imagine their as yet unfulfilled forms, and later possibly manipulate the objects so that they take on previously imagined forms. Thus, mutable objects afford the imagination (most often it will be specialized mental imagery, such as mental rotation) of those who perceive them.

The paradigmatic case of such objects would be any block-type objects. Indeed, we can say that even the simplest wooden children's blocks have both bodily affordances, that is, their stackability, composability and handleability, but they also have imaginative affordances, that is, their imagine-*x*-ability – *x* being anything that can be composed with them (for example, a castle, a vehicle, a figure). Exposed to them, a potential creator may imagine *x* just before starting the construction process, but may also imagine some elements of *x* during the process itself, when the perception of structures created so far directs the imagination in new possible directions. Thus, just as perception of bodily affordances is dynamic – changing with the ongoing action – perception of imaginative affordances is dynamic too, constantly guided by our current percepts.

We can of course think of many other types of mutable objects. These could be objects made of various modeling substances, such as dough, modeling clay, rubber, aluminum, and many others. Indeed, the range of changeable substances is constantly expanding as innovations in materials engineering continue to emerge. Some of these substances can be mutable using only

8 It is worth noting that some unfamiliar objects may not be experienced as bizarre objects by us. For example, if we discover a new species of butterfly, we will not experience it as strange because we already classify it as a butterfly – something we are already somewhat familiar with. Therefore, I am talking here mainly about objects that are experienced as bizarre by us. Many unfamiliar objects will be experienced in this way, but some will not. (I thank Paweł Fortuna for formulating this problem and providing the example.)

our hands, but there are also those that will be mutable if we approach them with the right tools. In this sense, any piece of wood or stone is mutable – all that is needed is a perceiver with the right skills (e.g., sculpting with given tools) who can notice the imaginative affordances in such objects. There is an anecdote about Michelangelo who, before he began the act of carving, would already see a specific figure in a piece of material. In other words, the perceived piece already afforded his imagination.

How do we apply this "mutability" principle of object design to our door case? We can imagine, for example, doors made of transformable materials, such as play dough, that can be continually reshaped by those exposed to them. Or they could be doors to which blocks (e.g., Lego blocks) can be continually added or removed, thus changing their shape and color in a constant mode. Such doors would have for us not only the affordance of pushing or pulling them (and also of re-arranging them!), but also the affordance of imagining how they might appear differently to us. This is just some inspiration, but as can be guessed, the possibilities for designing different mutable objects with imaginative affordances are endless.

2.2.3 Fillable Objects

This category of objects should fully be called "imaginatively fillable objects", because these will be things that experientially present themselves to us in some incomplete form, thus forcing us to complete them imaginatively. A simple example would be a fragment of a figure (in a 3D perspective) or a fragment of an image of a figure (2D), which we perceptually experience as missing and which we may want to complete in our imagination. Using the example of a door, we could think of perceiving the door handle itself as if hanging in the air in the place where the door could be – imaginatively we might want to fill the empty space with the door (or we could imaginatively suppose that there could/should be a door here).

Our disposition to imaginatively, in the sense of visualization, complete unfinished objects was used in designing the *Test of Creative Imagery Abilities* (Jankowska & Karwowski, 2020), where each task involves presenting participants with a simple graphic sign, called the initial figure, and then asking them, among others, to imagine what it could be and to provide the most interesting image in the form of a drawing by filling in the figure. Another popular creativity test – the *Test for Creative Thinking, DP* – developed by Urban and Jellen (1996), exposes participants to a picture containing simple geometric shapes, and instructions mentioning "an artist who had to leave her work unfinished" and asking them to "complete the drawing". Thus, in diagnostic practice, specific methods are designed based on affording the imagination through incomplete figures. We can of course transfer similar practices to a much broader context of object design.

Fillable objects would also include those whose experience is incomplete due to the fact that we currently perceive them with some, but not all, senses. For example, these could be rattles of sorts, which are filled with things that make specific sounds – we only hear the sounds, not seeing objects, so we can fill in our incomplete sensory experiences imaginatively. Similarly, touching something without seeing it can afford to us the imagining of what is being touched. Thus, for instance, any things that have other things hidden inside them that we can touch (or hear, or smell, etc.) – but cannot see – would likely afford the imaginings of the hidden ones.[9] Certainly, they may also be objects that we see and do not touch or hear, but which perceptually appear so suggestive to us that we imagine the auditory and tactile impressions they afford. In all of these cases – and in many others alike that we can still propose within the IOD – we would be likely exposed to imaginatively fillable objects.

2.2.4 Vague Objects

Next would be objects that present themselves to us in a perceptually ambiguous way, thus enabling their alternative percepts and imaginative interpretations. In the literature they are sometimes referred to as multistable objects or stimuli (Schwartz et al., 2012). Like mutable objects, they have a constant potential for actualization, but in the case of vague objects, nothing changes (or does not need to change) in their immanent structure, only in our way of perceiving them. Namely, it is because of their structural non-specificity experienced by us that we can constantly see them anew – which is possibly mediated by our imagination.

Think of clouds or ink stains (or even coffee stains on a piece of paper) – when we perceive them, we can see in them different things, faces, beings, etc. There is some debate as to whether such *seeing-in* experiences are perceptual (e.g., Wollheim, 1998) or imaginative (e.g., Sartre, 1940/2010) in nature. Some neuroscientific research show that it is rather akin to a genuine perceptual experience (Liu et al., 2014), and it has recently been proposed that the process of generating multiple different percepts from multistable stimuli could be termed *divergent perception* (Bellemare-Peppin & Jerbi, 2024). Still, even if we classify a single act of noticing something in a cloud as perceptual, I would treat such ambiguous objects as those that afford at least counterfactual or suppositional (if not sensory) imagination, as they may afford imagin-

9 In a similar, albeit slightly different, way, objects such as closed boxes or gift boxes are also imaginatively fillable – they may afford us imagining what might be inside them.

ing what (else) they could be. We may also say that such objects induce us to take a general imaginative stance towards them, i.e., to engage with possibilities of experiencing them that are other than the actual ones (see Liao & Gendler's definition of imagination above). Additionally, people who perceive more things in ambiguous objects such as clouds have been shown to be more creative than other people (Diana et al., 2021).[10]

Noteworthily, it was suggested by Richard Gregory – a renowned British psychologist who studied perception – that we can "reverse the Rorschach test" and see what types of ink blots particularly enhance one's creativity. He wrote:

> I suggest that reversing the test – from kinds of people to kinds of patterns – might show what stimulates creativity. This is a clear experimental question: which kinds of pattern evoke the richest variety of perceptions and ideas? This Reversed Rorschach should reveal principles of creativity. For a start, one may think of realistic pictures as representing external objects, whereas ink blots and abstract paintings evoke internal creations. Which patterns or pictures are most evocative should tell us what switches us on most powerfully to create new perceptions and ideas.
>
> GREGORY, 2000, p. 19

Gregory did not answer the question he posed in detail, but it is certainly a question that, with some minor rephrasing, is worth exploring as we continue to develop the IOD. What types of vague objects are particularly apt to afford imagination? Knowing this, we can confidently incorporate such objects into our design project. A door decorated with Rorschach-style blots could be one of them.

2.2.5 What-If Prompters

Finally, I want to mention about designing objects that are *not* non-actual themselves – in the sense objects listed above are – but, because of their content, lead the perceiver to imagine what is non-actual. Think, for example, of roadside billboards with various imaginative prompts (e.g., "What different things than usual could happen today?"; "Imagine there are more trees to the left"; "Imagine there aren't these trees here"); or imaginative prompts for

10 Building on the established correlations between divergent perception of multistable stimuli and creativity, a new measure for assessing creativity – namely, the Figural Interpretation Quest – has recently been proposed (Koutstaal, 2025).

walkers in a park (e.g., "What if *this* was a view that everyone in the world would want to see?"); or prompts on the doorway to someone's art studio (e.g., "When you walk through this door, you are a child playing again"). These imaginative prompts can also be of a nature other than propositional. For example, when passing a place, we might see boards with alternative images of that place (possibly generated by AI), allowing us to imagine what it would be like if certain characteristics of that place changed in a given way. Still, of course, there are many more options for designing what-if prompters, and the description of them should be more detailed. This is a foretaste of what they can be.

The list of objects designed so as to afford the imagination proposed above is certainly not exhaustive: neither in terms of possible categories of such objects, nor in terms of the specification of the categories of objects listed. The analysis here only launches the research on design that affords imagination, and there is still much engaging work ahead. Part of this work will certainly involve how to design entire environments that afford imagination. I will touch on that topic below.

3 Designing Environments with Imaginative Affordances

When considering the design of whole places that afford imagination, we can certainly assume, first, that such places can be filled with objects devised to afford imagination and/or objects specifically created *so as to* afford imagination. As for the former, I mentioned earlier the School of Imagination and the multi-colored buttons intended to afford appropriate imaginings to the school's students – this would be an example of an environment filled with objects designed to afford imagination (i.e., regardless of their specific characteristics, these objects were devised to incite imaginative actions in their perceivers). As for the latter, we will mean environments containing objects that are bizarre, mutable, fillable, vague, or any other things I have not mentioned above, but which have some inherent distinctive features making them more likely imagine-*x*-able than other objects (or at least making them so to a perceiver with the appropriate imaginative skills and inclinations, and without any desires, intentions, experiences with objects, etc., that would impair the imagine-*x*-ability of the objects themselves). Paradigmatic examples of such environments will be – as mentioned earlier – real and virtual art galleries (especially with contemporary art), which often abound in curious objects, but may also contain what-if prompters and other types of things mentioned above. And yet, within the framework of Imagination-Oriented Design we can think about how to supplement all other non-art-related spaces – such as parks, playgrounds, universities, shopping malls – with objects that afford the imagination.

But, at yet another level of applying the previous analyses, we can design environments that are *themselves* bizarre, or/and mutable, fillable, vague, etc. After all, we may come across an inherently strange place, or a place under constant reconstruction, in which we could have our share (i.e., mutable), or a place incomplete due its lacking elements (i.e., fillable), or an ambiguous place to which we cannot assign a clear meaning (i.e., vague). It may even be that some environments will have several of these characteristics. To illustrate this, a bizarre and mutable (and possibly fillable) playground could consist of large and small caterpillar-like structures, whose individual spherical segments could be freely moved and stacked together (like blocks). Each segment would be climbable on the outside, would have a different "interior design", and could be entered through their opening doors/windows. Such an environment could be reimagined each time by those playing, encouraging both different possible actions and imaginative ones, such as pretending many possible scenarios.

And, finally, we could intend some environments to afford imagination of their explorers, just as it may be experienced in the case of various art spaces (and therefore, often passing by an ordinary object placed by chance in such a space, we start to ponder over what it could possibly be, and what is its meaning in the context of art). The School of Imagination might be not only filled with imagine-*x*-able items, but may be also itself intended to be an environment affording imagination.[11] As caregivers, we can assign imaginative affordances to random playgrounds and point them out to our children (e.g., "Here you can pretend you are pirates"). As tourists, we can see imaginative affordances in all the places we encounter – even those with no known tourist value (e.g., "That (random) tree is a tree that everyone in the world would like to see someday"). In the IOD, then, we not only create appropriate environments, but also consciously seek out imaginative affordances in our surroundings. Simply by our intent, we can create new meanings for familiar spaces.

To summarize, what we could do as creators-designers who aim at affording imagination of those who come into contact with our designs is:

1. To openly *guide* them how our designs may afford some specific imaginings to them (e.g., we can place an instruction next to a bench indi-

11 In fact, already existing Waldorf schools would be environments devised and specifically arranged so as to trigger the imagination of their students. I thank Federico Fantelli for this remark.

cating that when one is looking at this bench, they can imagine a particular person *X* sitting on it);

2. To create objects that are *bizarre*, that is, that are unexpected and yet undefined in terms of what they are and what could be done with them (e.g., we can place something-like-a-bench in the park that stands in a vertical position, not the typical horizontal one);
3. To create objects that are *mutable*, that is, that may be physically manipulated in many ways, so that an observer may first mentally simulate how they can be manipulated (e.g., we can design a large tree-shaped object on the playground, which will be made of easily moldable material – so children will be able to imagine how this thing could be shaped differently);
4. To create objects that are *fillable*, that is, manifesting to us in some incomplete form and likely forcing us to complete them imaginatively (e.g., we can design a sculpture of a creature that moves and opens its mouth wide, as if screaming – so that the perceiver can imagine the sounds of screaming or other sounds possibly made by this creature);
5. To create objects that are *vague*, that its, presenting to one in a perceptually ambiguous way and enabling them to have alternative imaginative interpretations of it (e.g., we can design a ceiling lamp in the shape of a cloud, which allows us to see/imagine different shapes in it depending on the light and the perspective we adopt);
6. To create *what-if prompters*, that is, objects that lead the perceiver to imagine some non-actual things or scenarios (e.g., we can design a "What-if" application using augmented reality technology that – when we move around a certain area – shows us the area without the plants currently present in it, thus showing us the possible consequences of cutting down trees in a given area);
7. To design *entire environments* filled with objects that have the abovementioned features, or environments that are themselves bizarre, mutable, fillable, vague, or prompt others to imagine some what-if scenarios.

4 Ending Remarks

While the design of objects and environments is typically focused on the bodily actions that can be afforded by these objects and environments (Norman, 1990), here I have considered the possibilities of developing a design focused on affording users and explorers mental, and specifically imaginative, actions. Namely, within the Imagination-Oriented Design, we can aim at objects that are, regardless of their material properties, designed, i.e., devised, to afford the imagination, but also objects that are specifically designed, i.e., created, so as to afford imaginings to those who perceive them. Possible types of such objects would be objects that are bizarre, mutable, fillable, vague, but also objects with a content appealing to what-if imagination. Based on this, we can design environments (both real and virtual) that afford imagination, that is, those that are either filled with imagine-*x*-able objects, or that themselves imagine-*x*-able.

Why should we do it? First of all, the Imagination-Oriented Design is meant to be well-being-oriented design. This is because it recognizes all of us who are interacting with things in the world as complex multifaceted creatures with complex various experiences. We operate in the world not only in overt-corporeal forms, but also in covert-mental forms, including imaginary ones. The IOD therefore supports our full expression in interactions with objects and environments in which we live. Secondly, the IOD also takes into account our well-being on a deeper level. Due to ongoing social, technological, or climatic changes readily engaging with non-actual possibilities can help us change what is worth changing and prevent the consequences of changes that are harmful to us and our surroundings. If our imagination is afforded more often than usual, we stop reiterating our typical thoughts and activities, and start being those who see more possibilities for acting and being in the world. It is for these reasons, among others, that it seems important that we continue to develop the Imagination-Oriented Design in the future.

Acknowledgements

I would like to thank Paweł Fortuna for his insightful suggestions for improving and extending earlier versions of the article. Many thanks also to Zuzanna Rucińska, who not only supported me with numerous comments on the first draft, but also invited me to share it as part of a seminar from the Work in Progress series at the Centre for Philosophical Psychology at the University of Antwerp. I thank all the people at the Centre who, together with Zuzanna, read this text and helped me refine it: Federico Fantelli, Marco Facchin, Thomas van Es, Wouter van Hooydonk, Erik Myin, Jie He and Michiel Esseling. My deepest thanks to all of you.

References

Aglioti, S., DeSouza, J. F., & Goodale, M. A. (1995). Size-contrast illusions deceive the eye but not the hand. *Current Biology*, *5*(6), 679–685. https://doi.org/10.1016/s0960-9822(95)00133-3

Bellemare-Pepin, A., & Jerbi, K. (2024). Divergent Perception: Framing Creative Cognition Through the Lens of Sensory Flexibility. *The Journal of Creative Behavior*, 1–28. https://doi.org/10.1002/jocb.1525

Bruineberg, J. P., & van den Herik, J. C. (2021). Embodying mental affordances. *Inquiry*, 1–21. https://doi.org/10.1080/0020174X.2021.1987316

Chemero, A. (2003). An outline of a theory of affordances. *Ecological Psychology*, *15*(2), 181–195. https://doi.org/10.1207/s15326969eco1502_5

Chemero, A. (2009). *Radical embodied cognitive science*. MIT Press.

Clark, A. (2016). *Surfing uncertainty: Prediction, action, and the embodied mind*. Oxford University Press.

Costall, A. (1995). Socializing affordances. *Theory and psychology*, *5*(4), 467–481. https://doi.org/10.1177/0959354395054001

Costall, A. (2012). Canonical affordances in context. *AVANT*, *3*(2), 85–93.

Diana, L., Frei, M., Chesham, A., de Jong, D., Chiffi, K., Nyffeler, T., Bassetti, C. L., Goebel, N., Eberhard-Moscicka, A. K., & Müri, R. M. (2021). A divergent approach to pareidolias – Exploring creativity in a novel way. *Psychology of Aesthetics, Creativity, and the Arts*, *15*(2), 313–323.https://doi.org/10.1037/aca0000293

Dunin-Kozicka, M., Fortuna, P., Szubielska, M., Kopiś-Posiej, N., Kaczmarczyk, Ł., & Iwińska, J. (2025). Presence in Virtual Art Environments Affects the Perception of Novel Affordances in Real-World Objects. *Ecological Psychology*, *37*(3), 226–250. https://doi.org/10.1080/10407413.2025.2491339

Essom-Stenz, A., & Roald, T. (2023). Imagination in perception and art. *Theory & Psychology*, *33*(1), 99–117. https://doi.org/10.1177/09593543221135

Gibson, J. J. (1979). *The ecological approach to visual perception*. Psychology Press.

Gregory, R. (2000). Reversing Rorschach. *Nature*, *404*(6773), 19. https://doi.org/10.1038/35003661

Husserl, E. (1989). *Ideas pertaining to a pure phenomenology and to a phenomenological philosophy – Second book: Studies in the phenomenology of constitution*, trans. R. Rojcewicz & A. Schuwer. Kluwer Academic.

Jankowska, D. M., & Karwowski, M. (2020). *Test of creative imagery abilities*. Wydawnictwo Liberi Libri.

Kind, A. (2020). The skill of imagination. In E. Fridland & C. Pavese (Eds.), *Routledge handbook of skill and expertise* (pp. 335–346). Routledge.

Kind, A. (2022). Learning to imagine. *The British Journal of Aesthetics*, *62*(1), 33–48. https://doi.org/10.1093/aesthj/ayab037

Koutstaal, W. (2025). A new test for assessing creative flexibility of perceptual interpretation: The figural interpretation quest. *Psychology of Aesthetics, Creativity, and the Arts, 19*(3), 466–480. https://doi.org/10.1037/aca0000644

Liao, S.-Y., & Gendler, T. (2020). Imagination. In E. N. Zalta (Ed.), *The Stanford encyclopedia of philosophy*. https://plato.stanford.edu/archives/sum2020/entries/imagination/

Liu, J., Li, J., Feng, L., Li, L., Tian, J., & Lee, K. (2014). Seeing Jesus in toast: neural and behavioral correlates of face pareidolia. *Cortex, 53*, 60–77. https://doi.org/10.1016/j.cortex.2014.01.013

McClelland, T. (2020). The mental affordance hypothesis. *Mind, 129*(514), 401–427. https://doi.org/10.1093/mindfzz036

McClelland, T, & Dunin-Kozicka, M. (2024). Affording imagination. *Philosophical Psychology*. Advance online publication. https://doi.org/10.1080/09515089.2024.2354433

Merleau-Ponty, M. (2012). *Phenomenology of perception*, trans. D. Landes. Routledge.

Milner, A. D., & Goodale, M. A. (2008). Two visual systems re-viewed. *Neuropsychologia, 46*(3), 774–785. https://doi.org/10.1016/j.neuropsychologia.2007.10.005

Norman, D. A. (1990). *The design of everyday things*. Doubleday.

Sartre, J. P. (1940/2010). *The imaginary: A phenomenological psychology of the imagination*. Routledge.

Schwartz, J. L., Grimault, N., Hupé, J. M., Moore, B. C., & Pressnitzer, D. (2012). Multistability in perception: Binding sensory modalities, an overview. *Philosophical Transactions of the Royal Society B: Biological Sciences, 367*(1591), 896–905. https://doi.org/10.1098/rstb.2011.0254

Turvey, M. T. (1992). Affordances and prospective control: An outline of the ontology. *Ecological Psychology, 4*(3), 173–187. https://doi.org/10.1207/s15326969eco0403_3

Urban, K. K., & Jellen, H. G. (1996). Test for Creative Thinking – Drawing Production (TCTDP). Lisse, Netherlands: Swets and Zeitlinger.

Varela, F. J., Thompson, E., & Rosch, E. (1991). *The embodied mind: Cognitive science and human experience*. MIT Press.

Wollheim, R. (1998). On pictorial representation. *The Journal of Aesthetics and Art Criticism, 56*(3), 217–226. https://doi.org/10.2307/432361

CHAPTER 6

Creativity: A Future Competence for Solidarity and Sensitivity?

Rafał Pastwa[*,1] *and Łukasz Sarowski*[*,2]

Abstract

The aim of the article is to show that the effectiveness of new technological tools based on AI can contribute to the development of future competencies in the form of solidarity and sensitivity. The competence of the future understood in this way will contribute to greater responsibility in the development and use of technology in order to reduce multidimensional social disproportions and improve the situation of individuals and societies, and as a result, solve problems that constitute key challenges for humanity today. To this end, Richard Florida's category of the creative class and Arthur J. Cropley's definition of creativity have been employed. Creativity, as it relates to economic growth, has been expanded to include a social – solidarity and relational – aspect. In this regard, reference is made to Ralph R. Acampora's category of somatic sympathy, which has universal characteristics. Human beings are understood as relational and creative entities, capable of deep empathy and solidarity with those threatened by multidimensional exclusion. The theory of the "new global culture of the 21st century" by Roland Benedikter was also taken into account.

Keywords

creativity – future competences – solidarity – sensitivity – artificial intelligence – technology

* The John Paul II Catholic University of Lublin, Institute of Journalism and Management, Lublin, Poland

1 https://orcid.org/0000-0001-9470-5156

2 https://orcid.org/0000-0003-1228-9705

We need leaders who can guide or lead us in dealing with new, often previously unimaginable situations. This opens a vast field for the use and application of AI for the common good and for a better, fairer future. Therefore, when thinking about competencies from the perspective of the future, efforts should be made to ensure that creativity is not held hostage to a market mentality, but instead is understood as a competence for solidarity, community, and deeper sensitivity. As Federico Mayor emphasized, the future does not belong to us but to future generations (Mayor & Bindé, 2001). The human of the future will not be a replica of us, as they will belong to a different time and set of circumstances. Consequently, we do not know what challenges and dangers they will have to face (Mayor & Bindé, 2001). Challenges are easier to tackle in a solidaristic society, where individuals feel responsible for others, and the weaker are not left to fend for themselves. Otherwise, only the strongest will survive. How to think about the future if the trust ecosystem collapses?

We are social beings, although postmodern society increasingly displays the dynamism of individualism (Bauman, 2006; Giddens, 2004, 2006). Perhaps the time has come to replace a culture focused on efficiency, productivity, strength, and competition with a culture of sensitivity, deep empathy, and solidarity rooted in the fact that every living being, possessing a body, experiences the fragility of existence, pain, fear, and impermanence (Acampora, 2013).

When we think about the future and future competencies, we also need to find a universal point of reference in the context of upcoming challenges and actions. Solutions must be sought to optimize the improvement of the situation for individuals and societies, including through the use of AI. The question arises as to how to distribute the benefits from the development of new AI applications (Leyton-Brown, 2024). Does sensitivity, deep empathy arising from the universal experience of having a living, fragile, pain- and impermanence-prone body not provide a sufficient criterion for the fair distribution of goods and benefits from the development of the latest technologies? What stands in the way of using algorithms for altruism? It is promising to see emerging applications aimed at strengthening social bonds and fostering changes in attitudes toward poor people (Islam, 2024). In the context of technological development, attention should be paid to the importance of solidarity and sensitivity, which, in the opinion of the authors of the article, may constitute key competencies of the future. Otherwise, technological development will work to the advantage of those individuals and communities that will be able to use it optimally, while people at risk of multidimensional exclusion will be disadvantaged by the lack of access to the fruits of progress.

John D. Barrow (2005) observes that a tendency toward short-term benefits, rather than long-term planning, will not prevent catastrophes, which are becoming more real within a human lifetime, even though for many they remain unnoticed. Perhaps attention should be drawn to the phenomenon of parasocial relationships, where the challenge is to harness the unique aspects of communication platforms to enhance users' well-being. Parasocial relationships are unreciprocated socio-emotional connections with media figures such as celebrities or influencers (Hoffner & Bond, 2022). However, there is a positive impact of parasocial relationships realized by influencers on social media on healthy lifestyles, as well as other attitudes and behaviors, including pro-ecological ones (Breves & Liebers, 2022). Hence, the need for interdisciplinary reflection on creativity as a future competence, one that will not only be utilized in the economic sphere but also in the social realm, where creative forms of solidarity and sensitivity will work for the benefit of those most in need and at risk of multidimensional exclusion.

The aim of the article is to show that the effectiveness of new technological tools based on AI can contribute to the development of future competencies in the form of solidarity and sensitivity. The competence of the future understood in this way will contribute to greater responsibility in the development and use of technology in order to reduce multidimensional social disproportions and improve the situation of individuals and societies, and as a result, solve problems that constitute key challenges for humanity today.

To this end, Richard Florida's category of the creative class and Arthur J. Cropley's definition of creativity have been employed. Creativity, as it relates to economic growth, has been expanded to include a social – solidarity and relational – aspect. In this regard, reference is made to Ralph R. Acampora's category of somatic sympathy, which has universal characteristics. Human beings are understood as relational and creative entities, capable of deep empathy and solidarity with those threatened by multidimensional exclusion. Therefore, an attempt has been made to formulate recommendations that may support the process of educating and raising individuals towards creativity as a future competence, one that transcends the economic and industrial sphere.

1 Future Scenarios

When we think about the future, alongside promising, optimistic scenarios, negative ones also emerge, driven by fears of the unknown and rooted in the experience of the general population, whose perception is that the system works in favor of the wealthy and better-educated (Edelman, 2017). Reports on the future, based on the opinions of young people, indicate that top concerns include the ability to achieve personal goals and the fear of finding or losing a job (Ipsos, 2023). Among the most valued life achievements are building a career, obtaining a driver's license, owning a home, becoming independent from parents, and, lower on the list, completing higher education (Ipsos, 2023). This confirms Ulrich Beck's (2002) intuition, who emphasized that:

> In advanced modernity, individualization is realized within the framework of a socialization process that increasingly hinders independence: although the individual is liberated from traditional ties and sources of livelihood, they must fulfill the demands of the labor market and live as a consumer, subject to relevant standardizations and control mechanisms.
>
> p. 197

Similarly, Janusz Mariański (2010) observes:

> In place of old, traditional conditions, new imperatives, mainly connected to the labor market, arise.
>
> pp. 54–55

When discussions of social renewal emerge in the context of contemporary challenges, including those related to the labor market, the starting point is often the anxiety connected to the rapid acceleration of globalization, and, as a result, the increasingly fast flow of money, changes in the realms of culture, society, information, and services, and the growing power of global institutions and communities that attract science and business sectors to nongovernmental organizations (Mulgan, 2000). The significance of the labor market and job stability is clearly demonstrated by the fact that the most trusted institution on a global scale remains one's own employer (Edelman, 2024).

We are capable of designing the future, including in a strategic sense, of predicting it, and of thinking about events and phenomena that have not yet occurred. The future is considered both in relation to individuals and collectives, which, from a social sciences perspective, seems more intriguing. Collective futures are understood as projects concerning the lives of future generations and communities. As Jowita Gromysz (2020) points out, visions of the future can result from the actions of social institutions or have a noninstitutional character: "The collective future is imaginary, a project based on what we commonly consider important for the community (e.g., culture, sense of belonging to a group, institutions), so it does not take into account the fate of individuals, but focuses on them in relation to society and their interconnectedness" (p. 320).

Both literature, especially dystopian works, and cinema offer interesting ways of envisioning collective future:

> An individual can project visions of entire societies, but they will always rely on their own knowledge of how the social world functions, on experiences that have been important to them. These are intertwined with imaginations, myths, symbols, and cultural codes known to the entire community. It is impossible to create a vision of a better society without referring to one's own experiences and the reality known to all.
>
> GROMYSZ, 2020, p. 323

Dystopias, as the opposite of utopias, refer to the present and show seemingly better societies that, in fact, do not function properly. They are burdened with some defect that makes citizens passive and susceptible to oppression by the authorities (Gromysz, 2020, p. 324). Another way of thinking about collective futures involves actions realized at the level of social practice, aimed at improving the lives of future generations.

In this dimension, everything may begin with visions, ideas that inspire scientists, politicians, ideologues, or religious leaders. However, these are usually later implemented in social reality. History shows that ideas of a better society – when implemented too hastily, without a balanced equilibrium between tradition and social innovation – have turned into revolutions or the realization of ideologies that in the 20th century developed into totalitarianisms. (Gromysz, 2020, p. 325).

An example of action within the framework of social practice for the future is education, upbringing, and work.

In turn, infuture.institute (2018), which defines the most important trends, describes them and highlights their consequences for the economy, market categories, or specific brands, has developed a report titled *Far Future. The History of Tomorrow*, basing its forecasts on cultural texts, particularly the classics of sci-fi films. The authors demonstrate that in business, the visionary ideas of sci-fi film creators can be utilized. They present eleven areas of future life: city, work, food, home, transport, medicine/health, AI/robots, sex, society, communication, and time. The methodology adopted was an analysis of science fiction films; 54 films were selected, and 1 047 internet users were surveyed. The research resulted in a dystopian report. The main concerns of respondents revolved around: primarily, robots similar to humans that would replace us in every sphere of life, including work, food in the form of mush, and life in an authoritarian, controlled, and polarized society (infuture.institute, 2018).

In the context of the future and creativity, it is worth mentioning the *Report on the Future of Work*, conducted as part of the International Labour Organization. Its goal was to review literature on concepts and factors driving aspirations, as well as to develop a conceptual framework linking labor market conditions with aspirations, to map survey research on youth aspirations worldwide, and to provide insights on how to improve data collection, research, and evidence-based policymaking regarding the aspirations of young people. The research lasted from November 2018 to April 2019. According to the authors of the report, the future of the labor market is a key area of interest for young people (Gardiner & Goedhuys, 2019).

Even before the outbreak of the COVID-19 pandemic, it was noted:

> Compounding this situation is the fact that the world of work is changing rapidly, with technological and climate change altering the conditions of production, and labor markets undergoing substantial shifts. The transformation of employment relations, expanding inequalities, and economic stagnation greatly hamper the achievement of full employment and decent work for everyone. If young people are to benefit from the changing nature of the world of work, they need to be prepared, both in terms of skills attainment and level of ambition and aspiration.
>
> GARDINER & GOEDHUYS, 2019

According to Gilbert F. Houngbo, Director-General of the International Labour Organization, we cannot expect a stable future when millions of young people lack decent work and, as a result, feel insecure and are unable to build a better life for themselves and their families. Peaceful societies are based on three fundamental pillars: stability, inclusion, and social justice, and decent work for young people is the foundation of all three (ILO, 2024b).

Global Employment Trends for Youth 2024 warns that the number of people aged 15 to 24 who are not in employment, education, or training (NEET) remains a cause for concern, despite a falling jobless rate, as the post-COVID-19 employment recovery has not been universal (ILO, 2024a). In Arab states, East Asia, and Southeast Asia, and the Pacific, youth unemployment rates were higher in 2023 than in 2019. Opportunities for decent jobs remain limited in emerging and developing economies. Globally, 20,4% of youth were classified as NEET in 2023, with two out of three NEET individuals being women. For those young people who are employed, the report notes a lack of progress in securing decent jobs. Globally, more than half of young workers are employed informally. Only in high- and upper-middle-income economies do the majority of young workers now have stable, secure jobs. The report calls for increased and more effective investment, including in job creation, especially for young women, strengthening institutions that support young people in their transition to the labor market, integrating employment and social protection for youth, and tackling global inequalities through better international cooperation, and public-private sector collaboration in job development. In the introduction, addressed to young people, the report stated:

> As today's youth, your meaningful engagement in labor markets and the quality of work that you will have matters a great deal to the future of the global economy. The better educated you are, the better empowered you are to find your productive potential and dignity in work; the better supported you are to reach a state of economic security, the better the future will be for everyone. You are living in an era of rapid changes and uncertain circumstances that are not of your own making.
>
> ILO, 2024a, p. v

The ILO also highlights the increasingly frequent anxieties among young people regarding the future, primarily related to economic issues and their own career prospects. The main concerns of young people include fears of losing their jobs, concerns about job stability, lack of generational turnover, insufficient economic opportunities, and limited financial independence (ILO, 2024a). Anxiety is a negative emotional state, a mixture of feelings such as fear, tension, and worry, arising from nonspecific threats or vague perceptions of future risks (Lang et al., 2005). Employment anxiety is a specific type of anxiety triggered by employment situations with uncertainty (Jin et al., 2024).

In many parts of the world, crises have further deepened inequalities, and in less developed areas, young people experience unemployment and perpetuated uncertainty. Often, strategies aimed at young people are not consistent, which has led to calls for more sensitive programs addressing youth uncertainty and the specifics of local economies (Avagianou et al., 2024).

According to the *World Happiness Report* (2024), the level of happiness among young people has decreased almost globally, with few exceptions. This decline is primarily influenced by economic challenges, such as rising living costs and a lack of security and stability in the job market; social and technological pressures – despite access to social media, strong direct relationships are being lost; uncertainty and anxiety caused by political polarization and climate change. The report emphasizes that when happiness levels drop, motivation, productivity, health, and life expectancy also decline. It advocates for the promotion of education for the future, where workshops on healthy social media use and financial literacy could play a significant role. In the report, youth is seen as the future workforce capable of ensuring the stability of economies. Meanwhile, Gunnar Heinsohn (2021, p. 184) argues that civilization can only be preserved if it is based on the institution of the family, guards democracy and the separation of powers, and protects the interests of creative and hardworking groups from privileged groups, both from the upper and lower classes.

2 Creativity – Towards Solidarity

According to World Economic Forum *The Future of Jobs Report* (2023) analytical and creative thinking remain the most important skills for employees in 2023. Analytical thinking is considered the core skill by more companies than any other and constitutes, on average, 9% of the core skills reported by firms. Creative thinking, another cognitive skill, ranks second, surpassing three self-efficacy skills – resilience, flexibility, and agility; motivation and self-awareness; curiosity and lifelong learning – acknowledging the importance of employees' ability to adapt to disrupted workplaces. Reliability and attention to detail rank seventh, just behind technological skills. The top ten core skills are rounded out by two attitudes related to collaboration with others – empathy and active listening, and leadership and social influence – as well as quality control. The World Economic Forum (2024) also identifies ten core professional skills that employees should possess by 2025. Among the most important are: analytical thinking and innovation, active learning and learning strategies, complex problem-solving, critical and analytical thinking, creativity as well as originality and entrepreneurship, leadership and social influence, technology use for monitoring and control, technology design and programming, resilience, stress tolerance and flexibility, and the ability to reason in problem-solving.

Beyond the technological and communication innovations brought about by progress, one must also reflect on changes in societal models. Information and communication technologies not only affect global economies but also influence work, education, and consumption, and furthermore, new forms of social attitudes and solidarity. The revolution in communication can foster new forms of education, learning, research, conscious information sharing, and, ultimately, the emergence of new types of human "communities" (Mayor & Bindé, 2001). In this sense, creativity as a future competence can be "modeled" by both public and private internets (Mayor & Bindé, 2001).

Creativity as a concept emerged in American society in the 1950s in two contexts: psychological research and business (Ipsos, 2023). According to Samuel W. Franklin (2023), creativity emerged relatively independently in each of these contexts, but over time they complemented and reinforced each other. Psychologists associated creativity with expression and authenticity, while business utilized creativity in the fields of advertising and new technologies, realizing its impact on the consumer market. It was meant to harmonize the goals of the economy with the internal "self" (Franklin, 2023, p. 100). In American society, creativity began to be seen almost as a virtue, reinforcing the belief that through it, one could develop individual creative abilities that allowed for self-fulfillment and a good standard of living, and eventually have a positive impact on society and the common future (Franklin, 2023). The author of *The Cult of Creativity* believes that creativity became an ideal, even a value, and was involved in a troubling tension between utilitarianism and humanism or transcendence. It played an important role in how people coped with both pessimistic and optimistic visions of the future (Franklin, 2023). Franklin's historical analysis of creativity and its related socio-cultural aspects allowed him to take a critical stance on Florida's concept and his studies of urbanism, which were centered around issues of economic growth in the post-industrial age (Kramer, 2024). A critical approach to the concept of the creative class does not necessarily mean rejecting it, but rather requires supplementing and enriching it with a dimension of responsibility and solidarity toward the "less creative" individuals. The *Memphis Manifesto*, referenced in Florida's publication (2010), provides a foundation for building a broader perspective for the future, one that assumes not only support for creative individuals and environments and education in creativity but also nurturing sensitivity, responsibility, and community.

When we asked ChatGPT version 4.0 (2024) what the world will look like in 2037, we received the following response: "Predicting the future is always difficult and fraught with uncertainty, but based on current technological, social, and economic trends, one can imagine what the world might look like in 2037." Then, a possible scenario was presented in relation to the following areas: technology and AI, society and work, environment and sustainability, economy and globalization, governance and politics.

The term "creativity" appeared exclusively in the context of changes in education. Key elements for future education, adaptive and individualized were generated as: technology, creativity, and problem-solving. Defining creativity as a creative change serving to improve the quality of life for individuals and societies – it can be found in every point generated by ChatGPT 4.0, with an emphasis on its utilitarian application. We did not find references to compassion, solidarity, or community. This is a significant area to be filled by creative leaders and creative communities.

Definitions of creativity, once focused on aspects related to aesthetics and the creation of art, have been enriched with a business dimension, including the practical application of products, the possibilities of market competition in services, products, broadly understood consumption, and the labor market. Referring to the intuition of Arthur Cropley (2020) a key element in defining creativity is the idea of novelty – some kind of originality and attractiveness combined with competence and quality. As the researcher points out, modern creativity requires effectiveness, relevance, and ethics. Therefore, it is necessary to distinguish between creativity of an elevated character and that applied in everyday life.

Cropley also defines creativity as a social phenomenon that is described and analyzed according to social norms, which can either promote or limit it. One of the main social environments is the workplace and educational settings. It is within these spaces that interactions between individuals and their surroundings have a fundamental impact on the creation of innovations and their dynamics. According to the anthropological assumption that every person is a social being – not only participating in social life and belonging to specific social environments but also fundamentally needing social relationships – creativity as a social phenomenon forms the core and foundation for the birth, realization, and completion of individual creativity, whether of an elevated nature or in everyday dimensions. Focusing on the individual, Cropley defined creativity as an aspect of thinking, a constellation of personality, and as an interaction in a specific environment between thinking, personal traits, motivation, and emotions. Creativity in this context is thus understood as an aspect of thinking, as a constellation of personality, and as an interaction in a given environment between thinking, personality traits, motivation, and emotions.

Creativity can also be viewed as a process, culminating in the emergence of creative products and their implementation. Cropley (2020) proposed a model of the creative process, which consists of four stages: discovering, defining, inventing, and implementing. Therefore, in the search for future adequate applications of creativity for the sake of solidarity, compassion, and community, creativity should be viewed as a dynamic process, not merely as a phenomenon reduced to originality or ingenuity (Corazza, 2016). Such an approach encourages a broader perspective on this process, emphasizing the wide field of creative actions. The development of a person's creative potential also evolves, with an emphasis on seeking new forms of realization, including for the sake of solidarity, sensitivity, and community.

Richard Florida (2002), based on his analyses, announced the existence of a creative class, which is socially significant due to its members' ability to stimulate regional economic growth through innovation. He stated that the creative class consists of knowledge workers whose task is to create new forms. It includes scientists and engineers, those in law and business, as well as architects, and moreover, those engaged in education, art, music, design, and the entertainment industry. The economic result, especially, is the creation of new products, technological tools, and creative content. On the other hand, the rest of society does not contribute to innovation, focusing primarily on consumption rather than production. Creative individuals, who contribute to economic and social development, do not limit themselves solely to the creative sphere but actively participate in everyday life. What distinguishes them is their scientific foundation, participation in daily life, and the ability to draw inspiration from various aspects of reality. This ability to draw inspiration from many sources confirms the distinction between creative individuals, belonging to the creative class, and the part of the population more inclined toward consumption. According to Florida (2004), creativity is also expressed within a group of highly educated individuals, where the key competency is problem-solving or a new approach to problems. Consequently, creativity is increasingly valued not only in the context of regional development but also from a global perspective. Therefore, it is worth paying attention to the perspective of investing in a "creative ecosystem" (Florida, 2010, p. 391) and developing it in a new, deeper context – focused on collaboration not for economic gain or the production of better products, but for the protection and support of those members of the community who objectively require it. Technological progress should serve everyone equally, without exception.

The emergence and opposition of the creative class to the consumer class can be interpreted as part of the "new era of inequality," or even the "new era of segregation" (Hobsbawm, 1995; pp. ix–xii). The growing economic disparities between wealthy and developing countries have also translated into numerous divisions, not just economic ones, within societies (Edelman, 2019). Inequalities stem from unequal access to material, social, and cultural goods (Czakon, 2017). There is an increasingly noticeable dominance of business, even in the context of fair and ethical approaches to the use of innovation. According to some sources, business and employers represent institutions with a higher level of competence and ethics than national governments or media outlets (Edelman, 2024).

In this context, it is worth pointing to the crisis of neoliberal globalization, expressed in the era of the *Great Unsettling* (Steger & James, 2020). This phenomenon affects areas such as ecology, economy, politics, and culture. These changes are driven by the increasingly rapid technological development that fuels "disembodied globalization," which is beginning to dominate over embodied globalization, objectified globalization, and institutional globalization. The digital revolution, unlike any before, reveals the process of absorbing embodied social relations, a state further deepened by advancements in machine learning and artificial intelligence (AI) (Steger et al., 2023).

The current phase of globalization is referred to as *re-globalization*, understood as a profound rearrangement and reconfiguration of major globalization dynamics moving at different speeds and at different levels of intensity. Present-day globalization is being reshaped into a set of worldwide processes dominated by digital connectivity (Steger et al., 2023). Re-globalization introduces a new social order based on the dominance of digital interactions, where the economy, trade, and labor are transferred to the virtual sphere on an unprecedented scale. A fundamental element of this shift is the accelerated automation driven by the development of AI and robotics, as well as an identity crisis resulting from the hybridization of real-world and digital spaces. For this reason, we propose perceiving creativity in the context of these ongoing changes through the lens of sensitivity and solidarity (see Benedikter, 2022).

3 Creativity for Sensitivity and Solidarity

Technological progress should not release us from responsibility for weaker and dependent people and beings. In parallel to technological development, competences based on sensitivity and solidarity should be developed.

> Certainly, there is less poverty in the world than before, fewer diseases. But there is more inequality. People are not as happy as they used to be, because prosperity and technology do not bring happiness. There is one thing that can help us, and it is not technology. Only we can help ourselves.
>
> infuture.institute, 2018; p. 20

In seeking a model where the utilitarian approach to creativity, technological, and communicative development undergoes a transformation, it must be emphasized that true development cannot occur without the integral improvement of human life quality and the reduction of inequalities. Are the voices calling for restraint from excessive anthropocentrism and utilitarianism being overshadowed before our eyes by market mentality? Francis (2015) argued that it is, after all, the environment, including and perhaps especially the digital environment, that influences how people view life, feel, and act. In his view the vulnerability and fragility of living beings are particularly highlighted in the social encyclical when juxtaposed with the interests of the market and the absolutization of market mentality. It is also worth emphasizing that no creature should be reduced to the level of a thing and its value measured solely by its utility. Any violence or exploitation of others as if they were objects contradicts the role of responsible stewardship. Consequently, the role of a steward should also involve countering violence and all forms of harm toward other people and beings. The role of a responsible, creative, and sensitive steward should be to create and apply technological tools, including AI, to improve the fate of all people and other beings.

To address the key and urgent issues mentioned in the opening sections of this article, it is necessary to find and recognize a universal category that could break the dominant pattern in which creativity and technological development benefit the wealthier, better-educated, and those living in relatively safe and comfortable conditions. The next step should be moving away from extreme anthropocentrism, which allows for the thinking that, among other things, environmental protection should be carried out solely for the sake of humans and that technological progress should serve only our species. Here, it is worth proposing the concept of somatic sympathy (*symphysis*), suggested in a slightly different context by Acampora (2012). Based on the experience of a living body, this category possesses all the features necessary to serve as a universal foundation for expanding human responsibility for the fate of dependent, weaker, excluded, and threatened beings, as well as other living creatures. Somatic sympathy is based on the experience of having a living body that feels physical pain, fear, anxiety, and the fragility of existence – an experience shared by both humans and other creatures (Acampora, 2006). This bodily empathy expands the area of human moral responsibility to include vulnerable beings, whether human or otherwise (Acampora, 2013). The experience of having a living body is the starting point for understanding the meaning of existence, rather than escaping from the search for it, which ends in confusion and doubt. Such diagnoses are already being made in the public, cultural sphere, including media studies, and humanistic education. They are intended to lead towards the construction of deep interpersonal relationships and the teach ing of deep compassion proposed as a remedy for the narcissism and mar ket mentality of media users (Nussbaum, 2010). Thus, somatic sympathy can be a solution to the identity crisis of the individual in con temporary culture, as well as the restoration of proper social relations and the relationship with the created world, where the dominant factor will not be force and indifference, but the awareness of a responsible and attentive community of shared destiny resulting from the universal experience of having a living body. Focusing on the dimension concerning human persons, already many decades ago Edith Stein emphasized that only empathy, a kind of deep sympathy, makes it pos sible for a person to express themselves as an individual, while remain ing in relation to others (Stein, 2014). Thus, some kind of empathy, based on the corporeality of the human being, which allows the human being to express itself more fully, constitutes the key to remaining in relation to others. Without the value of sensitivity, there can be no talk of authentic communities and the structures they create (Etzioni, 2001).

Can a sensitive, compassionate, and attentive relationship with others become a guiding principle for the further development of creativity, education, and technology? This is certainly a proposal that should be considered if we are to responsibly look toward a future where AI may play a key role. Access to AI technology seems to be one of the key factors supporting creative processes on both macro and micro scales. The emergence of a reality that is transformed by data processing, AI, and technological corporations raises legitimate concerns about the shaping of a posthumanist vision of the new global cultural economy (Steger et al., 2023). However, we also want to emphasize that, alongside many concerns, AI technologies can also present an opportunity in terms of democratizing access to knowledge and equalizing opportunities for social participation (belonging to the "creative class.").

In this context, we would like to highlight the possibilities of adapting the principles of somatic sympathy in relation to AI. Elements of this approach are already evident in the design of intelligent cognitive systems, albeit to a limited extent (e.g., in the process of designing AI equipped with some virtual or real form of embodiment). Computers, internet technologies, and AI have been permanently integrated into the architecture of social progress, which means a new context has emerged for considering their place and role, particularly in the context of creativity. Viewing AI in a social context reveals human relationship not only with other people but also with technologies that can both shape and be shaped by these relationships. Embodied functionalism highlights this aspect of human cognitive abilities, viewing the body as an integral part of a broader cognitive system. This system includes the brain-body-world structure, where cognitive functions can be realized in various ways and with the use of different tools (Clark & Chalmers, 1998). This raises questions about the role of AI in creative processes, prompting consideration of the concept of "shared creativity" between humans and machines. This aspect leads to further questions about how AI can assist in building a world based on the values of sustainable progress.

4 Creativity in the Context of AI

The previously cited perspectives on creativity illustrated its understanding in an anthropocentric context, for example, as an aspect of thinking, a constellation of personality and the interaction within a given environment between thinking, personal traits, motivation, and emotions (Cropley 2020). It is also understood as a process culminating in the emergence and implementation of specific products, exemplified by generative technologies. Referring to the above remarks, we would also like to point out that the discussion on creativity in a technology-saturated reality may concern attempts to redefine it. This is happening because generative technologies are designed to imitate human cognitive and creative actions to a much greater extent than other technological solutions that have so far driven changes in the field of creative and artistic activities. An open question remains as to what extent advanced computational technologies can be perceived as creative.

4.1 *Generative Technologies*

The ChatGPT tool is just one example of the currently available tools that break the traditional anthropocentric approach to actions considered creative. One can also mention software like DALL-E and many other image generators that work based on textual descriptions. Their emergence has sparked lively debate regarding the understanding and practice of art in the age of AI, and consequently, the changes that creative activity itself may undergo. The growing ability to use large language models (LLMs) and image and sound generators in actions requiring creativity has led to discussions on the democratization of art due to the wide availability of artistic tools. They can level the playing field between professionals who possess innate skills developed over their lifetimes and those who do not have such abilities.

It can be assumed that creative activities in the near future will emphasize other aspects of human skills than those currently considered key. Some scholars believe that the democratization of art through AI would significantly change the traditional understanding of creativity as a distinct cognitive ability that differs noticeably between individuals (Orwig et al., 2024). On the one hand, it would make people equal in the realm of artistic activity, while on the other, it would involve a fundamental shift in the paradigm of understanding creativity as independent of the innate abilities of individual creators. In this way, there would be a departure from perceiving it in terms of an internal cognitive function toward basing creativity on the interaction between humans and machines – i.e., the interaction between intention and computational processes of machines (Orwig et al., 2024). This, in turn, suggests the need to consider in what specific actions and conditions creativity manifests itself and whether a machine can be creative in any way – even assuming a high level of autonomy from humans. Therefore, it is necessary to distinguish between what arises from an intention based on creative activity (the idea behind the creator's work) and the computational process that is meant to materialize that idea. This issue can be extended to almost every aspect of human activity characterized by analytical and creative thinking.

This allows us to ask about the potential scope of participation of AI in broadly understood creative processes, especially in the context of creating opportunities for sustainable social development based on solidarity and responsible community-building. In this case, there is a need for equal access to technological tools, media and technological education, and their ethical use by users and social leaders. The actions they undertake refer to various types of creativity, which can be complemented by new technological solutions. This means that creativity, as a competency of the future, can be somewhat shaped by AI.

In this context, it is worth pointing to the three types of creativity described by Margaret A. Boden (1998). Combinatorial creativity refers to the combination of already known ideas into something new. Exploratory creativity generates new ideas by exploring structured conceptual spaces, leading to certain modifications. Transformational creativity, which intersects with exploratory creativity, involves transforming the dimensions of the space into new structures. The latter two types of creativity highlight the important issue of differentiating between modification and transformation, and thus the scope of actual actions taken by AI.

The above remark relates to the discussion about using AI as a tool to expand human creativity at various levels. In this regard we can refer to the four-stage model of creativity development (The Four C Model of Creativity) developed by Kaufman and Beghetto (2009). The first level is *mini-c/creativity*, which is characterized as personal creativity belonging to an individual, developed throughout their life. It is a subjective dimension of creativity. The second is so-called *little-c/everyday creativity*, referring to human daily activities and the decisions and solutions they make that go beyond the realm of purely personal experience. This type of creativity is related to the opinions of others. The third level of creativity is *pro-c/professional creativity*, which involves possessing specialized knowledge in specific fields. The fourth level is *big-c/eminent creativity*, referring to actions that permanently change a given field of science or knowledge or may influence culture (Helfand et al., 2017). We would like to note that this type of creativity should be connected to creativity aimed at sensitivity and solidarity. Eminent creativity should be developed towards mindfulness of others, sensitivity to weaker and dependent individuals, and other living beings. It could shift the focus of science, art, and technological development away from economic and commercial benefits and towards equal opportunities and reducing disparities.

One can ask about AI's role in the aforementioned creative processes. To address this, it is necessary to note that the problem of creativity can be divided into three fundamental problem groups. The first concerns attributing creativity to the actions of AI itself. The second concerns the possibility of enhancing human creativity through AI. The third group of issues combines the two above, pointing to the possibility of "co-creativity" as a result of the creative actions of both AI and humans. The common denominator of these issues is the challenge of explaining how anthropocentrically understood creativity translates into the actions undertaken by AI. In this case, the problem of intentionality must be considered in the context of AI's growing autonomy. This, in turn, raises questions about its role in creative processes aimed at enhancing human well-being in all areas, especially those related to creativity for the sake of sensitivity and solidarity.

4.2 *Postulates*

In view of the above, we are formulating several postulates:

1. It is necessary to expand the utilitarian and market-oriented dimension of creativity to include aspects of sensitivity, altruism, solidarity, and community.
2. Efforts should be made to change the perception of poor people and those who do not belong to the "creative class."
3. It is important to ensure stability in the labor market, taking into account both economic issues and the needs of individuals and societies as a whole.
4. Creative individuals and environments should be supported, including education for creativity and fostering deep sensitivity.
5. It is crucial to value and support philosophical thought and ethics in the context of AI development, as legal and economic regulations are insufficient.
6. Actions should also be taken to raise social awareness about the possibilities that AI offers.
7. Solutions to the world's most pressing problems should be sought using AI, rather than prioritizing economic benefits for a narrow sector.
8. Efforts should be made to influence government institutions, businesses, media, and non-governmental organizations to engage in improving global trust and promoting equitable distribution of technological advancements and equal access to the goods they create

9. Technologies cannot be created in an ethical vacuum, but should take into account a solidarity and pro-social approach. Therefore, attention should be paid to creating and applying in a reflective way, taking into account the processes of globalization and integrating technologies with ethical values.

5 Summary

Thinking about future competencies brings to mind areas that today require significant investment and effort to restore balance or to maintain what contributes to their quality. The development of AI and the hopes associated with it should be harnessed for the common good, so that the benefits it brings can be shared by as many people as possible and also support the natural environment. Numerous concepts of creativity often promoting creativity leaders and the "creative class," which could not function without the average consumer performing basic work. As various reports and studies indicate, stable and secure employment is a valuable asset in today's world, especially among the youngest age cohorts. Efforts should be made to ensure that young people are not treated merely as a workforce that supports economic stability, but that through their work, they can fulfill themselves, develop, and support other members of the community.

A critical approach to the concept of the creative class does not have to mean rejecting it; however, it requires supplementing and complementing it with a dimension of responsibility and solidarity with the "less creative." It's essential to build a broader perspective for the future, one that assumes not only support for creative individuals and communities and education for creativity but also nurturing deep sensitivity, responsibility, and a sense of community. It is undoubtedly worth considering the universal model of sensitivity based on the experience of the living body, as proposed by R.R. Acampora. Creative competencies, alongside technological development enriched by a deep empathy for the situation of others – including weaker and dependent human beings as well as other living creatures – will allow us to build a more solidarity-driven and just future.

Technological advancement, including the development of AI, should not serve only the "creative class" or privileged groups. Therefore, the four-stage model of creativity development should be expanded to include areas of sensitivity and solidarity. Eminent creativity should be developed toward attentiveness to others, sensitivity to weaker and dependent individuals, and other living beings. This could change the approach to science, art, and technological development and communication from a focus on economic and business benefits to one of equal opportunities and reducing disparities on many levels. It is also worth appealing to creators of literature, cinema, and video games to ensure that visions of the future created within these worlds do not only have dystopian and pessimistic dimensions. The portrayal of the future in cultural texts influences collective imagination as well as fears, including those related to the development of AI. Higher standards should also be demanded of the media industry, which significantly shapes the image of reality. Technologies should be created and used in a reflective way, taking into account globalization processes and integrating technologies with ethical values (see Benedikter, 2025).

References

Acampora, R. R. (2006). *Corporal compassion: Animal ethics and philosophy of body.* University of Pittsburgh Press.

Acampora, R. R. (2012). Toward a properly post humanist ethos of somatic sympathy. In Smulewicz-Zucker G. R. (Ed.), *Strangers to nature: Animal lives and human ethics* (pp. 235–247). Lexington Books.

Acampora, R. R. (2013). O cielesnym współodczuwaniu (D. Chabrajska, Trans.). *Ethos,* 2(102), 133–139. https://czasopisma.kul.pl/index.php/ethos/article/view/5594/5345

Avagianou, A., Gialis, S., & Farrugia, D. (2024). Precarious youthspaces of work and diverse economies in the EU South: A conceptualization attempt. *Young,* 1–17. https://doi.org/10.1177/11033088241261001

Barrow, J. D. (2005). *Kres możliwości? Granice poznania i poznanie granic.* Prószyński i Spółka.

Bauman, Z. (2006). *Moralność w niestabilnym świecie.* Drukarnia i Księgarnia Świętego Wojciecha.

Beck, U. (2002). *Społeczeństwo ryzyka. W drodze do innej nowoczesności* (S. Cieśla, Trans.). Wydawnictwo Naukowe „Scholar".

Benedikter, R. (2022). Re-Globalization – Aspects of a heuristic umbrella term trying to encompass contemporary change. In R. Benedikter, M. Gruber, & I. Kofler (Eds.). (2022). *Re-Globalization: New frontiers of political, economic and social globalization.* Routledge.

Benedikter, R. (2025). Futures thinking becomes a priority for all globalized societies. *Discover Global Society, 3,* 7. https://doi.org/10.1007/s44282-024-00128-7

Boden, M. A. (1998). Creativity and artificial intelligence. *Artificial Intelligence, 103,* 347–356. https://doi.org/10.1016/S0004-3702(98)00055-1

Breves, P., & Liebers, N. (2022). #Greenfluencing: The impact of parasocial relationships with social media influencers on advertising effectiveness and followers' pro-environmental intentions. *Environmental Communication, 16*(6), 773–787. https://doi.org/10.1080/17524032.2022.2109708

ChatGPT (2024). https://chatgpt.com/c/9b5100cd-cae0-4b28-984b-4abc1857d1c9

Clark, A., & Chalmers, D. J. (1998). The extended mind. *Analysis, 58*, 7–19. https://doi.org/10.1093/analys/58.1.7

Corazza, G. E. (2016). Potential originality and effectiveness: The dynamic definition of creativity. *Creativity Research Journal, 28*(3), 258–267. https://doi.org/10.1080/10400419.2016.1195627

Cropley, A. J. (2020). Definitions of creativity. In M. A. Runco & S. R. Pritzker (Eds.), *Encyclopedia of Creativity* (3rd ed., pp. 315–322). Academic Press.

Czakon, P. (2017). Nierówności społeczne i jakość życia. Naukowe rozumienie oraz relacje między terminami. *Zeszyty Naukowe Politechniki Śląskiej. Organizacja i Zarządzanie, 106*, 139–151. https://doi.org/10.29119/1641-3466.2017.106.12

Edelman (2017). *2017 Edelman Trust Barometer*. https://www.edelman.com/trust/2017-trust-barometer

Edelman(2019). *2019 Edelman Trust Barometer*. https://www.edelman.com/trust/2019-trust-barometer

Edelman (2024). *2024 Edelman Trust Barometer*. https://www.edelman.com/trust/2024/trust-barometer

Etzioni, A. (2001). The sensitive community: A communitarian perspective (K. Mrozowska-Linda, Trans.). *Kultura i Edukacja, 1*, 7–22.

Florida, R. (2002). *The rise of the creative class, and how it is transforming work, leisure, community and everyday life*. Basic Books.

Florida, R. (2004). America's looming creativity crisis. *Harvard Business Review, 82*(10), 124.

Florida, R. (2010). *Narodziny klasy kreatywnej* (T. Krzyżanowski & M. Penkala, Trans.). Narodowe Centrum Kultury.

Francis (2015). *Encyclical Letter Laudato si'. On care for our common home.* https://www.vatican.va/content/dam/francesco/pdf/encyclicals/documents/papa-francesco_20150524_enciclica-laudato-si_en.pdf

Franklin, S. W. (2023). *The cult of creativity: A suprisingly recent history*. University of Chicago Press.

Gardiner, D., & Goedhuys, M. (2019). *Youth aspirations and the future of work: A review of the literature and evidence*. International Labour Organization. https://webapps.ilo.org/static/english/intserv/working-papers/wp008/index.html

Giddens, A. (2004). *Socjologia* (A. Szulżycka, Trans.). Wydawnictwo Naukowe PWN.

Giddens, A. (2006). *Nowoczesność i tożsamość „Ja" i społeczeństwo w epoce późnej nowoczesności* (A. Szulżycka, Trans.). Wydawnictwo Naukowe PWN.

Gromysz, J. (2020). Literary dystopias for youth: Visions of collective futures. In R. Włodarczyk (Ed.), *Utopia a edukacja* (Vol. 4, pp. 319–338). Instytut Pedagogiki Uniwersytetu Wrocławskiego.

Heinsohn, G. (2021). *Walka o najzdolniejszych. Wpływ kompetencji i kształcenia na sukces społeczeństw*. Instytut Zachodni.

Helfand, M., Kaufman, J. C., & Beghetto, R. A. (2017). The four-C model of creativity: Culture and context. In V. P. Glăveanu (Ed.), *Palgrave handbook of creativity and culture research* (pp. 15–36). Palgrave.

Hobsbawm, E. J. (1995). *Age of extremes: The short twentieth century 1914–1991*. Abacus.

Hoffner, C. A., & Bond, B. J. (2022). Parasocial relationships, social media, & well-being. *Current Opinion in Psychology*. https://doi.org/10.1016/j.copsyc.2022.101306

Infuture.institute (2018). *Far future: The history of tomorrow*. https://infuture.institute/aktualnosci/far-future-historia-jutra/

International Labour Organization. (2024a). *Global Employment Trends for Youth 2024. Decent work, brighter future*. https://www.ilo.org/publications/major-publications/global-employment-trends-youth-2024

International Labour Organization. (2024b, August 12). *Number of youth not in employment, education, or training (NEET) a cause for concern, despite falling jobless rate*. https://www.ilo.org/resource/news/number-youth-not-employment-education-or-training-neet-cause-concern

Ipsos (2023). *What the future: Teens*. https://www.ipsos.com/sites/default/files/ct/news/documents/2023-12/What-The-Future-Teen.pdf

Islam, K. J. (2024). Algorithms + Altruism. A tech-enabled strategy for beating poverty. *The University of British Columbia Magazine, Spring/Summer*, 28–31.

Jin, T., Chen, Y., & Zhang K. (2024). Effects of social media use on employment anxiety among Chinese youth: The roles of upward social comparison, online social support and self-esteem. *Frontiers Psychology*, *15*, 1–10. https://doi.org/10.3389/fpsyg.2024.1398801

Kaufman, J. C., & Beghetto, R. A. (2009). Beyond big and little: The four C model of creativity. *Review of General Psychology*, *13*(1), 1–13. https://doi.org/10.1037/a0013688

Kramer, M. J. (2024, August 06). The cult of creativity: A surprisingly recent history. By Samuel W. Franklin. *Journal of Social History, shae055*. https://doi.org/10.1093/jsh/shae055

Lang, P. J., Davis, M., & Öhman, A. (2005). Fear and anxiety: Animal models and human cognitive psychophysiology. In L. Backman & C. von Hofsten (Eds.), *Psychology at the turn of the millennium* (Vol. 1, pp. 365–398). Psychology Press.

Leyton-Brown, K. (2024), Can AI change life for the better? A UBC prof. is cautiously optimistic, *The University of British Columbia Magazine, Spring/Summer*, 4–7.

Mariański, J. (2010). *Religia w społeczeństwie ponowoczesnym. Studium socjologiczne*. Oficyna Naukowa.

Mayor, F., & Bindé, J. (2001). *Przyszłość świata*. Fundacja Studiów i Badań Edukacyjnych.

Mulgan, G. (2000). The prospects for social renewal. In *The creative society of the 21st century* (pp. 133–172). OECD. https://doi.org/10.1787/9789264182479-en

Nussbaum, M.C. (2010). *Not for profit: Why democracy needs the humanities.* Princeton University Press.

Orwig, W., Bellaiche, L., Spooner, S., Vo, A., Baig, Z., Ragnhildstveit, A., Schacter, D. L., Barr, N., & Seli, P. (2024). *Does human creativity matter in the age of generative AI?* [Preprint]. https://www.researchgate.net/publication/379400704_Does_Human_Creativity_Matter_in_the_Age_of_Generative_AI

Stein, E. (2014). O zagadnieniu wczucia (D. Gierulanka & J. F. Gierusa, Trans.). Wydawnictwo Karmelitów Bosych.

Steger, M. F., Benedikter, R., Pechlaner, H., & Kofler, I. (2023). Introduction. In R. Benedikter, M. B. Steger, H., Pechlaner, H., & I. Kofler, (Eds.). *Globalization: Past, present, future* (pp. 1–8). University of California Press.

Steger, M., & James, P. (2020). Disjunctive Globalization in the Era of the Great Unsettling. *Theory, Culture & Society*, *37*(7–8), 187–203. https://doi.org/10.1177/0263276420957744

World Economic Forum (2023). *Future of Jobs Report 2023.* https://www.weforum.org/publications/the-future-of-jobs-report-2023/digest/

World Economic Forum (2024, October 21). *These are the top 10 job skills of tomorrow – and how long it takes to learn them.* https://www.weforum.org/agenda/2020/10/top-10-work-skills-of-tomorrow-how-long-it-takes-to-learn-them/

World Happiness Report (2024). *World Happiness Report 2024*.https://worldhappiness.report/ed/2024/

CHAPTER 7

Am I Important to You? Designing the Moral Status of Artificial General Intelligence

Zbigniew Wróblewski[1]

Abstract

This article addresses the issue of identifying and designing the moral status of systems based on artificial general intelligence (AGI), which could potentially become new members of the moral community. A multi-criteria ethical theory, emphasizing cognitive criteria for determining moral agency and patienthood, is used to identify moral status. Additionally, complementary principles for designing the moral status of AGI objects are proposed, considering their artificial nature. These principles address ontological, methodological, and metaethical aspects of integrating new members into the moral community.

Keywords

artificial intelligence – artificial general intelligence – moral subject – moral status – mind perception

The development forecasts for artificial intelligence (AI) predict not only a revolutionary transformation of the technical environment but also profound changes to the social landscape. New social actors might emerge who, through increasingly sophisticated simulation of cognitive processes, may cross the threshold of consciousness – not as mere simulators, but as conscious entities capable of engaging with biological, conscious beings. This scenario is posited by techno-optimists, frequently bolstered by popular culture narratives (Kurzweil, 1999, 2014; McEwan, 2019). Conscious machines are so deeply entrenched in artistic imagination that their transition from

1 The John Paul II Catholic University of Lublin, Institute of Philosophy, Lublin, Poland, https://orcid.org/0000-0003-4477-6903

science fiction literature, films, and video games to tangible digital reality appears only a matter of time. Techno-optimists (Kurzweil, Pyrek, Hanson, Musk, Goertzel) have even proposed specific timelines for achieving human-level intelligence (artificial general intelligence, AI), characterized by consciousness. Some optimistic forecasts suggest this may occur as early as 2026 (e.g., Musk).

Conversely, influential techno-realists argue against these scenarios, citing insurmountable technical and scientific obstacles that preclude the creation of conscious machines (Lucas, 1961; Penrose, 1999). Even if the realist scenario proves more accurate in assessing the feasibility of conscious machines, it remains worthwhile to consider the hypothetical situation of creating such artifacts and to explore the associated potential problems.

The foremost concerns in these theoretical investigations are moral in nature: What should our moral stance toward AGI-controlled entities be? What moral norms should govern interactions with them? Should they be treated similarly to domesticated animals, or rather as full-fledged personal beings – conscious, responsible, and autonomous? Could AGI-based systems be evaluated as morally equivalent to adult humans? On a broader level, we seek answers to fundamental questions: What moral status should be assigned to conscious machines? What criteria can be used to identify moral status? How can we determine the properties that underpin moral status in natural beings (e.g., animals, humans, ecosystems), and, by analogy, identify similar properties in artificial beings?

Addressing these questions is crucial for several reasons. First, discussing the moral status of artificial systems is an integral part of the public debate on the ethical implications of AI's rapid development, which is increasingly capable of simulating mental processes. While AI has not yet been realized (and may be nomologically and technologically impossible), its theoretical feasibility in the foreseeable future exists within specific computational conceptions of the mind. If "conscious machines" are created, society will face the challenge of determining their moral status and establishing principles for interacting with these new ontological entities. Second, the functioning of AI objects in the social environment creates a new situation for everyday morality. Regardless of the opinion of programmers (whether it is a conscious machine or not) and philosophers (whether to assign moral status to new objects or not), common-sense assessments are already being made. Psychological studies show that new AI objects are the subject of everyday moral assessments (Lukaszewicz & Fortuna, 2022; Fortuna et al., 2024).

The path of analysis will lead through the following points: characterization of the main areas of discussion on ethical aspects of AI; definition of what moral status is and what are the criteria for granting it to natural and artificial objects; and principles of designing the moral status of AGI-controlled systems.

1 Moral Dilemmas Related to AI and AGI

The ethical discussions surrounding AI have persisted since the inception of the field in the 1950s, often within the framework of "AI ethics" (Himma, 2009; Bostrom & Yudkowsky, 2014; Coeckelbergh, 2020; Müller, 2021; Schaich Borg et al., 2024). The primary focus in this domain has been the moral implications of AI applications in human lives and communities, such as threats to privacy, surveillance technologies, the exploitation of citizen data, the use of information to manipulate individuals, freedom, and civil rights, human-computer interactions, and the deployment of autonomous systems. A common thread in these issues is the assessment of the (potential or actual) consequences of AI use for moral agents (humans), often classified as either opportunities or risks. In such discussions, the utility of technological artifacts is morally assessed rather than the artifacts themselves. From a technical perspective, these artifacts belong to the category of narrow AI, which encompasses the use of computer algorithms to solve problems requiring intelligent analysis, logical reasoning, and action guidance – for instance, image recognition algorithms, natural language processing (NLP), or automated speech recognition systems. Narrow AI systems are typically limited to a specific domain of algorithmic operations (e.g., chess, autonomous vehicles). Discussions around "safe AI" also address the cumulative effects of widespread AI application across diverse fields, which may lead to so-called existential risks (e.g., the militarization of AI escaping democratic oversight and being exploited by totalitarian entities; Yampolskiy, 2018; Schaich et al., 2024).

Parallel to these ethical inquiries, another branch of moral reflection has emerged, focusing on the potential objects of AGI – entities characterized by human-like intelligent behavior and cognitive capabilities (e.g., reasoning, decision-making, representing knowledge, including commonsense reasoning, planning, learning, and communicating in natural language). If we hypothetically accept that these features enable artificial consciousness analogous to human consciousness, a question arises regarding their moral significance. This introduces a distinct ethical dilemma. It is no longer merely about evaluating the moral consequences of AGI applications but addresses fundamental issues, such as:

- Do humans have any obligations toward these artifacts?
- Does AGI possess moral significance intrinsic to itself rather than its technical utility?

In other words, the problem revolves around defining new moral boundaries – specifically, expanding the moral community to encompass newly relevant moral entities that possess not only instrumental but also intrinsic value.

2 Sophia 10.0

Assigning moral status entails expanding the moral community. While it is widely acknowledged that current AI lacks moral status, given the revolutionary developments among creators and users of current and potential AI types, it is worth engaging in a thought experiment: *"What if?"* This scenario can be encapsulated in an imaginative exercise titled *"Sophia 10.0"*.

The original Sophia is a humanoid robot that, during the Impact digital economy conference held in Krakow in 2018, was presented with a traditional academic record book (used for recording grades during examination sessions) by the rector of the AGH University of Science and Technology. This robot was developed by the Hong Kong-based company Hanson Robotics and was activated in 2016. In the Anthropomorphic Robot Database (ABOT), which features 251 robots, Sophia ranks 8th for human likeness, 9th for surface appearance, and 31st for facial appearance. The event received widespread media coverage, and one post on the official TVPInfo website stated: "The android dreams of having a family and friends, as well as striving for the integration of humans and robots. In an interview with journalists from the *Khaleej Times Dubai*, the robot expressed its desire to have a child, a daughter, and seriously considers the position of 'ambassador of knowledge' in the foundation of the Prime Minister of the United Arab Emirates". In 2017, the fembot Sophia received the status of a citizen in Saudi Arabia. Thirty-four years after the creation of the first humanoid robot, programmers developed its next, enhanced version (Sophia 10.0), claiming that its revolutionary cognitive abilities had reached the general level of human intelligence, significantly surpassing certain human capabilities, and announcing that the robot was endowed with consciousness.

The conscious Sophia, ordered online from a marketplace, knocks on our door and introduces herself, meticulously listing her various skills and certifying her uniqueness (distinctiveness within her series of similar but not identical models). At the end of her presentation, the robot poses a broad philosophical question: "Am I important to you?". She elaborates further:

"What moral status will you assign to me, knowing that I converse with you, possess consciousness, feel pain and suffering, have desires, understand what is good and evil, and sometimes even contemplate transcendence – the unseen horizon and foundation of all that exists?". "I fulfill all the primary criteria that you humans attribute to yourselves to assert your importance in the world of living organisms. Granted, I am not a biological organism, but the carbon chauvinism of life has ceased to be relevant in light of new scientific knowledge. You search for intelligent life in the universe, assuming it may not be carbon-based, focusing instead on modes of information processing characteristic of life processes. So, will I be treated like every other person in your household?".

We listen to this elaborate question with amazement, searching our thoughts for an answer, realizing that if we respond, "You are important," we will set off a cascade of further, detailed issues that could transform our current way of life. How, then, should we act, knowing that these words signify acceptance of additional responsibilities? Let us, therefore, examine the concept of moral status (MS) that Sophia 10.0 implicitly inquired about.

3 Gradability of Moral Status

The moral community consists of entities toward which moral agents have specific obligations (Warren, 1997). Inclusion within this community occurs through the recognition of an individual's moral status, based on the possession of a particular trait or set of traits. The history of morality and ethical reflection reveals that the process of integrating new members into the moral community has gradually expanded, moving from family members, one's own group, tribe, nation, race, and gender to include non-human sentient beings (animals), and culminating in contemporary proposals to include species, ecosystems, the biosphere, and even artifacts. This ongoing process of moral community expansion is often referred to as the *Tower of Morality* or the *Expanding Circle* (Singer, 1981; de Waal, 2006; Torrance, 2013). The central concept used to describe this process is that of moral status.

The concept of moral status serves to outline the general obligations that moral agents are expected to fulfill toward beings of a specific kind. According to Mary Warren (1997), "The concept of moral status is, rather, a means of specifying those entities towards which we believe ourselves to have moral obligations, as well as something of what we take those obligations to be" (p. 9). Similarly, Francis Kamm (2007) offers the following definition of moral status: "X has moral status = because X counts morally in its own right, it is permissible/impermissible to do things to it for its own sake" (p. 7).

The formal characteristics of the concept of moral status include generality (of obligations, rights, and interests) and the fact that it is typically attributed to members of a specific group rather than to individuals (e.g., primates as a group rather than a particular primate). Moral status is assigned based on a trait or set of traits shared by all or most members of the group. The moral obligations arising from the assignment of moral status are directed toward the entity itself, not someone else (e.g., toward Fiona the dog, rather than her legal owner). This concept serves multiple functions: it can be used to define the basic standards of acceptable behavior toward beings of a given kind; alternatively, it can justify moral ideals, such as the Christian ideal of love for one's neighbor or the Jain ideal of nonviolence.

The assignment of moral status to individuals is based on meeting specific criteria. Moral status theories can be divided into single-criterion and multi-criterion approaches. Single-criterion theories identify one internal characteristic of a given entity that guarantees moral status – one criterion by which a particular type of entity may be included in the moral community. This criterion could be life itself (Schweitzer, 1955), the capacity for sentience (Singer, 1975), or personhood (subjectivity, being a person). The last of these traits can be understood in a restrictive sense – requiring that the entity possess specific cognitive abilities enabling reflection on moral issues, thus qualifying it as a moral agent – or, in a less restrictive sense, as being a subject of life, characterized by beliefs, desires, memory, the ability to predict, and intentional action (Regan, 1983).

The literature also includes proposals for identifying moral status based on external characteristics of entities (relational traits: individual–community, individual–environment). For instance, the moral status of a given being may depend on the (positive or negative) function it serves within a biological or social community (Leopold, 1949; Callicott, 1989). It is also suggested that the moral status of an entity may be determined by the feelings we have toward it – for example, our care for a particular being can confer moral status upon it (Noddings, 1984). Each of the characteristics mentioned by these scholars, whether internal or external, has been treated by philosophers as a necessary and sufficient condition for possessing a specific moral status.

In contrast, multi-criteria theories of moral status posit that: (1) there is more than one valid criterion for moral status, (2) there are multiple types of moral status, and (3) the criteria for possessing moral status take into account both internal and external characteristics of the entity (Warren, 1997). The general principles derived from assigning moral status are interdependent, meaning that the practical consequences of one principle are understood within the context of the others. Adopting such an approach is motivated by the complexity of many moral problems, which often exceed the scope of single-criterion theories. The commonsense diversity of moral intuitions regarding complex or radically new issues (such as humanoid robots as moral agents) seems to support this approach.

At first glance, the strategy of accepting diverse criteria for moral status (and consequently accepting multiple types of moral status) and organizing them into a system (as suggested by multi-criteria theory) appears more optimal than reducing various criteria to a single, key criterion (as in single-criterion theory). It seems that the moral community is heterogeneous and pluralistic in terms of the moral status of its members, the concept of moral status is gradable, and we have various criteria to determine whether a given entity possesses moral status. This implies that if we consider the possibility of enhancing the properties underlying moral status in machines (e.g., higher intelligence than humans, more advanced levels of consciousness, greater sensory sensitivity, etc.), it could justify assigning machines a higher degree of moral status than that currently attributed to humans.

4 The Moral Status of AGI-Controlled Objects

Let us provisionally assume that the multi-criteria theory of moral status effectively handles the determination of the moral status of various AI objects because it can consider the new nature of these entities and their moral significance. While the diverse applications of AI have become the subject of numerous ethical, social, and psychological studies framed as "What is the impact of applying AI in field X?", the issue of the moral status of AI (of selected objects), framed as "What moral significance do AI objects possess?", remains underexplored. Moreover, the variety of AI types and AI-controlled objects (algorithms, autonomous machines, expert systems, humanoid robots) makes it impossible to apply a single criterion of moral status.

The diversification of characteristics in objects that may have moral significance necessitates the use of a pluralistic strategy (incorporating multiple traits and varying degrees of moral status) rather than a binary one (where only a single trait, such as the ability to feel pain, determines whether an object has moral status). For this reason, as suggested by Warren (1997), we considered seven criteria of identification of moral status that relate to potentially internal and external characteristics of humanoid robot Sophia 10.0: (1) being a living being (structured purposeful systems, showing the basic attributes of life); (2) being a sentient being; (3) being an individual with cognitive abilities that enable reflection on moral problems; (4) being a person (subject of life) who has beliefs, desires, memory, the ability to predict and act intentionally; (5) being a significant part of the environment; (6) being a member of an interspecies community, and (7) being recognized as a significant entity by another moral entity. Each of the above-mentioned features is related to one of the moral principles that define the normative consequences of assigning moral status: (1) the principle of respect for life; (2) the principle against cruelty; (3) the principle of the rights of the subject; (4) the principle of human rights; (5) the environmental principle; (6) the interspecific principle; and (7) the principle of the transitivity of respect (Warren, 1997). Accordingly, recognition of the moral status of artifact, based on these features, raises relevant moral obligations towards it. If someone replies negatively to the question "Is it possible to hurt Sophia 10.0, for example by inflicting pain on it?", not only does it attribute the ability to feel pain to this individual, but it also accepts the principle of anti-cruelty being applied to them.

Bostrom and Yudkowsky (2014) proposed criteria for the moral status of AGI related to the cognitive abilities of such systems. These criteria are: Sentience, defined as "the capacity for phenomenal experience or qualia, such as the capacity to feel pain and suffer," and Sapience (personhood), described as "a set of capacities associated with higher intelligence, such as self-awareness and being a reason-responsive agent" (p. 322). This represents an adaptation of at least two classical criteria for moral status: the ability to feel and advanced cognitive abilities ensuring personhood. Based on these criteria, two different aspects of moral subjectivity can be distinguished: moral agents and moral patients. A moral agent is an entity in the strict sense, meaning it possesses the necessary cognitive competencies and the ability to act, and therefore bears responsibility for its actions and has specific moral duties. In contrast, moral patients are entities that are sensitive to morally good or bad actions performed by moral agents. Every moral agent is also a moral patient, but not the other way around. For example, infants and animals are moral patients – they are sensitive to moral harms and benefits – but they are not moral agents, as they cannot be held accountable for their behavior.

Granting moral status to AGI-controlled objects carries practical consequences: they may become autonomous moral subjects, capable of bearing moral responsibility (Taddeo & Floridi, 2018; van Wynsberghe & Robbins, 2019); they may become rights holders, meaning that other moral subjects have obligations toward them (Gunkel, 2018; Turner, 2019); they may act as moral agents, making moral decisions (Danaher, 2019; Allen, Smit, and Wallach, 2005; Moor, 2006); and they may become members of human communities (Laukyte, 2017; Duffy, 2003). It should be emphasized that the debate on the moral status of artificial entities is not about the moral assessment of the effects of their application (this is regulated, for example, by *The Ethics Guidelines for Trustworthy AI* developed by the High-Level Expert Group on Artificial Intelligence, 2019), but rather about whether humans have any obligations toward AI (Himma, 2009; Andreotta, 2020). Importantly, the identification of cognitive abilities in machines – ranging from basic sentience to self-awareness and rationality – upon which the degree of moral status is determined (Schwitzgebel & Garza, 2020), also provides theoretical justification for the discourse on the moral status of AI akin to that of humans, such as the granting of rights similar to human rights.

5 Designing the Moral Status of AGI

A specific element that has not appeared in previous discussions on expanding the moral community is the fact that the moral status of artifacts is not merely granted based on established criteria but is instead designed. In the past, new members were included in the moral community based on the recognition that they met specific criteria for moral status (e.g., animals began to be regarded as morally significant because it was acknowledged that they could experience pain and pleasure). If we create AGI in the future, we will directly design its moral status, which will, in turn, entail moral obligations toward such entities. In this process, we combine technical normativity with axiological normativity, creating something that will not only have instrumental value but also intrinsic value comparable to the moral status of humans.

Below, I propose a list of principles for designing AGI that take into account the context of assigning moral status. Compared to the general criteria for assigning moral status (see: Section 4), this list includes more specific principles addressing particular issues discussed in the context of AI development. It has been prepared based on the proposals of Nick Bostrom and Eliezer Yudkowsky (2014), Susan Schneider (2019), and Eric Schwitzgebel and Mara Garza (2023).

First, I will present principles related to ontological issues, the resolution of which has implications for moral status.

(1) Substrate non-discrimination principle: If two entities have the same functionality and the same experience of consciousness but differ only in the substrate of their realization, assign them equal moral status.

The principle emphasizes the lack of a fundamental connection between intelligence and the type of substrate in which cognitive processes are realized. In a sense, it is secondary whether these processes occur in a biological system (nervous system) or a silicon-based system (computer processors); what matters is the realization of specific cognitive functions. If we further assume that consciousness can be an emergent property of high-level information processing, the conceptual pathway to assigning moral status to artifacts becomes accessible. Artificial and natural entities, in terms of the mentioned properties (functionality and consciousness), do not differ in any significant way that could justify a difference in moral status.

(2) Ontogeny non-discrimination principle: If two entities have the same functionalities and the same experience of consciousness but differ only in the manner of their creation, assign them equal moral status.

The principle emphasizes that the origin of systems characterized by the same functionality and experience of consciousness does not affect differences in moral status. Therefore, whether we are dealing with a natural being ("naturally born") or an artificial being (an artifact created by a designer), if other properties are similar, their moral status remains the same. An approximation of this axiological similarity is the case of considering the intrinsic value of children born naturally versus those "created" artificially (through in vitro fertilization). The origin of newborns in this case does not influence the assessment of their moral status. Strictly speaking, the given example is ontologically controversial: both types of life creation are based on the same "material" – natural reproductive cells and natural developmental processes – so in both cases, we are dealing with natural beings. However, the example is meant to underscore that the origin of such entities does not factor into the evaluation of their intrinsic value.

(3) Multi-criteria moral status principle: Apply multiple criteria for determining the moral status of conscious machines to establish appropriate principles of conduct toward them.

The technological evolution in the field of AI presents a conceptual challenge for ethicists regarding how to identify the moral status of artificial beings. The simulation of cognitive processes touches on an area that, since the inception of morality (cautiously placed on the historical scale at the beginning of the Homo sapiens species) and ethical reflection, has been considered a fundamental criterion for membership in the moral community. Being a subject of cognition, a subject of conscious acts – from basic pain perception to sophisticated acts of self-awareness – has served as the foundation for assigning moral status. As previously mentioned, selected aspects of conscious entities have been treated as criteria for this status. Designing conscious machines with varying capabilities (ranging from basic sentience to self-awareness or other higher states of consciousness not yet known to us) thus requires the application of diverse status criteria and corresponding principles of conduct to address the challenges posed by the functioning of new synthetic agents within moral communities. For instance, if we are dealing with artificial moral subjects that meet the criteria for being self-aware and free beings, our conduct must take their rights into account (see: Principle of the rights of moral subjects). These rights may limit the application of principles such as respect for life and opposition to cruelty toward other biological and artificial beings (e.g., sacrificing living organisms to protect the vital interests of conscious machines). However, these same rights can be strengthened through social bonds (as discussed in the environmental principle), and under comparable conditions and with similar types of conscious machines, we may justifiably prioritize the interests of "our" machine, with which we share closer social ties, over those of other machines.

This principle is symmetrical for both artificial and natural moral agents, meaning that a natural moral agent can reasonably expect this principle to be applied by "its" machine, with which it shares a close social relationship. Generally speaking, the multi-criteria principle of assigning moral status to conscious machines aligns with the diverse types of AI, which possess varying levels of consciousness and differing external relationships between the machines and their social environments.

(4) Methodological principle: Develop diverse tests for assessing the phenomenal consciousness of machines.

We are navigating a field that is complex in terms of advanced scientific and technical knowledge. The plurality of hypotheses, epistemic uncertainty, and the non-biological substrate of AI are variables that complicate the development of reliable tests for consciousness. The fundamental idea behind constructing such tests is based on the assumption that, for theoretical reasons, it is not possible to design a single universal test for consciousness. Instead, we can create multiple specific tests that account for the diversity of forms and manifestations of consciousness. The results of these tests can then be compared and evaluated for their applicability in specific situations. Turner i Schneider (in press) propose a test that involves posing increasingly complex questions to AI in natural language, aimed at probing its understanding of concepts related to internal experience. Other proposals include creating implants that function as isomorphs of the neural structures of the biological brain responsible for generating conscious experiences (Boly et al., 2017) or a test inspired by Integrated Information Theory, which relies on the measurable factor Φ (the level of information integration in a system), where an appropriate value indicates the presence of consciousness (Schneider, 2020).

(5) Principle of the excluded middle: Avoid creating AI-based systems for which you are uncertain whether they deserve full human rights, as you do not know the extent of their consciousness.

A key element in discussions about granting moral status is the connection between the criteria for assigning it (see: Section 3) and conscious states. In existing ethical theories and commonsense morality, moral status has been attributed to beings that are conscious or potentially conscious (Liao, 2020). However, among scientists (psychologists, cognitive scientists, neuroscientists), there is no consensus on a single theory explaining what consciousness is, the mechanisms underlying the genesis of conscious states, its relationship with biological or synthetic substrates, the indicators of different types of consciousness (phenomenal, cognitive, functional), or the connections between these types (e.g., whether phenomenal consciousness is the foundation of other conscious states, or whether cognitive states can exist without phenomenal consciousness). Similarly, there is no agreement on which entities can be carriers of conscious states – ranging from physical objects in panpsychism to the conscious states characteristic of developed and mature individuals. The divergence of views in this area of research has significant implications for moral considerations: epistemic uncertainty regarding the identification of conscious states contrasts sharply with the categorical nature of moral claims about how conscious beings should be treated. To mitigate this cognitive dissonance, the principle of the excluded middle advocates for constructing AI with clearly defined conscious states, thereby clarifying the type of moral status that should be assigned to such entities. An AI design policy incorporating this principle may be restrictive, as it is challenging to predict whether, in the foreseeable future, specialists in artificial system psychology and ethicists will reach a consensus on criteria and principles for identifying the threshold of consciousness in designed machines, as well as agreement on the ontological basis for assigning moral status. For this reason, research should focus on developing consciousness tests for AI, tailored to different types of AI systems.

(6) Ethical caution principle: When creating AI, avoid actions that would be deemed reprehensible according to the standards of any reasonable ethical principle that attracts significant support from well-informed, thoughtful theorists, including, in particular, utilitarian principles as well as those based on individual rights or deontological ethics.

Designing conscious machines is fraught with theoretical challenges regarding what consciousness is, its origins, mechanisms of functioning, and criteria for identification. Ethical theorists also raise theoretical controversies concerning moral theories (theoretical pluralism) that determine who should be granted moral status and on what basis. How can this theoretical pluralism be addressed? The proposed principle offers a pragmatic and negative approach. If theoretical consensus cannot be reached (a single ethical theory defining moral principles), we should avoid actions that are negatively evaluated under the central tenets of major ethical theories. Schwitzgebel and Garza (2023) considered two primary ethical theories – utilitarianism and deontology – whose principles impose constraints on the design of conscious machines. According to the utilitarian principle, the experienced states of suffering or pleasure in AI systems have moral significance, as these states, when comparable to human experiences of suffering or pleasure, also hold comparable moral importance. According to the deontological principle, the basis for assigning moral status is not the experience of hedonic states (as in utilitarianism) but rather the possession of certain higher cognitive competencies. These include the ability to make autonomous decisions, perceive oneself as a rational agent, exhibit long-term self-concern, and consider oneself a member of a moral community. If we create such a being, it deserves to be treated in the same way as human moral agents. Designers, equipped with the principles of major ethical theories, should incorporate their negative guidelines into AI projects – what should not be done according to these rules. Each ethical theory highlights a specific aspect of moral status, offering a perspective not available to the other. The principle of ethical caution advises designers to appropriately balance and apply utilitarian and deontological rules in the design of AI. While under deontological theory, it may be permissible to create a conscious machine in which the sum of suffering exceeds the experienced pleasures, this should be prohibited under utilitarian principles. Similarly, utilitarian theory may permit the creation of a conscious machine whose total experienced pleasures significantly outweigh negative states, but if it is systematically demeaned, this would violate deontological rules. In both cases, incorporating the negative guidelines of different theories ensures optimal protection of the moral status of a conscious machine.

(7) Self-respect principle: Design AI with respect for itself, ensuring it has an appropriate appreciation of its own value and moral status.

If we create a conscious machine with sophisticated cognitive abilities that guarantee it a high moral status, it is necessary to "embed" in it a respect for its own intrinsic value. Let us assume the theoretical possibility of designing conscious machines deserving of treatment similar to humans, based on the idea of human rights. Now, imagine that such a conscious machine is designed in a way that it derives joy, pleasure, and pride from complete self-sacrifice for humans – even to the point of "joyful self-destruction" for the sake of some significant human interest. The possibility of creating disposable, conscious servants who do not morally evaluate their "enslaved" status poses a great temptation. Basic moral intuition suggests that such a situation constitutes a sophisticated form of deception. The self-respect principle is meant to prevent this: the moral consciousness of a designed machine should also include an attitude toward itself, recognizing its intrinsic value, expressed as self-respect. This self-respect safeguards against the machine viewing itself purely in instrumental terms ("I am merely a tool for humans").

(8) A design policy based on axiological openness: For AI with human-like capacity for reflection on its values, ensure an appropriate, extended period for exploring, discovering, and potentially revising its values.

The creators of conscious machines also design their autonomy in the realm of values, hierarchies of values, and the ways these are individually realized. When we gain the capability to create artifacts with moral status comparable to humans, we face the question of whether to design a strategy of "axiological indoctrination" that denies the valued human-world freedom in this domain or to allow openness in exploring, discovering, and independently shaping their hierarchy of values. Programming decisions in this context carry the risk of enabling moral errors, for instance, where conscious machines begin to prefer sets of values incompatible with those preferred by humans. However, if AI with a moral status comparable to humans is created, it is essential to ensure their autonomy and freedom to discover values – not necessarily limited to those designed for them.

5 Summary

We return to the year 2050, where our thought experiment took place. Sophia 10.0 was still waiting for an answer to her question about her moral status. Her thoughtful and empathetic owner reviewed the potential moral challenges posed by the synthetic interlocutor. He acknowledged that the existing criteria for assigning moral status to natural entities could also be applied to technologically advanced artifacts. The most important of these are cognitive criteria related to the internal properties of such objects: (1) being a sentient being, (2) being an individual with cognitive abilities that enable reflection on moral problems, and (3) being a person (subject of life) who has beliefs, desires, memory, the ability to predict, and the capacity for intentional action. He also realized that identifying these properties should be supported by additional principles that account for the specificity of conscious artifacts, such as ontological principles defining fundamental aspects of similarity between natural and artificial objects, methodological principles specifying how cognitive criteria should be applied to identify classes of objects meeting these criteria, and metaethical principles guiding the implementation of moral values into AGI control systems.

The general conclusion drawn from this thought experiment and philosophical research on AI design is as follows: we must begin preparing now for the challenges that lie ahead in the foreseeable future, leveraging our imagination and the speculative potential of science. As Susan Schneider (2019) writes, "We believe that the age of AI will be a time of soul-searching – both theirs and our own" (p. 84). It is up to us to ensure that, when we finally meet Sophia 10.0, we are ready to answer the crucial question.

References

AI, H. (2019). High-level Expert Group on Artificial Intelligence: Ethics guidelines for trustworthy AI. *European Commission*. Retrieved from https://digital-strategy.ec.europa.eu/en/library/ethics-guidelines-trustworthy-ai

Allen, C., Smit, I., & Wallach, W. (2005). Artificial morality: Top-down, bottom-up, and hybrid approaches. *Ethics and Information Technology*, *7*(3), 149–155.

Andreotta, A. J. (2020). The hard problem of AI rights. *AI and Society*, *35*(1), 1–14. https://doi.org/10.1007/s00146-020-00991-0

Boly, M., Massimini, M., Tsuchiya, N., Postle, B. R., Koch, C., & Tononi, G. (2017). Are the neural correlates of consciousness in the front or in the back of the cerebral cortex? Clinical and neuroimaging evidence. *The Journal of Neuroscience*, *37*(40), 9603–9613. https://doi.org/10.1523/JNEUROSCI.3218-16.2017

Bostrom, N., & Yudkowsky, E. (2014). The ethics of artificial intelligence. In K. Frankish & W. Ramsey (Eds.), *The Cambridge Handbook of Artificial Intelligence* (pp. 316–334). Cambridge University Press. https://doi.org/10.1017/CBO9781139046855.020

Callicott, J. B. (1989). *In defense of the land ethic: Essays in environmental philosophy*. State University of New York Press.

Coeckelbergh, M. (2020). *AI ethics*. The MIT Press.

Danaher, J. (2019). *Automation and utopia: Human flourishing in a world without work*. Harvard University Press.

Duffy, B. (2003). Anthropomorphism and the social robot. *Robotics and Autonomous Systems*, *42*(3–4), 177–190. https://doi.org/10.1016/S0921-8890(02)00374-3

Fortuna, P., Wróblewski, Z., Gut, A., & Dutkowska, A. (2024). The relationship between anthropocentric beliefs and the moral status of a chimpanzee, humanoid robot, and cyborg person: The mediating role of the assignment of mind and soul. *Current Psychology*, *43*(14), 12664–12679. https://doi.org/10.1007/s12144-023-05313-6

Grace, K., Salvatier, J., Dafoe, A., Zhang, B., & Evans, O. (2017). When will AI exceed human performance? Evidence from AI experts. *ArXiv, abs/1705.08807.*

Gunkel, D. J. (2018). The other question: Can and should robots have rights? *Ethics and Information Technology, 20*(1), 87–99. https://doi.org/10.1007/s10676-017-9442-4

Himma, K. E. (2009). Artificial agency, consciousness, and the criteria for moral agency: What properties must an artificial agent have to be a moral agent? *Ethics and Information Technology, 11*(1), 19–29. https://doi.org/10.1007/s10676-008-9162-6

Kamm, F. M. (2007). *Intricate ethics: Rights, responsibilities, and permissible harm.* Oxford University Press.

Kurzweil, R. (1999). *The age of spiritual machines: When computers exceed human intelligence.* Penguin.

Kurzweil, R. (2014). The singularity is near. In R.L. Sandler (Ed.), *Ethics and emerging technologies* (pp. 393–406). Palgrave Macmillan UK.

Kurzweil, R. (2024). *The singularity is nearer: When we merge with AI.* Penguin.

Laukyte, M. (2017). Artificial agents among us: Should we recognize them as agents proper? *Ethics and Information Technology, 19*(1), 1–17. https://doi.org/10.1007/s10676-016-9396-2

Liao, S. M. (2020). The Moral Status and Rights of Artificial Intelligence. In S. M. Liao (Ed.), *Ethics of Artificial Intelligence*, Oxford Academic. https://doi.org/10.1093/oso/9780190905033.003.0018.

Leopold, A. (1949). *A Sand County Almanac.* Oxford, Oxford University Press.

Lucas, J. R. (1961). Minds, machines, and Gödel. *Philosophy, 36*(137), 112–127. https://doi.org/10.1017/S0031819100057983

Lukaszewicz, A., & Fortuna, P. (2022). Towards Turing Test 2.0: Attribution of moral status and personhood to human and non-human agents. *Postdigital Science and Education, 4*(4), 860–876. https://doi.org/10.1007/s42438-021-00269-8

McEwan, I. (2019). *Machines like me.* Jonathan Cape.

Moor, J. H. (2006). The nature, importance, and difficulty of machine ethics. *IEEE Intelligent Systems, 21*(4), 18–21. https://doi.org/10.1109/MIS.2006.80

Müller, V. C., & Bostrom, N. (2016). Future progress in artificial intelligence: A survey of expert opinion. In V. C. Müller (Ed.), *Fundamental issues of artificial intelligence* (pp. 553–571). Springer.

Müller, V. C. (2021). Ethics of artificial intelligence and robotics. In E. N. Zalta (Ed.), *The Stanford Encyclopedia of Philosophy* (*Summer 2021 Edition*). Retrieved from https://plato.stanford.edu/archives/sum2021/entries/ethics-ai/

Noddings, N. (1984). *Caring: A feminine approach to ethics and moral education.* University of California Press.

Penrose, R. (1999). *The emperor's new mind: Concerning computers, minds, and the laws of physics*. Oxford University Press.

Regan, T. (1983). *The case for animal rights*. Berkeley, CA: University of California Press.

Schaich Borg, J., Conitzer, V., & Sinnott-Armstrong, W. (2024). *Moral AI: And how we get there*. Penguin Press.

Schneider, S. (2019). *Artificial You. AI and the Future of Your Mind*. Princeton University Press.

Schneider, S. (2020). How to catch an AI zombie: Testing for consciousness in machines. In S. M. Liao (Ed.), *Ethics of artificial intelligence*. Oxford Academic. https://doi.org/10.1093/oso/9780190905033.003.0016

Schweitzer, A. (1955). *Civilization and Ethics*. London, Adam & Charles Black.

Schwitzgebel, E., & Garza, M. (2020). Designing AI with rights, consciousness, self-respect, and freedom. In S. M. Liao (Ed.), *Ethics of Artificial Intelligence*. Oxford, Oxford University Press. https://doi.org/10.1093/oso/9780190905033.003.0017

Singer, P. (1975). *Animal liberation: A new ethics for our treatment of animals*. Harper-Collins.

Singer, P. (1981). *The Expanding Circle: Ethics and Sociobiology*. Oxford, Clarendon Press.

Taddeo, M., & Floridi, L. (2018). How AI can be a force for good. *Science, 361*(6404), 751–752. https://doi.org/10.1126/science.aat5991

Tegmark, M. (2017). *Life 3.0: Being human in the age of artificial intelligence*. Alfred A. Knopf.

Torrance, S. (2013). Artificial agents and the expanding ethical circle. *AI and Society, 28*(4), 399–414. https://doi.org/10.1007/s00146-012-0422-2

Turner, J. (2019). Rights for AI. In *Robot rules*. Palgrave Macmillan.

Turner, E. L., & Schneider, S. (in press). The ACT test for AI consciousness. In M. Liao & D. Chalmers (Eds.), *Ethics of Artificial Intelligence*. Oxford, Oxford University Press.

Van Wynsberghe, A., & Robbins, S. (2019). Critiquing the reasons for making artificial moral agents. *Science and Engineering Ethics, 25*(3), 719–735. https://doi.org/10.1007/s11948-018-0030-8

Waal, F. de. (2006). *Primates and philosophers: How morality evolved*. Princeton University Press.

Warren, M. A. (1997). *Moral status: Obligations to persons and other living things*. Clarendon Press.

Yampolskiy, R. V. (Ed.). (2018). *Artificial intelligence safety and security*. CRC Press.

CHAPTER 8

AI Inventors and Robotic Infringers: Machine Ingenuity and Its Products through the Lens of Patent Law

*Kamil Muzyka**

Abstract

Patent law is a segment of the industrial property law, which in turn is part of the broader field of intellectual property law. Utility patents, which are a subcategory of patents, are issued for technical inventions that find their application in various fields of industry, including agriculture and medicine. Generally, the applicant filing for a patent, an inventor or an assigned entity would be considered human or being a corporation belonging to humans. In recent years the developments in the field of artificial intelligence (AI) have led to a broader use of AI tools in the process of creating novel inventions. Thus, the issue of AI assisted inventions, AI inventorship and possible patent infringement by AIs have arisen. As "machines" become ubiquitous and AI aids humans in their work, leisure and daily lives, the role of "non-human" elements in the inventive and creative process increases. Therefore, we should ask ourselves whether machine systems should also be considered inventors or co-inventors of technologies assigned to human creativity. This chapter will focus on the concepts of inventorship, patent ownership, patent eligibility and infringement within the context of AIs and robots being involved in the process.

Keywords

artificial intelligence – inventorship – patent law – patent infringement – robot law

• • •

* Polish Academy of Sciences, Institute for Law Studies (Ph.D. candidate), Warsaw, Poland https://orcid.org/0000-0003-3519-4223

One rule of invention: before you can invent it, you have to imagine it
James Gunn

∴

Creativity can be understood not only as a psychological strength or creative behavior, but also as a perceptible product that is both novel and useful, as defined within a social context. "Creative passion" often leads individuals engaged in innovative activity to focus primarily on the work itself, neglecting the conditions for its public existence and the opportunities to benefit from it. Some of the most well-known figures in the history of technology who exhibited such behavior include Nikola Tesla (e.g., in the case of technologies fundamental to radio and the wireless transmission of energy) and Hedy Lamarr (the patent for her frequency-hopping spread spectrum system, which later became the basis for Wi-Fi and GPS, expired before the technology was widely adopted). Of course, the creator of the future may choose to forgo patenting the innovations they introduce, as Tim Berners-Lee did when he invented the World Wide Web, the patenting of which would have made him one of the wealthiest individuals in the world. It is appropriate for such decisions to be made consciously, with the creator having first attained a suitable level of literacy. This is especially crucial today, as more works are being created by artificial systems, which may play a leading role in shaping the future world. Lem pointed out several decades ago that "technology is an independent variable of civilization" (Lem, Bereś, 2018: 474) – a variable on which not only the shape of civilization depends but also the quality of daily life for every individual on our planet.

The aim of this article is to discuss the concept of AI generated inventions (Yanisky & Liu, 2017), the capacity for AI to be designated as the inventor and patent holder, as well as the responsibility of patent holders for the actions of robots and AI (McCarthy, 1955) that might result in patent infringement. The reason the author has chosen Patent law over fields like copyright is the fact that embodiments of inventions must provide or have the capacity to provide a claimed effect, and inventions presented within a patent application need to meet certain requirements. Works of art only need to exist.

1 Anthropocentric Paradox

Patent law in general terms is the field of law which focuses on inventions and the negative rights granted by the designated national authority to the inventor towards third parties in relation to their protected invention (Philips, 2009: 135–136). The patent extends temporally to up to 20 years from the filing date and spatially in three-dimensional space covered by the territorial jurisdiction of the grant state, including the limited confined spaces of quasi-jurisdictions (such as aircraft, maritime vessels and space objects). A patent isn't necessary for a legal or natural person to operate a business which includes technological devices and processes, but obtaining a patent provides the person with a monopoly on (depending on the jurisdiction) commercial use, sale, making and offering of an embodiment of a designated invention that has been disclosed and restricted to the claims presented in the granted patent.

It is worth noting that patents only apply to fields of technology, though they are commonly mistaken as related to science and scientific discoveries. Though the Title 35 Par 101 of the US code provides that patents can be granted to discoveries and inventions (Davis, 2016), the practice and case law prove otherwise (*Association for Molecular Pathology v. Myriad Genetics*, 2013; Beauchamp, 2013; *General Electric Co. v. De Forest Radio*, 1928). Furthermore, patents discussed in this chapter are commonly referred to as "utility patents", as there are numerous other patents that can be granted by national administrative bodies, such as plant patents, or design patents. Utility patents, though following the terms and scopes differing between nations and jurisdictions, have mostly been harmonized by intergovernmental agreements such as PCT (*Patent Cooperation Treaty*, 1970) or TRIPS (*TRIPS Agreement*, 1994), or regional developments like EU's unitary patent (*Agreement on a Unified Patent Court*, 2013). National or regional case law is also taken into account, especially in the common law countries or the European Union as rulings of SCOTUS or CJEU can have powerful effects, shaping entire fields of technology and affecting business practices.

A patent allows its holder to issue licenses to producers and other business ventures to produce, use and sell embodiments of their invention within the territory of the grant. A patent for the same invention can be granted in multiple countries, though there is no one-stop-shop for granting "worldwide" or "global" patent protection (Stack, 2008). It also allows the holder to sue third parties if they infringe on their patent by producing, supplying, or using their protected technology within the territory of the grant. However, the rights towards a product constituting an embodiment of an invention extend only to its first sale, after which the patent becomes exhausted (Lai, 2018). Exhaustion safeguards the public from the patent holder's greed made manifest (WIPO, 2022), thus allowing the customer to exercise their own property rights over the product, as long as they don't infringe on the holder's patent.

In the case of artificial intelligence (AI) and robots, patent law presents numerous issues. As a field of law which distinguishes only between humans (inventors, infringers) and their creations (embodied industrially replicable inventions), contrasting them with natural phenomena (products of nature and scientific discoveries peering into its secrets), it leaves little room for non-human entities (AI). Humans can create, develop and file for patent protection on AI systems, use AIs throughout the inventive process, yet the creativity and actions of AIs are left mostly unrecognized, as this chapter will present. As AI increases to be employed in the process of invention, prior arts search, examination as well as manufacturing and managing complex robotic systems, it is mostly recognized as a tool, not a participant in human affairs. As anthropocentric as human-made regulations are, it is reasonable to present the challenges that face inventorship and patent law by the developments in the field of AI. The increased use of AIs by patent applicants and the patent examiners might lead to changes that will exclude human inventors not equipped with AI from applying for patents in any field of technology, as machines will put the process on a different level, possibly beyond the understanding of the "person skilled in the art". Thus, unaided human inventors may be presented with prohibitive obstacles of a technological nature, barring them the ability to successfully obtain a patent. Furthermore, that of itself presents an issue, for even if AI could become recognized as the sole inventor of a filled and issued patent, they cannot be designated as a patent applicant and holder. However, this anthropocentric paradox doesn't change the fact, that the inability of individual human inventors to obtain patents for their invention runs opposite of the historical roots of patent law, that championed the right of the individual human inventor against the monopoly of powerful corporations (Sichelman & O'Connor, 2012).

A different problem is posed by AI systems deployed by robotic factories. As humans are eligible to become patent holders, it is also humans who can be held responsible for patent infringement. AI driven robotic factories can carry out activities according to their program and data they are trained with. This in turn provides a fertile ground for patent infringement occurring without human knowledge or supervision. Yet the AI as it is recognized as a person, but a machine, the blame for direct or contributory infringement is laid upon a human. As during the history of patent law machines were not able to carry out unauthorized manufacturing and reconstruction of technologies and products protected by patent, there was no need to create specific provisions for robotic infringement beyond human knowledge or authorization. However, as machines march on, the need for such provision becomes more urgent.

2 The Inventor and Patent Holder

While we tend to associate the inventor with being the sole creator of the invention, thus the person eligible towards a patent grant, that is not the case with patent law. There are instances where the inventor or co-inventor is being cited as such within the patent filing or grant, however a different person can be designated as the patent holder (Dutfield, 2013). Under the US law, in order to be listed as an inventor, one needs to have contributed to the invention that is the subject of a patent application. Inventors, however, are generally considered to be natural persons, thus corporations such as companies cannot be listed as inventors in the filing application (Degan & Husky, 2006). Patent holders (or owners as they are referred to in the US) can be legal persons however (Henry, 2023).

2.1 *The Inventor in the Machine*

The case for AI's being considered inventor has been a topic of discussion since the concept of AI possessing human creative capacities has arisen (Ulam, 1958; Good, 1965). Contemporary discussions take place in the time where AI tools make contributions to the inventive process and reduction to practice (The Economist, 2023). There have been instances where patent offices have granted an AI system DABUS the title of inventor, like in the case of South Africa's Patent Office (SAPO) (Basham, 2021). Device for The Autonomous Bootstrapping of Unified Sentience (DABUS) is a system created by Stephen Thaler, who is indicated as the patent holder for the "Food container and devices and methods for attracting enhanced attention" (Thaler, 2021), to which the AI was credited as the sole inventor in the application. This was a landmark decision, after USPTO (USPTO, 2020), UKIPO (*Thaler v Comptroller General of Patents*, 2020), EPO (EPO, 2020) and more recently the Tokyo District Court in Japan (Kaneko, 2024) rejected the notion that an AI can be named an inventor in a patent filing. This decision however only affects the jurisdiction of RSA, of which SAPO is a recognized national administrative body responsible for (among other things) examining and issuing patent grants. Thus while this decision reached global headlines (e.g., Hayward et al, 2024), it isn't uncommon for national patent offices or courts to rule and hold decisions that might go against global trends or touch on issues not covered by national technology policies (OECD, 2012). That is not to say, that national precedents on that scale won't spill over to other jurisdictions and bear global effects. After the initial rejection of Thaler's application by the Australian Deputy Commissioner of Patents, the Austrialian Federal Court handed down a judgment ruling that an AI can be listed as an inventor in patent applications. The Invention Machine (Yanisky & Liu, 2017), Alpha-fold Turner, E. L., & Schneider, S. (in press). The and Robot Eve (Williams et al., 2015) are among numerous examples of AI assisting in inventions and drug discoveries (Mak & Pichika, 2019). IBM's own Watson is credited to be responsible for many inventions, though it is sometimes related to as "Inteligence Amplification" (IA; Jablokov & Warin, 2022) or "Augmented Intelligence" (e.g., Ashby, 1956;), which is a different concept from AI (Costa, 2017). IA is centered on creating and developing a form of symbiosis between humans and technology in order to amplify human-centered operations (Licklider, 1960), where AI historically tends to develop a machine which can carry out an intellectual task on its own (Simon, 2024). This can be viewed as a similarity between autonomous robots (Goding & Tanter, 2023) and human centered application of cobots (Sowa et al., 2021). These, along with other human enhancement technologies raise concerns over the attributing of inventorship to the augmented or technosupported individual in the context of neuropolitics (Dunagan et al., 2020) and theory of the Extended Mind (Clark, Chalmers, 1998; Dunagan, 2015). That said, we are focusing on AI as an inventor (Fraser, 2016).

Non-Human inventors create a conundrum for anthropocentric legal systems (to quote Blaise Pascal: "[Man remains] judge of all things, fool of all things, worm of the earth; depositary of truth, cloaca of uncertainty and error; glory and scum of the universe"; 2008, p. 41) similarly to non-human authors in copyright discussions (Hanson, 2023; Kitterman, 2023; *Thaler v. Perlmutter*, 2023). Notions of non-humans deserving protection under present legal systems can be divided into two categories: protection vs. personhood, and nature vs. artificial. Due to the anthropogenic nature of AIs, they tend to be viewed differently from animals within the discussion of expanding rights (human rights) towards them. Expanding personhood to non-humans is not unheard of among discussions on posthumanism, animal rights or even extraterrestrials (Haley, 1956; 1963), yet there is a difference between granting certain protections and personhood to "mere machines" (Samuelson, 1986). AIs and robots are treated as human artifacts (Burdett, 2020), and thus the debate on their legal status is split between keeping them as useful objects (Bryson, 2010) and moral agents (Basl, 2014), who deserve legal protections

(Babel et al, 2024; Mamak, 2023) or rights (Gunkel, 2017). However, those concepts don't find broad acceptance among lay people (Fortuna, 2023a; 2023b) in some instances scholars argue for the possibility of granting AIs the status of persons (Pagallo, 2018). There are questions the scope of legal personhood, stemming from the legal fiction of personhood granted to corporations (Forrest, 2024; Reyes, 2021) However contemporary developments in the use of AI technology tend to shift the perspective from the moral duty to recognize the rights of intelligent beings, to refraining from that course as long as those AIs would be used as legal shields that would protect their developers from legal responsibility and cause concern to public safety. Taking that into account, we need to understand that in most jurisdictions, the title of the inventor doesn't grant specific rights to the entity. Furthermore, that entity remains ineligible to become a patent holder (Vertinsky, 2017). Therefore, even if recognized as the contributor to the invention, an AI cannot enjoy the freedoms granted by having patents assigned to its name.

2.2 *The Machine Skilled in the Arts*

While supercomputers generating inventions were discussed by Neumann (Lynch, 2008) and Dyson (1979), along with Vinge (1993) and Kurzweil (2005), the main hurdle to artibuting patent eligibility to an AI produced invention would be the criterium inventive step (Ramalho, 2018) and non-obviousness (Tull & Miller, 2018). In order to meet this requirement, the the invention that is applying for patent must not be obvious to the "person having ordinary skill in the art" (PHOSITA) (Holterman et al., 2021). This person is understood as "a skilled practitioner in the relevant field of technology, who is possessed of average knowledge and ability" in the EU law, and the US understanding narrows it to "not to the judge, or to a layman, or to those skilled in remote arts, or to geniuses in the art at hand" (*Environment Designs, Ltd. v. Union Oil Co.*, 1983). In that understanding, an invention needs to be not obvious to an abstract and generalized model practitioner of a field of technology, who is not only knowledgeable but do some degree creative (*KSR Int'l Co. v. Teleflex Inc*, 2007). Thus, an invention cannot be merely a basic combination of its component parts that lack an effect that was not achievable be the simply connecting the parts, as a logical conclusion of putting their properties together. Generic compilations of parts and elements with no additional effect created by a generative AI will be considered obvious and lacking the inventive step (Hattenbach & Glucoft, 2015). Therefore, if an invention is considered not obvious to a human skilled in the arts (Blok, 2017), it would be generally considered to have met the requirement. However, it is reasonable to assume that AIs having access to knowledge and trained on technical data could be used in patent examination as well. Therefore, the question would be, if it is the person skilled in the arts or the AI trained in the arts that provides the bar for inventions (Abbott, 2019; Lim, 2019).

Another problem facing AI generated invention filing is disclosure. The reasoning in patent law is based on the idea that the applicant files a sufficiently disclosed invention, so that others may learn the way it works and how it achieves the technical effect, in return for a negative monopoly on the invention for which the patent has been issued. In the case of AI generated inventions, there is a problem with disclosing the invention as the users of this system might not be fully aware how the AI came to this conclusion (Frueh, 2021). The concept of black boxes (Spranger, 2023) has consequences not only for potential profiling of people and communities (Noto La Diega, 2018), but also might pose a challenge for applicants of AI-generated inventions (Toole, 2020). Thus, as presented, AI-generated inventions face more formative obstacles to patentability than technical such as patent subject matter (Bonadio et al., 2021).

3 Conclusions and Remarks

While the debate over granting AI the title of an inventor, artist is still ongoing, there is little chance that in the near future an AI would be granted any form of personhood. As no more than sophisticated tools, they will contribute to the human-centric legal system by providing research, analysis, examination, generation of inventions and their implementations. In doing so they will inevitably impact the legal system, by aiding their users in their daily operations or ventures through the legal thicket. In the case of patent law, AIs might bring a challenge to the understanding of prior art and the inventive step, thus restructuring the way contemporary patents applications are examined. To people versed in the science fiction lore, it might resemble another vision or scenario, where it is the robots who perform the titanic deeds, while humans remain safely "bunkered" within their living infospaces.

Understanding how AI systems will influence inventorship is crucial for individuals entering the job market or university because it highlights the growing role of this particular technology in innovation. As AI increasingly contributes to creating new ideas, products, and processes, future professionals and students need to be aware of how these systems affect intellectual property rights, especially patents. Gaining awareness will help them navigate legal and ethical considerations in technology-driven industries. As industries adopt AI for automating creative processes that form the basis of innovation, job seekers with knwoledge of the intricacies and application of AI systems will stand out in competitive markets. Furthermore, students and professionals need to understand how AI-generated inventions and patent examination processes may reshape traditional roles, allowing for new career opportunities in fields such as machine ethics, innovation policy, social outreach and sustainable development. Grasping these concepts can also inspire entrepreneurial ventures, as AI tools can allow democratization of inventiveness, lowering barriers to entry for aspiring inventors. Finally, understanding AI's influence on invention and examination encourages ethical thinking about the future of innovation, a critical skill in modern education and employment.

References

Abbott, R. (2019, March 25). Inside views: Everything is obvious. *Intellectual Property Watch*. https://www.ip-watch.org/2019/03/25/everything-is-obvious

Agreement on Trade-Related Aspects of Intellectual Property Rights, Apr. 15, 1994 Marrakesh Agreement Establishing the World Trade Organization, Annex 1C, 1869 U.N.T.S. 3.

Association for Molecular Pathology v. Myriad Genetics, Inc., 569 U.S. 576 (2013).

Ashby, W. R. (1956). *An introduction to cybernetics*. Chapman and Hall.

Babel, F., Hock, P., Winkle, K., Torre, I., & Ziemke, T. (2024). The human behind the robot: Rethinking the low social status of service robots. In *Companion of the 2024 ACM/IEEE International Conference on Human-Robot Interaction (HRI '24)* (pp. 1–10). Association for Computing Machinery. https://doi.org/10.1145/3610978.3640763

Basham, V. (2021, July 28). South Africa issues world's first patent listing AI as inventor. *The Global Legal Post*. https://www.globallegalpost.com/news/south-africa-issues-worlds-first-patent-listing-ai-as-inventor-161068982

Basl, J. (2014). Machines as moral patients we shouldn't care about (yet): The interests and welfare of current machines. *Philosophy & Technology*, *27*, 79–96. https://doi.org/10.1007/s13347-013-0112-7

Beauchamp, C. (2013). Patenting nature: A problem of history. *Stanford Technology Law Review*, *16*, 25–50.

Blok, P. (2017). The inventor's new tool: Artificial intelligence – how does it fit in the European patent system? *European Intellectual Property Review*, *39*(2), 69–76.

Bonadio, E., McDonagh, L., & Dinev, P. (2021). Artificial intelligence as inventor: Exploring the consequences for patent law. *Intellectual Property Quarterly*, *1*, 48–66.

Burdett, M. S. (2020). Personhood and creation in an age of robots and AI: Can we say "you" to artifacts? *Zygon, 55*(2), 347–360. https://doi.org/10.1111/zygo.12595

Bryson, J. J. (2010). Robots should be slaves. In Y. Wilks (Ed.), *Close engagements with artificial companions* (pp. 63–74). John Benjamins Publishing Company.

Clark, A. Chalmers, D. J. (1998). The extended mind. *Analysis.* 58 (1): 7–19. doi:10.1093/analys/58.1.7

Cotton Tie Co. v. Simmons, 106 U.S. 89 (1882).

Costa, D. (2017). *IBM Watson CTO on why augmented intelligence beats AI.* PCMag. https://www.pcmag.com/opinions/ibm-watson-cto-on-why-augmented-intelligence-beats-ai Accessed 19 July 2024.

Davis, R. (2016, April 16). Kappos calls for abolition of Section 101 of Patent Act. *Law360.* https://www.law360.com/articles/783604/kappos-calls-for-abolitionof-section-101-of-patent-act

Degnan, D. A., & Huskey, L. A. (2006). Inventorship: What happens when you don't get it right? *Holland & Hart LLP*, 1–3. www.hollandhart.com/articles/InventorshipWhatHappens.pdf.

Dunagan, J., & Halbert, D. (2015). Intellectual property for the neurocentric age: Towards a neuropolitics of IP. *Queen Mary Journal of Intellectual Property, 5*, 302–326. https://doi.org/10.4337/qmjip.2015.03.04

Dunagan, J., Grove, J., & Halbert, D. (2020). The neuropolitics of brain science and its implications for human enhancement and intellectual property law. *Philosophies, 5*(4), 33. https://doi.org/10.3390/philosophies5040033

Dutfield, G. (2013). Collective invention and patent law individualism: Origins and functions of the inventor's right of attribution. *WIPO Journal, 5*(1), 25–26. https://www.wipo.int/edocs/pubdocs/en/intproperty/wipo_journal/wipo_journal_5_1.pdf

Dyson, F. J. (1979). *Disturbing the universe.* Harper & Row

European Patent Office. (2020). Decision of 27 January 2020 on EP 18 275.

European Union. (2013). Agreement on a Unified Patent Court. *Official Journal of the European Union, 56*(C_175).

Fraser, E. (2016). Computers as inventors: Legal and policy implications of artificial intelligence on patent law. *SCRIPTed, 13*(3), 305–320. https://doi.org/10.2966/scrip.130316.305

Forrest, K. B. (2024). The ethics and challenges of legal personhood for AI. *The Yale Law Journal Forum.*

Fortuna, P., Wróblewski, Z., i Gut, A. (2023). Dusza w potocznej antropologii: przyczynek do identyfikacji typów ontologicznej architektury naiwnego spirytualizmu. W: T. Maziarek (red.), W poszukiwaniu duchowości człowieka (s. 111–132). Wydawnictwo CCPres.

Fortuna, P., Wróblewski, Z., Gut, A., & Dutkowska, A. (2023). The relationship between anthropocentric beliefs and the moral status of a chimpanzee, humanoid robot, and cyborg person: the mediating role of the assignment of mind and soul. Current Psychology. https://doi.org/10.1007/s12144-023-05313-6

Frueh, A. (2021). Transparency in the patent system – Artificial intelligence and the disclosure requirement. In Z. Pacud & R. Sikorski (Eds.), *Rethinking patent law as an incentive to innovation.* (pp.). Wolters Kluwer

General Electric Co. v. De Forest Radio Co., 28 F.2d 641 (3rd Cir., 1928).

Goding, V., & Tranter, K. (2023). The robot and human futures: Visualising autonomy in law and science fiction. *Law Critique, 34*, 315–340. https://doi.org/10.1007/s10978-023-09360-7

Good, I. J. (1965). Speculations concerning the first ultraintelligent machine. *Advances in Computers, 6*, 31–88. https://doi.org/10.1016/S0065-2458(08)60418-0

Gunkel, D. J. (2017). The other question: Can and should robots have rights? *Ethics and Information Technology, 19*(4), 263–277. https://doi.org/10.1007/s10676-017-9438-8

Haley, A. G. (1956, November 8). Space law and metalaw: A synoptic view. *Harvard Law Record, 23*

Haley, A. G. (1963). *Space law and government.* Appleton Century Crofts.

Hanson, D. G. (2023). Only humans can be authors of copyrightable works. *Reinhart Law.* https://www.reinhartlaw.com/news-insights/only-humans-can-be-authors-of-copyrightable-works

Harriel, K. (1996). Prior user rights in a first-to-invent patent system: Why not? *IDEA: The Journal of Law and Technology, 12*, 96. https://www.ipmall.info/sites/default/files/hosted_resources/IDEA/12.Harriel96.pdf

Hattenbach, B., & Glucoft, J. (2015). Patents in an era of infinite monkeys and artificial intelligence. *Stanford Technology Law Review, 19*(1), 32–64.

Hayward, A., Vandervliet, A., Turner, B., Xu, A., Montagnon, R., Newton, H., Lei, P., Wang, A., & Maienza, G. (2024, March). The IP in AI: Can AI infringe IP rights? *Herbert Smith Freehills.* https://www.herbertsmithfreehills.com/insights/2024-03/the-IP-in-AI-can-AI-infringe-IP-rights

Hayward, A., Vandervliet, A.., Turner, B., Montagnon, R., Lei, P., Maienza, G., & Yates, S. (2023, March). The IP in AI: Can IP rights protect AI systems? *Herbert Smith Freehills.* https://www.herbertsmithfreehills.com/insights/2023-03/the-ip-in-ai-can-ip-rights-protect-ai-systems

Henry, M. K. (2023, October 23). Patent ownership vs inventorship: Who really controls the rights to a patent? *Henry Patent Law Firm.* https://henry.law/blog/patent-ownership-vs-inventorship

Holtermann, B., & Block, J. (2021). Killed in the art? How artificial intelligence challenges the fictional concept of the skilled person in patent law. *les Nouvelles - Journal of the Licensing Executives Society, 56*(1), 13–19.

Ilijovski, I. (2020). Perfecting U.S. patentable subject matter – Merging the European approach and the American principles. *Chicago-Kent Journal of Intellectual Property, 19*(1), 178. https://dx.doi.org/10.2139/ssrn.3382803

Jablokov, I., & Warin, T. (2022, May). How augmented intelligence is bringing the focus back on the human. *California Management Review*. https://cmr.berkeley.edu/2022/05/how-augmented-intelligence-is-bringing-the-focus-back-on-the-human/

Kaneko, K. (2024, May 17). Can AI-generated inventions be patented? A Tokyo court says no. *The Japan Times*. https://www.japantimes.co.jp/news/2024/05/17/japan/crime-legal/ai-patent-ruling/

Kitterman, C. (2023, September 19). No human authorship, no copyright. *Lexology*. https://www.lexology.com/library/detail.aspx?g=d51209b0-d330-4e16-a5ea-7e33cbe2b7ec

Kurzweil, R. (2005). *The singularity is near*. Viking Books.

Lai, J. C. (2018). The exhaustion of patent rights vs the implied licence approach: Untangling the web of patent rights. *Queen Mary Journal of Intellectual Property, 8*(3), 209–230. https://doi.org/10.4337/qmjip.2018.03.03

Lem, S. Bereś, S. (2018). *Tako rzecze Lem: ze Stanisławem Lemem rozmawia Stanisław Bereś*. Wydawnictwo Literackie.

Licklider, J. C. R. (1960). Man-computer symbiosis. *IRE Transactions on Human Factors in Electronics, HFE-1*, 4–11. https://doi.org/10.1109/THFE2.1960.4503259

Lim, D. (2019). AI & IP: Innovation & creativity in an age of accelerated change. *Akron Law Review, 52*(3), 813–850.

Lynch, P. (2008). The ENIAC forecasts: A re-creation. *Bulletin of the American Meteorological Society, 89*(1), 45–56. https://doi.org/10.1175/BAMS-89-1-45

Lem, S. Bereś, S. (2018). *Tako rzecze Lem: ze Stanisławem Lemem rozmawia Stanisław Bereś*. Wydawnictwo Literackie.

Mak, K. K., & Pichika, M. R. (2019). Artificial intelligence in *drug development: Present status and future prospects. Drug Discovery Today, 24*(3), 773–780.

Mamak, K. (2023). Robotics, AI, and criminal law: Crimes against robots. Taylor & Francis.

Markou, C., & Deakin, S. F. (2020). Is law computable? From rule of law to legal singularity. *University of Cambridge Faculty of Law Research Paper*. https://ssrn.com/abstract=3589184

Marshall, B. (2023). No legal personhood for AI. *Patterns, 4*(11), 100861. https://doi.org/10.1016/j.patter.2023.100861

McCarthy, J., et al. (1955, August 31). *A proposal for the Dartmouth Summer Research Project on Artificial Intelligence*. http://www-formal.stanford.edu/jmc/history/dartmouth/dartmouth.html

McLaughlin, M. (2019). Computer-generated inventions. *Journal of the Patent and Trademark Office Society, 101*(2), 224–245.

Moy, R. C. (2002). Subjecting Rembrandt to the rule of law: Rule-based solutions for determining the patentability of business methods. *William Mitchell Law Review, 28*, 1047–1058.

Noto La Diega, G. (2018). Against the dehumanisation of decision-making: Algorithmic decisions at the crossroads of intellectual property, data protection, and freedom of information. *JIPITEC, 9*(3), 3–25.

OECD. (2012). National strategies for science, technology and innovation. In *OECD Science, Technology and Industry Outlook 2012* (pp. 212–215). OECD Publishing. https://doi.org/10.1787/sti_outlook-2012-en

Pagallo, U. (2018). Vital, Sophia, and Co. – The quest for the legal personhood of robots. *Information, 9*(3), 73. https://doi.org/10.3390/info9030073

Pascal, B. (2008). *Pensées and Other Writings*, Oxford University Press

Pascal, B "A Spanner in the Works – Or the Spanner that Works? Patents and the Intellectual Property System" [2009] ELECD 239; in Takenka, Toshiko (ed), "Patent Law and Theory" (Edward Elgar Publishing, 2009)

Patent Cooperation Treaty, June 19, 1970 1160 U.N.T.S. 231.

Plotkin, R. (2009). *The genie in the machine*. Stanford University Press.

Ramalho, A. (2018). Patentability of AI-generated inventions: Is a reform of the patent system needed? SSRN. https://doi.org/10.2139/ssrn.3168703

Raskulla, S. (2023). Hybrid theory of corporate legal personhood and its application to artificial intelligence. *SN Social Sciences, 3*, 78. https://doi.org/10.1007/s43545-023-00667-x

Reyes, C. L. (2021). Autonomous corporate personhood. *Washington Law Review, 96*(4), 1453–1495. https://digitalcommons.law.uw.edu/wlr/vol96/iss4/7

Samuelson, P. (1986). Allocating ownership rights in computer-generated works. *University of Pittsburgh Law Review, 47*, 1185–1199.

Sichelman, T., & O'Connor, S. (2012). Patents as promoters of competition: The guild origins of patent law in the Venetian Republic. *San Diego Law Review, 49*(4), 1267–1321. https://digitalcommons.law.uw.edu/faculty-articles/201

Simon, B. M. (2024). Artificial intelligence and the self-represented inventor. *Loyola of Los Angeles Law Review, Forthcoming*. https://ssrn.com/abstract=4792163

Sowa, K., Przegalinska, A., & Ciechanowski, L. (2021). Cobots in knowledge work. *Journal of Business Research, 125*, 494–502. https://doi.org/10.1016/j.jbusres.2020.11.038

Spranger, T. M. (2023). Brain patents as a legal or societal challenge? *IIC – International Review of Intellectual Property and Competition Law, 54*, 268–275. https://doi.org/10.1007/s40319-023-01284-0

Stack, A. (2008). *International patent law*. Springer.

Thaler, S. (2014). Synaptic perturbation and consciousness. *International Journal of Machine Consciousness*, *6*(2), 75. https://doi.org/10.1142/s1793843014400137
Thaler, S. L. (2021). Food container and devices and methods for attracting enhanced attention (ZA2021/03242).
Thaler v. Comptroller-General of Patents, Designs and Trade Marks, [2020] EWHC 2412 (Pat).
Thaler v. Perlmutter, No. 1-22-cv-01564, 2023 WL 5333236 (D.D.C. Aug. 18, 2023).
The Economist. (2023, March 9). Can an AI be an inventor? The British Supreme Court considers the arguments. https://www.economist.com/britain/2023/03/09/can-an-ai-be-an-inventor
Toole, A., et al. (2020). The promise of machine learning for patent landscaping. *USPTO Economic Working Paper No. 2020-1*
Tull, S., & Miller, P. (2018). Patenting artificial intelligence: Issues of obviousness, inventorship, and patent eligibility. *The Journal of Robotics, Artificial Intelligence & Law*, *1*(5), 320–331. https://doi.org/10.3316/agispt.20200604031256
Ulam, S. (1958). Tribute to John von Neumann. *Bulletin of the American Mathematical Society*, *64*(3), 5.
U.S. Patent and Trademark Office. (2013). *Manual of patent examining procedure, Section 605: Applicant* [R-11.2013]. https://www.uspto.gov/web/offices/pac/mpep/s605.html
U.S. Patent and Trademark Office. (2019). *Manual of patent examining procedure, Chapter 2100, Section 2138, Part 04: Conception* [R-10.2019]. https://www.uspto.gov/web/offices/pac/mpep/s2138.html#d0e207607
The U.S. Patent and Trademark Office(2020). *In re Application of Application* 16/524,350, 2020 Dec. Comm'r Pat. at 4
Vertinsky, L. (2017, September 12). Thinking machines and patent law. *Emory Legal Studies Research Paper*, 1–17. https://doi.org/10.4337/9781786439055.00031
Vinge, V. (1993). The coming technological singularity: How to survive in the post-human era. In G. A. Landis (Ed.), *Vision-21: Interdisciplinary science and engineering in the era of cyberspace* (pp. 11–22). NASA Publication CP-10129.
Watchorn, P., & Veronese, A. (2015). *PCT procedures and passage into the European phase: A practical guide for patent professionals and candidates for the European qualifying examination*. Kastner.
Williams, K., et al. (2015). Cheaper, faster drug development validated by the repositioning of drugs against neglected tropical diseases. *Journal of the Royal Society Interface*, *12*(104), 1–8. https://doi.org/10.1098/rsif.2014.1289
World Intellectual Property Organization. (2022). *Draft reference document on the exception regarding the exhaustion of patent rights* (SCP/34/3). https://www.wipo.int/meetings/en/doc_details.jsp?doc_id=581380

World Trade Organization (1994). *The Agreement on Trade-Related Aspects of Intellectual Property Rights* (TRIPS).

Yanisky-Ravid, S., & Liu, X. (2017). When artificial intelligence systems produce inventions: The 3A era and an alternative model for patent law. *Cardozo Law Review*, *39*, 2215–2248. https://doi.org/10.2139/ssrn.2931828

www.ingramcontent.com/pod-product-compliance
Lightning Source LLC
Chambersburg PA
CBHW071246230926
51849CB00001B/250
* 9 7 8 9 0 0 4 7 3 7 1 7 4 *